POVERTY AMID PLENTY
A POLITICAL
AND ECONOMIC
ANALYSIS

POVERTY AMID PLENTY
A POLITICAL AND ECONOMIC ANALYSIS

HARRELL R. RODGERS, JR.
UNIVERSITY OF HOUSTON

ADDISON-WESLEY PUBLISHING COMPANY
Reading, Massachusetts • Menlo Park, California
London • Amsterdam • Don Mills, Ontario • Sydney

*For Micah and Jimmy
and those who love them*

Public welfare ... must be more than a salvage operation, picking up the debris from the wreckage of human lives. Its emphasis must be directed increasingly toward prevention and rehabilitation—on reducing not only the long-range cost in budgetary terms but the long-range cost in human terms as well. Poverty weakens individuals and nations. Sounder public welfare policies will benefit the nation, its economy, its morale, and most importantly, its people.

John F. Kennedy

Neither misery nor squalor is inevitable so long as the people and government are one.

Lyndon B. Johnson

PREFACE

This book is based on data gathered primarily by various agencies of the federal government. Over the last six years many members of Congress and the executive branch have helped me obtain literally hundreds of published studies and unpublished reports. Congressional committees routinely sent any study I requested, and the staffs of numerous members of Congress traced down particular studies and bits of information. While more persons deserve thanks than I could ever name, the staffs of William R. Archer (R.-Tex.), Bob Eckhardt (D.-Tex.), and Barbara Jordan (D.-Tex.) were particularly helpful. I often take exception to the studies on poverty and welfare programs conducted by the Congressional Budget Office, but, in fairness, I should say that employees of the CBO supplied me with a great deal of data and clarified any point that I raised with them.

Much of the data used in the book was collected and analyzed by the United States Bureau of the Census, located in the Department of

Commerce. I had to depend on the Census Bureau for dozens of studies, many of which were made available to me before being released for public consumption. It would be impossible for me to state strongly enough my appreciation to Arno I. Winard, Staff Assistant for Poverty Statistics, of the Bureau of the Census for all of his and his staff's help. Mr. Winard not only provided me with dozens of studies, but he and his staff understood my needs well enough to send materials that I had not yet requested. They also checked a number of points that were not contained in published reports. Mr. Winard and his staff were excellent representatives of the dozens of dedicated federal employees that it was my pleasure to meet and communicate with while writing this book.

My understanding of American poverty and the bewildering array of state and federal programs designed to administer to the poor was aided very considerably by two people. Leonard Derden and Judy Cox, both dedicated employees of the Texas Department of Welfare, spent many hours discussing issues and programs with me. Cox and Derden supplied me with documents and data, took me on field tours, and introduced me to many other persons in state and federal welfare organizations who became my friends and advisors. Both of them, along with others they suggested, also lectured to my classes on poverty and furnished my students with research assistance. Judy Cox took time to read the entire manuscript. Her help was very important. To both of these compassionate people I owe a considerable debt.

Three fellow political scientists also read the manuscript and helped me more than I can express. John C. Donovan, DeAlva Stanwood Alexander Professor of Political Science at Bowdoin College, and himself author of an excellent book on poverty, provided a thoughtful critique that led to many important additions to the book. Larry L. Berg, the University of Southern California, provided an exceptionally detailed and helpful critique that also led to many solid improvements.

Michael Harrington, whose book *The Other America* probably played a larger role than any other single factor in bringing poverty in modern America to the attention of the nation, was extremely gracious in taking time away from his own busy schedule to provide a critique of this book. His comments reflected the brilliance of his insights into this national shame, and helped me improve the manuscript in a number of ways.

The various drafts of the book were typed by Sandra Walsh, whose skill and dedication can hardly be repaid by the small sums the university provides such excellent people. Needless to say, I owe her a considerable debt.

I do not usually bother to exonerate those who have assisted me on a book, even though it is a time-honored practice. Generally I think the tradition silly, but a book such as this requires an exception. It should be clear that none of the federal officials who supplied me with data have read this book or have any idea how I used the data. They bear no responsibility for my conclusions.

My wife, Lynne, took time out from her own busy schedule to read this book in its many stages, discussed my developing ideas with me, and gave me both her critical insights and love and support. For her uncommonly beautiful love and goodness, I am both grateful and inspired.

Houston, Texas   H.R.R.
September 1978

CONTENTS

1

AMERICAN POVERTY

In the richest and most powerful country on earth, poverty still plagues millions of people. In 1976, even after the expenditure of billions in cash assistance, the federal government calculated that 25 million Americans remained poor. As staggering as this number is, it still falls short of accurately reflecting the enormity of the problem. As we will learn in Chapter 2, the yearly poverty count undoubtedly seriously underestimates the extent of poverty in the United States. Additionally, the poverty count does not include those who, while not utterly destitute, suffer the type of severe economic hardship that dooms them to live far below society's modal standards.

Poverty in America is not restricted to a few "outcast" groups. It affects all races, all ages, and every region of the country. The poor can be found in the tar-paper shacks of Appalachia, the migrant-labor camps of Florida, Texas, and California, the sharecropper shanties of the Mississippi Delta, the Mexican-American slums of the Southwest, the declining neighborhoods of the aged, the Indian reservations of every section of the country, and the ghettos of every major American city.

As numerous as the American poor are, they are mostly invisible. Often, they are segregated in neighborhoods that the nonpoor have no reason to enter, and many are children and the elderly—those persons least visible in our society. The poor are politically invisible as well. As Michael Harrington has observed:

> It is one of the cruelest ironies of social life in advanced countries that the dispossessed at the bottom of society are unable to speak for themselves. The people of the other America do not, by far and large, belong to unions, to fraternal organizations, or to political parties. They are without lobbies of their own; they put forward no legislative programs. As a group they are atomized. They have no face; they have no voice.[1]

The poor are invisible because we want them to be. Poverty is an affront to the American image of unlimited bounty and opportunity.

"Where? Here? Goodness knows I can't see it"

Hugh Haynie and *The Courier-Journal,* Louisville, Ky.

Americans have long been taught that the poor are simply the lazy, those who through flaws of character fail to have the requisite initiative and self-discipline to improve their lot. But the recent struggles over civil rights and women's equality have documented a fundamental truth: opportunity has never been equal in America. Those persons born black, Mexican-American, Oriental, American Indian, female, or poor in America have faced overwhelming obstacles to education, good jobs, promotions, and prosperity. As Kotz has said:

> The poorest Americans who have been buried in the Deep South, the Appalachian hills, the Indian reservations, the barrios of the Southwest, and the big city ghetto did not fail to make it in America simply because they lacked ambition or ability. The plantation system, the migrant system, the mining system, the Indian welfare system all created long odds against a man's breaking out of a cycle of abject, dependent peonage.[2] *

Thus, as later chapters detail, much of the current poverty in America is the legacy of hundreds of years of discrimination against large numbers of American citizens. And many of the political biases that have permitted slavery, Jim Crowism, discrimination, economic exploitation, and sexism to continue for 200 years in America still survive to limit the political influence of many Americans. The underlying philosophy that defined America as an unqualified success, the greatest of all nations—even during periods when millions were poor, unemployed or grossly underpaid, uneducated, ill-housed, and hopeless—continues to provide justification for conditions that emasculate the dreams and ambitions of the poor, spawn social ills, destroy families, and ultimately poison the fabric and soul of our society.

THE DISCOVERY OF POVERTY

Poverty and hunger in America only became a matter of national political concern in the 1960s. During his campaign for the presidency, John Kennedy saw poverty at its bleakest in West Virginia. Touched and concerned by what he saw, Kennedy implored the public to help eradicate such human suffering. Once in office Kennedy quickly expanded the food commodity program and initiated a pilot food-stamp program. In 1962

---

* This material and the quotes on pp. 5–8 are from the book *Let Them Eat Promises* by Nick Kotz. © 1969 by Nick Kotz. Published by Prentice-Hall, Inc., Englewood Cliffs, N.J. 07632.

Michael Harrington published *The Other America,* a book about the American poor that sent a shock wave through the nation. In 1963 Dwight MacDonald's "Our Invisible Poor" appeared in *The New Yorker* and added considerably to public concern about severe poverty, hunger, and deprivation in the United States.

During the summer of 1963, President Kennedy ordered various federal agencies to develop a case for a full-scale attack on poverty. Also during the summer of 1963, a 200,000-strong civil rights demonstration in Washington, D.C. led by Dr. Martin Luther King, Jr. focused national attention on racism, unemployment, hunger, and poverty. By the time of President Kennedy's assassination in November of 1963, concern about American poverty had gained considerable momentum.

President Lyndon Johnson decided to expand on Kennedy's efforts and, in 1963, declared a War on Poverty.[3] The thrust of the "war" was the Economic Opportunity Act of 1964, which consisted primarily of job and work-experience programs and small-business loans. The Office of Economic Opportunity (OEO) was created to coordinate the attack on poverty. In 1964 the war was launched with a miniscule budget of only $800 million.

The War on Poverty never really got off the ground, because funds were diverted to the undeclared war in Southeast Asia. Donovan calculated that "the [funding for OEO] from fiscal years 1965 to 1973 cost approximately $15.5 billion. Expenditures for the war in Vietnam during the same period totalled some $120 billion."[4] Investigations of poverty and hunger in the mid- and late 1960s confirmed the need for a reversal in American priorities.

In early 1967 the Senate Subcommittee on Employment, Manpower, and Poverty held hearings to determine whether hunger and malnutrition were serious problems in America.[5] The testimony, primarily by civil rights leaders and workers, portrayed severe conditions of poverty, unemployment, and hunger in many areas of the South. The hearings were widely publicized and prompted two subcommittee members, Robert Kennedy of New York and Joseph Clark of Pennsylvania, to tour the Mississippi countryside personally. The senators returned to Washington to tell of squalid poverty among blacks living and working on plantations, as well as among blacks placed outside the job market by farm automation.

The initial hearings by the subcommittee had also prompted the Field Foundation, a privately financed group long interested in the plight of the poor, to send a delegation of four doctors to Mississippi to study the medical conditions of Head Start children. The medical team issued a report

"This Is War?"

From *The Herblock Gallery* (Simon & Schuster, 1968).

entitled "Children in Mississippi," which described extensive disease among poor children, hopelessly inadequate diets, and pervasive hunger. In part the report said:

> We saw children being fed communally—that is by neighbors who give scraps of food to children whose own parents have nothing to give them. Not only are there children receiving no food from the government, they are also getting no medical attention whatsoever. They are out of sight and ignored. They are living under such primitive conditions that we found it hard to believe we were examining American children of the twentieth century![6]

During the summer of 1967 the subcommittee held additional hearings on hunger and malnutrition. The Field Foundation's medical team and numerous other experts testified. Among other points, researchers provided the following testimony, indicating that, in 1967:

1. we knew more about the nutritional status of persons in 31 underdeveloped countries of the world than of Americans, rich or poor;

2. we were better informed about the nutritional content of the food fed to our dogs, cattle, and pigs than about human food;

3. the diet of the poor in Mississippi was uniformly worse than had been that of the average southern family with less than $2,000 annual income in 1955—twelve years earlier;

4. poverty children lagged from six months to two-and-a-half years behind their peers in physical development; 34 percent were badly anemic; 33 percent suffered severe shortages of Vitamin A (of which fortified milk is a primary source); and 16 percent lacked adequate amounts of Vitamin C.[7]

During these hearings, Dr. Raymond Wheeler, a North Carolina physician and one of the Field Foundation's medical team, charged that black poverty in Mississippi was so shameful that he had concluded, along with many others, that white politicians were trying to drive poor blacks out of the state before they became powerful enough to vote whites out of power. Mississippi Senators John Stennis and James Eastland, both of whom had been particularly vocal in their denunciation of "hunger fighters" and the subversive idea that hunger was a serious problem in Mississippi or any other part of America, fumed at the charges. "Gross libel and slander," charged Stennis; "Totally untrue," replied Eastland. Nick Kotz described the scene that followed:

Dr. Wheeler looked straight at the Mississippi senators and stated softly: "I am distressed and concerned that Senators Stennis and Eastland interpret my remarks as libelous to the state of Mississippi. I was born and reared and educated in the South. I love the region.

"Throughout these years my heart has wept for the South as I have watched the southern Negro and the southern white walk their separate ways, distrusting each other, separated by false and ridiculous barriers, doomed to a way of life tragically less than they deserve, when by working together, they could achieve a society finer and more successful than any which exists today in this country.

"Throughout all that dreadful pageant of ignorance and suspicion and mutual distrust, the most distressing figure of all has been the southern political leader who has exploited all our human weaknesses for his own personal and selfish gains, refusing to grant us the dignity and capability of responding to courageous and noble leadership when all of us had nothing to lose but the misery and the desolation which surrounds all our lives.

"The time has come when this must cease, for we are now concerned with little children whose one chance for a healthy, productive, dignified existence is at stake.

"I invite Senators Eastland and Stennis to come with me into the vast farmlands of the Delta, and I will show them the children of whom we have spoken. I will show them their bright eyes and innocent faces, their shriveled arms and swollen bellies, their sickness and pain, and the misery of their parents.

"Their story must be believed, not only for their sakes, but for the sake of all America."

The huge auditorium of the New Senate Office Building was silent. Then Senator Clark, his voice unsteady, asked, "Senator Eastland, would you care to ask any questions?"

"I have no questions," Senator Eastland replied.

"Senator Stennis?" Clark asked.

"I have no questions," answered Stennis.[8]

The publicity surrounding the subcommittee's hearings had stimulated the interest of The Citizens' Crusade Against Poverty, a group founded in 1965. The group's main backers were the United Auto Workers, the National Council of Churches, the United Presbyterian Church, and the Ford Foundation. Under the leadership of Richard Boone, the Citizens' Crusade began to conduct preliminary research into the extent of poverty in America. The initial investigation convinced the group that the problem was a real one and that an in-depth study of poverty and hunger should be carried out. The Field Foundation, under the direction of Leslie Dunbar, decided to finance the study and join forces with the Citizens' Crusade to carry out the project. The two groups combined their efforts to form the Citizens' Board of Inquiry into Hunger and Malnutrition in the United States.

The Citizens' Board conducted investigations, held hearings, and reported its findings in late 1967 and 1968. What the Citizens' Board found confirmed the worst suspicions. They discovered, within America's larger population, a population that might best be described as an underdeveloped nation. They reported "concrete evidence of chronic hunger and malnutrition in every part of the United States where we have held hearings or conducted field trips."[9] Those living in poverty suffered a high incidence of anemia, growth retardation, protein deficiencies, and other signs of malnutrition. Parasites and worm infestation among the poor were common. Rickets and even marasmus and kwashiorkor, diseases caused by severe malnutrition and hunger, were found. Poor children were described as often having distended bellies, bulging, dull eyes, falling hair, and severely decreased alertness. Senator Robert Kennedy summarized some of the findings of board members:

1. They found that American babies die in infancy, because their mothers cannot nurse them and cannot buy the milk to keep them alive.

2. They found that thousands of American children are anemic and listless, their physical growth stunted because they lack adequate protein.

3. They found that scurvy and rickets, surely diseases of an alien past, cripple American children who never drink citrus juice, and who rarely drink milk.

4. They found that American children in large numbers suffer from hookworms and roundworms, parasitic infections that drain what strength these children have.

5. They found that hundreds of thousands of school children cannot learn their lessons, because they go to school without breakfast, have no money for lunch, and return to a supper without meat or green vegetables.

6. And they found that countless old people in America exist almost entirely on liquids, because they cannot buy or find a decent meal.[10]

Despite these terrible findings, many of the most powerful members of Congress remained unconvinced. In late 1967, W.A. (Bob) Poage (D.-Tex.), Chair of the House Agriculture Committee, railed against an emergency food program for the hungry poor. Poage literally shouted that the bill was so loosely drawn that he could get "food when his wife was out of town."[11] Poage managed to get his committee to kill the bill, keeping it from going to the House floor for debate. Late that month in another hearing for the poor, Poage revealed his own plan for dealing with America's hungry poor. In response to a startled Urban Coalition witness, Poage asked why he was "so concerned in maintaining a bunch of drones. You know what happens in the beehive? They kill those drones. That is what happens in most primitive societies. Maybe we have just gotten too far away from the situation of primitive man."[12]

Despite continuing hostility toward the poor by some members of Congress, the revelations of acute poverty and hunger in America had made an indelible impression on many political leaders and the media and had activated numerous private groups on behalf of the poor. Additionally, while the war in Asia stalled the attack on poverty, the hundreds of hostile outbursts and riots that occurred in U.S. cities between 1964 and 1969[13] prompted increased attention to the needs of the poor. To put out the fires that were literally burning down parts of the nation's major cities, Congress passed several important civil rights bills in the 1960s and increased allocations for employment training, job creation, and public-assistance programs.[14]

Still, poverty programs grew very slowly. As late as 1970, the major cash-assistance program, Aid to Families with Dependent Children (AFDC), had total expenditures of only $4.8 billion. The food-stamp program had a total budget of only $577 million in 1970. Medicaid and Medicare were established in 1965, but funding was very low until the early 1970s (see Chapter 6). The Supplemental Security Income (SSI) program for the aged, disabled, and blind was not enacted until 1973.

By 1973, however, funding for all the major programs had increased substantially, with considerable increases occurring in 1974 and 1975 (see Chapter 5). In 1975, the federal, state, and local governments were spending six times as much for cash and in-kind programs to aid the poor as they had in 1968. But, according to the government's official poverty count, the number of poor has not steadily decreased with increased expenditures. Using a back-dated standard, the Social Security Administration (SSA) calculated that 40 million Americans were impoverished in 1959. By 1968 the number of poor had dropped to 25.4 million. In 1973 and 1974 the poverty count showed about 23 million poor. Then, in 1975, the poverty count actually rose to 25.9 million, the largest number of poor since 1967 and the largest increase in poverty for any one-year period during the years of SSA's official poverty count (see Table 2.1, pp. 19). In 1976, 25 million Americans were counted among the poor, about the same number of poor counted in 1971.

THE CONTINUATION OF POVERTY

Why in the face of increased funding has poverty remained so high and even shown signs of increasing? Much of the discussion in this book focuses on that question. Briefly, we can identify three reasons for the continuation of poverty. These topics will be dealt with in more depth in later chapters.

The Root Causes of Poverty

While welfare expenditures have increased substantially in the 1970s, the basic causes of poverty are often not affected by these expenditures, or they may be affected in only a limited, incremental manner. For example, as noted in Chapter 7, much poverty in America is caused by unemployment. Unemployment has affected as many as eight to ten million persons per month in recent years. In 1975 the increase in the poverty count was caused by an unemployment rate that averaged 8.5 percent. Underemployment also causes poverty. Millions of Americans work full-time year-round at jobs that simply do not pay a living wage. Welfare programs are generally not designed to expand the job market or eliminate the large number of poverty jobs.

Discrimination against certain Americans in the housing market, in education, and in job selection and promotion also causes some persons to be poor. The Civil Rights Act of 1964 prohibited such discrimination, but enforcement has been slow.[15] In a slack job market, enforcement is particularly difficult. As figures presented later in the text show, minorities and women are still represented very poorly in the better-paying jobs in America and their median earnings are far below those of white males. The trend in recent years for more women to head families has elevated the impact of sexual discrimination as a cause of poverty.

Problems with Welfare Programs

For the most part, welfare programs are not designed to end poverty, and they serve only some of the poor. The major cash-assistance program is AFDC. Cash grants under AFDC vary from state to state, but even in the most generous states the grants are not large enough to help families escape poverty. In many states the grants are pitifully small. The same is true of SSI and state general assistance. Even multiple aid from a number of programs is often not enough to help the poor escape poverty.

The benefits are purposefully kept low, because poverty is generally regarded as a self-inflicted condition. To give the poor too much aid is thought to be tantamount to rewarding sin. Assistance to many impoverished groups is so low that it is a major cause of poverty.

Poverty among some groups is considered particularly inexcusable. Single persons (especially males), two-parent, male-headed families, and childless couples are generally excluded from cash-assistance programs, regardless of the reasons for their poverty or how hard they have tried to make it on their own. Even during periods of extremely high unemployment, only twenty-eight states allow an intact, male-headed family to receive AFDC benefits. Even in those states that allow male-headed families to qualify for aid, only a small proportion of all such impoverished families are actually assisted. Regardless of the state of the economy, none of the states allows single persons or childless couples to draw AFDC.

At worst, the combination of low benefits and exclusion creates a crisis situation for many of the poor. At best, the welfare programs only institutionalize poverty. It is the rare exception when poverty programs actually help the poor permanently break out of a cycle of abject poverty.

The Web of Poverty

Poverty creates mutually reinforcing conditions that handicap, and even sometimes debilitate, the poor. Even with the most forthright of efforts, many of the conditions created by poverty are not amenable to change over a short period of time. Equally important, without an honest appraisal of the factors that cause poverty and a change in the basic policy approach to the problem, the most serious societal conditions created by impoverishment are not likely to be overcome and the condition of poverty is not likely to be eradicated.

The entangling, reinforcing nature of poverty is often referred to as the cycle of poverty.[16] The 1964 *Economic Report of the President* describes this cycle:

A poor individual or family has a high probability of staying poor. Low incomes carry with them high risks of illness; limitations on mobility; limited access to education, information, and training. Poor parents cannot give their children the opportunities for better health and education needed to improve their lot. . . . Thus the cruel legacy of poverty is passed from parents to children.[17]

Welfare programs have had little effect on this vicious cycle. In many American cities the continuation of the cycle is distressingly obvious. The most concentrated and intensified poverty in America exists in the inner cities of major metropolitan areas. In 1976, 16.8 percent of all St. Louis residents were on welfare, as were 15.6 of all residents of Baltimore, 14.5 percent in Philadelphia, 14.2 percent in Washington, D.C., 14 percent in Boston, 13.2 percent in Newark, 11.5 percent in Detroit, 11.2 percent in New Orleans, 11 percent in New York, and 10.9 percent in Chicago.

It would not be too much to describe the urban cores of many of

America's largest cities as veritable seas of misery. A substantial proportion of all the housing in inner cities is substandard and/or severely over-crowded. In many cities, such as St. Louis, Detroit, Washington, D.C., Newark, and Cleveland, much of the central city is commonly referred to as the slums or the ghetto. Surrounding the slums are aging, stagnating neighborhoods that are seriously deteriorated and well on their way to ex-panding the slum area. These neighborhoods frequently house large num-bers of elderly persons who are trying desperately to hold onto their homes. Such peripheral neighborhoods are generally called "grey areas," or even grey ghettos.

Once neighborhoods reach a certain level of deterioration, they are almost beyond rehabilitation. Much of the housing in slum areas would cost more to repair than the property is worth. Many landlords make this calculation, renounce ownership, and simply have all services to a home or apartment turned off. A survey by the National Urban League found that as much as 20 percent of the housing in some central cities has been aban-doned.[18] Abandoned housing in a block can cause problems severe enough to drive citizens out of whatever livable housing may still be left in the neighborhood. Such buildings become the haunt of vandals or criminals, or even a source of entertainment for bored teenagers who set them on fire for the excitement of a visit by the local fire department. Thus, the devas-tation spreads, leaving literally block after block of housing with bashed-down doors, broken windows, ripped-out plumbing, and rubble-cluttered yards. The scene is often reminiscent of cities ravaged by war. The Urban League report concluded that: "The abandonment process has reached the stage where it poses a clear threat to the survival of certain central cities as viable environments for human habitation."[19]

For various reasons, even senior politicians are frequently unaware of the advanced state of deterioration of many American cities. In the fall of 1977 both President Carter and the majority leader of the United States House of Representatives toured the absolutely devastated East Harlem and South Bronx areas of New York City. Majority Leader Wright's reac-tions were revealing: "It was incredible, stark, unbelievable," Wright said, his voice quavering with emotion. "It's far worse than I ever imagined. I thought I understood the problems of the cities but I didn't fully compre-hend them. I don't understand them and very few of the members of Congress really do. And that also goes for the general public. . . . What I saw was too devastating to even be adequately described. But anyone would be shaken by it if they walked through that rubble and ruin."[20]

The severity of the impact of poor housing and deprived

neighborhoods on residents can hardly be exaggerated, but it is not widely appreciated by politicians or the public. As Anthony Downs has said:

> Most Americans have no conception of the filth, degradation, squalor, overcrowding, personal danger, and insecurity which millions of inadequate housing units are causing in both our cities and rural areas. Thousands of infants are attacked by rats each year; hundreds die or become mentally retarded from eating lead paint that falls off cracked walls; thousands more are ill because of unsanitary conditions resulting from jamming large families into a single room, continuing failure of landlords to repair plumbing or provide proper heat, and pitifully inadequate storage space.[21]

Quite naturally, such neighborhoods become a breeding ground for alienation, crime, and personal and economic exploitation. They not only severely limit opportunities for personal advancement, they often erect insurmountable barriers to even the most heroic efforts to better one's condition. The National Advisory Commission on Civil Disorders identified conditions in the ghetto as the *immediate* cause of numerous social problems. They concluded that ghetto conditions cause unemployment, crime, family disintegration, and

> generate a system of ruthless, exploitative relationships. . . . Prostitution, dope addiction, and crime create an environmental "jungle" characterized by personal insecurity and tension. Children growing up under such conditions are likely to participate in civil disorder.
>
> A striking difference in environment from that of white, middle-class Americans profoundly influences the lives of residents of the ghetto.
>
> Crime rates, consistently higher than in other areas, create a pronounced sense of insecurity. For example, in one city one low-income Negro district had 35 times as many serious crimes against persons as a high-income white district. Unless drastic steps are taken, the crime problems in poverty areas are likely to continue to multiply as the growing youth and rapid urbanization of the population outstrip police resources.
>
> Poor health and sanitation conditions in the ghetto result in higher mortality rates, a higher incidence of major diseases, and lower availability and utilization of medical review. The infant mortality rate for nonwhite babies under the age of one month is 58 percent higher than for whites; for one to twelve months it is almost three times as high.

The level of sanitation in the ghetto is far below that in high-income areas. Garbage collection is often inadequate. Of an estimated 14,000 cases of rat bite in the United States in 1965, most were in ghetto neighborhoods.

Ghetto residents believe they are exploited by local merchants; and evidence substantiates some of these beliefs. A study conducted in one city by the Federal Trade Commission showed that higher prices were charged for goods sold in ghetto stores than in other areas.[22]

In addition to all these problems, ghetto areas usually feature the highest rates of unemployment; inadequate transportation links to suburban neighborhoods where the better jobs are located; the worst educational systems; and, because of a declining tax base, very poor public services. Obviously these conditions perpetuate poverty from one generation to the next and contribute to crime, personal violence, broken families, and illiteracy.

Children born into these environments begin life waist deep in the quicksand of poverty and deprivation. As Birch and Gusson point out:

> Children who live in poverty live lives which are not merely intellectually depressing but physically destructive. Poor children are exposed to poor food, poor sanitation, poor housing, and poor medical care. The same homes which lack toys and games are the homes in which hunger and disease abound. To be poor in America . . . is to be assailed by a whole range of physical conditions which by endangering life, growth, and health, depress mental development and educational potential.
>
> For poor children are not merely born into poverty; they are born of poverty, and are thus at risk of defective development even before their births. The mothers of these children—exposed during their own childhoods to poor life conditions—come to maturity less well-grown and at greater biological risk as reproducers than do their more fortunate sisters. Beginning too young to bear children, such mothers repeat childbearing too often and continue it too long, through pregnancies in which their health is often poor, their nutrition suboptimal, and their medical care frequently nonexistent.[23]

Poverty, unrelenting and unmerciful, handicaps its victims severely and is rarely, as the American myth maintains, a builder of character. It is undeniably a part of our heritage, a problem that, over the course of two hundred years, has become a series of interrelated problems with a multiformity of victims. It is in no way exclusive in its impact; it devastates not just the poor but all of society. It wastes human potential, spawns social ills that affect everyone, and costs greatly in social programs designed to administer to the poor. Poverty can effectively be dealt with only through a series of coordinated programs carefully designed to deal with its diverse and deadly manifestations.

In the chapters that follow, we attempt to dissect American poverty, examine its causes, note the legislative and public response to it, and suggest some of the policies that will have to be enacted and carried out if poverty in the United States is to be eliminated.

NOTES

1. Michael Harrington, *The Other America: Poverty in the United States* (Baltimore: Penguin Books, 1963), p. 11.

2. Nick Kotz, *Let Them Eat Promises: The Politics of Hunger in America* (New York: Doubleday, 1971), p. 232.

3. For an overview, see John C. Donovan, *The Politics of Poverty* (Indianapolis: Bobbs-Merrill, 1973).

4. Ibid., p. 178.

5. No one has told the story of the struggle against hunger in the 1960s as well as Nick Kotz. Much of the discussion here is drawn from Kotz's book, *Let Them Eat Promises: The Politics of Hunger in America,* pp. 1–18.

6. Ibid., pp. 8 and 9.

7. Ibid., pp. 63–68.

8. Ibid., pp. 69–70.

9. *Hunger, USA: A Report by the Citizens' Board of Inquiry into Hunger and Malnutrition in the United States* (Boston: Beacon Press, 1968), p. 16.

10. Excerpts from a speech given by Robert F. Kennedy at Valparaiso University, Valparaiso, Indiana, April 29, 1968. Reprinted in *Hunger, USA,* p. 7.

11. Cited in Mark J. Green, James M. Fallows, and David R. Zwick, *Who Runs Congress?* (New York: Bantam Books, 1972), p. 79.

12. Ibid.

13. Bryan T. Downes reported that from 1964 to 1968 there were 225 hostile outbursts in American cities with 49,607 persons arrested, 7,942 wounded, and 191 killed. See "Social and Political Characteristics of Riot Cities: A Comparative Study," *Social Science Quarterly* 49 (December 1968): 509.

14. This thesis is documented in Francis Fox Piven and Richard A. Cloward, *Regulating the Poor: The Functions of Public Welfare* (New York: Vintage Books, 1971).

15. See Harrell R. Rodgers, Jr. and Charles S. Bullock, III, *Law and Social Change: Civil Rights Laws and Their Consequences* (New York: McGraw-Hill, 1972), pp. 113–139.

16. The concept was introduced by Gunnar Myrdal, *An American Dilemma: The Negro Problem and Modern Democracy* (New York: Harper & Row, 1942).

17. *The Economic Report of the President—1964* (Washington, D.C.: Government Printing Office, 1965), p. 7.

18. The Center for Community Change, The National Urban League, *The National Survey of Housing Abandonment,* 3d ed. (New York: The National Urban League, 1972), p. 88.

19. Ibid., p. 92.

20. Arthur Wiese, "Harlem, Bronx Visibly Shake Wright on Trip," *The Houston Post,* 16 October 1977, 4A.

21. Anthony Downs, "Housing," in Kermit Gorden, *Agenda for the Nation* (Washington, D.C.: Brookings Institution, 1968), pp. 141–142.

22. *National Advisory Commission on Civil Disorders, Report* (Washington, D.C.: Government Printing Office, 1967), pp. 6–7.

23. Herbert C. Birch and Joan Dye Gusson, *Disadvantaged Children: Health, Nutrition and School Failure* (New York: Harcourt, Brace & World, 1970), pp. xi–xii. Reprinted by permission.

2
POVERTY AND THE DISTRIBUTION OF WEALTH IN AMERICA

No one really knows exactly how much poverty there is in America. There is, in fact, no agreement about how poverty should be defined or measured. Any attempt at accurately defining and measuring poverty would have to consider dozens of variables and, consequently, would be quite complex. The federal government's poverty standards are defined and measured strictly in terms of dollar income. As we shall see, the calculations are flawed and provide only a crude approximation of the extent of poverty in the United States.

Poverty may be defined in absolute or relative terms. An absolute standard attempts to define some basic set of resources necessary for adequate existence. A relative standard attempts to define poverty in terms of the median standard of living in a society. A relative standard shows not only how many people cannot hope to live close to the average standard of a society, but also how evenly income is distributed among the population.

ABSOLUTE STANDARDS

The federal government defines poverty in absolute terms. Surprisingly perhaps, the government did not attempt to develop a poverty standard until the 1960s. The earliest poverty standard was developed by the Council of Economic Advisors (CEA) in 1964. The CEA standard relied on a Social Security Administration (SSA) study of the income needs of four-person, nonfarm families. The SSA study first used as its base a "low-cost" food budget prepared by the Department of Agriculture. The low-cost food budget was designed to provide a poor family with the minimum diet required to avoid basic nutritional deficiencies. The budget allowed twenty-eight cents per person per meal, or $3.36 per family per day. Since a 1955 Department of Agriculture study had shown that poor families spend about one-third of their budget on food, the food budget was multiplied by three to determine the poverty standard. This calculation produced a poverty threshold of $3,955.

Since $3,955 was considerably higher than welfare expenditures for poor families, SSA formulated a lower poverty standard. The new standard was based on an "economy" budget, which equalled about 80 percent of the low-cost diet. The new budget allowed expenditure of twenty-three cents per person per meal, or $2.74 per family per day.* When the new budget was multiplied by three, the poverty threshold was $3,165. Relying on this less expensive budget, CEA set the poverty standard for families at $3,000, and decided that half this amount would serve as the poverty line for a single individual.[1] Using this crude standard, the CEA found that 35 million people (about 20 percent of the total population) were poor in 1962.[2]

In 1965 the Social Security Administration published another study which updated and extended the poverty standard based on the economy food budget to various types of households.[3] This standard, known as the Orshanksky index after its author, was quickly adopted as the federal government's official measure of poverty. Table 2.1 shows the SSA poverty threshold for a nonfarm family of four back dated to 1959, and the number of persons counted as poor by year using the standard. Until 1969, the

---

* While theoretically the economy budget could adequately meet the nutritional needs of a family, its limitations were severe. For a meal for all four members of the family, only ninety-five cents could be spent. Meat had to be limited to one pound per day for all four members, and less than two dozen eggs could be purchased per month for all purposes. This, of course, would not even allow one egg per day per family member.

yearly changes in the poverty standard reflect changes in the cost of the economy budget. Since 1969 the standard has been adjusted yearly according to changes in the consumer price index.

TABLE 2.1

Poverty standard for family of four (nonfarm): 1959–1976

Year	Standard	Millions of poor	% of total population
1959	$2,973	39.5	22%
1960	3,022	39.9	22
1961	3,054	39.6	22
1962	3,089	38.6	21
1963	3,128	36.4	19
1964	3,169	36.1	19
1965	3,223	33.2	17
1966	3,317	30.4	16
1966*	3,317	28.5	15
1967	3,410	27.8	14
1968	3,553	25.4	13
1969	3,743	24.1	12
1970	3,968	25.4	13
1971	4,137	25.6	12.5
1972	4,275	24.5	12
1973	4,540	23.0	11
1974	5,038	24.3	12
1974*	5.038	23.4	11.5
1975	5,500	25.9	12
1976	5,815	25.0†	12†

Source: Derived from U.S. Bureau of the Census, "Characteristics of the Low-Income Population," *Current Population Reports,* Series P-60, various years.
* Revision in Census Calculations.
† See U.S. Bureau of the Census, "Money Income and Poverty Status of Families and Persons in the United States: 1976 (Advance Report)," *Current Population Reports,* Series P-60, no. 107, September 1977, p. 20.

Table 2.2 shows the poverty standard for various family sizes for 1976. Unlike CEA's fixed-dollar standard, the SSA standard varies by family size, the sex of the family head, and the family's place of residence. Farm families are presumed to need only 85 percent of the cash income required by nonfarm families (until 1969 they were presumed to need only 70 percent as much). The rate for single persons is adjusted up to compensate for the higher cost of living alone (the food budget is multiplied by 5.92 rather than by 3.0). The food budget for couples is multiplied

TABLE 2.2

Poverty standard: 1976

Size of family unit	Total	Nonfarm			Farm		
		Total	Male head	Female head	Total	Male head	Female head
1 person (unrelated individual)	$2,877	$2,884	$3,016	$2,788	$2,438	$2,532	$2,348
14 to 64	2,954	2,959	3,069	2,840	2,542	2,608	2,413
65 years and over	2,720	2,730	2,758	2,722	2,322	2,344	2,313
2 persons	3,688	3,711	3,721	3,660	3,128	3,133	3,033
Head 14 to 64 years	3,806	3,826	3,846	3,733	3,267	3,271	3,159
Head 65 years and over	3,417	3,445	3,447	3,428	2,928	2,928	2,922
3 persons	4,515	4,540	4,565	4,414	3,858	3,864	3,734
4 persons	5,786	5,815	5,818	5,790	4,950	4,953	4,840
5 persons	6,838	6,876	6,884	6,799	5,870	5,871	5,847
6 persons	7,706	7,760	7,766	7,709	6,585	6,584	6,607
7 persons and more	9,505	9,588	9,622	9,375	8,072	8,068	8,428

Source: U.S. Bureau of the Census, "Money Income and Poverty Status of Families and Persons in the United States: 1976 (Advance Report)," *Current Population Reports*, Series P-60, no. 107, 1977, p. 20.

by 3.88 to compensate for their higher costs. Female-headed families receive slightly less and elderly, two-person families are presumed to need 8 percent less than nonelderly, two-person families.

The SSA standard indicates that substantial progress toward eliminating poverty was made in the 1960s, with some reversal occurring in the 1970s. In 1959 there were almost 40 million American poor, but the count dropped to 25.4 million by 1968. In 1973 and 1974 (revised figures) poverty declined to about 23 million. However, in 1975, poverty increased by 2.5 million persons over 1974, and actually exceeded the poverty count for every year back to 1967. In 1976 there were 25 million poor.

The 10.7 percent increase in poverty in 1975 represented the largest increase in the seventeen years that SSA had been calculating a standard (see Table 2.1). The increase was brought about by record unemployment (8.5 percent in 1975), serious inflation, and the fact that 4.3 million persons exhausted their unemployment benefits in 1975 (up from 2.0 million in 1974). In addition, the buying power of families fell 2.6 percent, even though median family income rose by $818 to $13,720. This followed a 3.5 percent decline in consumer purchasing power in 1974, the fourth drop in a six-year period. The decrease of some 900,000 in the poverty count for 1976 reflected some improvement in the economy. In 1976 median family income was $14,960, an increase of about 9 percent over the 1975 median. The inflation rate was 6 percent in 1976, leaving an increase of 3 percent in real median family income in 1976.

Table 2.3 shows the breakdown of the poverty population by state in both 1970 and 1975. Most of the increase in poverty between those years occurred in the Northeast, the mid-Atlantic states, the West, and the Pacific states. Still, the largest number of poor live in the South. As Table 2.3 shows, in 1975 some 10 percent of the population in the Northeast were poor, compared to 9.2 percent in the Midwest, 11.7 percent in the West, and 16.4 percent in the South. In the eight states in the south central United States, an average of 19.3 percent of all citizens were poor, with a high of 32.2 percent of the population of Mississippi living in poverty.

While the standard shows a large number of poor even in recent years, it is undoubtedly not an accurate reflection of poverty in the United States. One major reason is that the standard is set unrealistically low. For example, in 1976 the poverty threshold for a nonfarm family of four was $5,815. This standard allowed $1,454 per person per year, or $3.98 a day, one-third being the allotment for food ($1.32). The family could spend a

TABLE 2.3

Poverty by state, 1970, 1975

	Total population 1975 (thousands)	Poverty population 1970 (thousands)	Est. poverty population 1975 (thousands)	Percent of total in poverty
Northeast	49,461	4,822	4,939	10.0%
New England	12,198	1,034	1,032	8.5
Maine	1,059	131	114	10.8
New Hampshire	818	65	63	7.7
Vermont	471	52	41	8.7
Massachusetts	5,828	473	489	8.4
Rhode Island	927	100	93	10.0
Connecticut	3,095	212	233	7.5
Mid-Atlantic	37,263	3,788	3,908	10.5
New York	18,120	1,986	2,208	12.2
New Jersey	7,316	574	601	8.2
Pennsylvania	11,827	1,228	1,099	9.3
Midwest	57,669	5,951	5,329	9.2
Great Lakes	40,979	3,886	3,563	8.7
Ohio	10,759	1,041	947	8.8
Indiana	5,311	493	400	7.5
Illinois	11,145	1,112	1,109	9.9
Michigan	9,157	819	715	7.8
Wisconsin	4,607	421	393	8.5
Great Plains	16,690	2,065	1,766	10.6
Minnesota	3,926	398	326	8.3
Iowa	2,870	319	251	8.7
Missouri	4,763	672	579	12.2
Kansas	2,267	275	256	11.3
Nebraska	1,546	188	164	10.6
South Dakota	683	120	109	16.0
North Dakota	635	93	80	12.6
South	68,113	12,288	11,159	16.4
South Atlantic	33,715	5,142	4,531	13.4
Delaware	579	58	57	9.8
Maryland	4,098	387	336	8.2
DC	716	123	128	18.0
Virginia	4,967	691	536	10.8
West Virginia	1,803	380	361	20.0
North Carolina	5,451	996	765	14.0
South Carolina	2,818	595	488	17.3
Georgia	4,926	924	754	15.3
Florida	8,357	1,088	1,107	13.2
South Central	34,399	7,146	6,628	19.3
Kentucky	3,396	718	649	19.1
Tennessee	4,188	836	709	16.9
Alabama	3,614	857	770	21.3
Mississippi	2,346	767	755	32.2

	Total population 1975 (thousands)	Poverty population 1970 (thousands)	Est. poverty population 1975 (thousands)	Percent of total in poverty
Louisiana	3,791	933	926	24.4%
Arkansas	2,116	523	474	22.4
Oklahoma	2,712	465	444	16.4
Texas	12,237	2,047	1,900	15.5
West	37,878	3,965	4,450	11.7
Mountain	9,644	1,137	1,194	12.4
Montana	748	92	98	13.1
Idaho	820	92	107	13.0
Wyoming	374	38	46	12.3
Colorado	2,534	263	176	6.9
Utah	1,206	118	143	11.9
Nevada	592	43	53	8.9
Arizona	2,224	264	291	13.1
New Mexico	1,147	227	280	24.4
Pacific	28,234	2,828	3,256	11.5
California	21,185	2,153	2,521	11.9
Oregon	2,288	235	280	12.2
Washington	2,544	336	356	14.0
Alaska	352	35	38	11.0
Hawaii	865	69	61	7.0
Total U.S.	213,121	27,026	25,877	12.0

Source: Joel Havemann and Linda E. Demkovich, "Making Some Sense Out of the Welfare 'Mess,' " *National Journal,* January 8, 1977, p. 50. Reprinted by permission.

total of $1.76 per meal for all four persons, or $36.96 per week on food. A budget for a four-person family would look like this:

$1,938.33 for food: $1.32 a day (44 cents per meal) per person; $9.24 per week per person.

$1,938.33 for shelter: $162.53 a month for rent or mortgage for four persons.

$1,938.33 for necessities: $40.63 a month per person for clothing, furniture, transportation, health care, utilities, taxes, entertainment, etc.

Quite obviously, it would take herculean efforts for a family of four to survive adequately on this budget. The food budget is too small and, as we shall see, more recent studies show that the relationship between food costs and other family needs should have been adjusted years ago. One dollar and seventy-six cents per meal for four persons is simply unrealistic. The budget for shelter and other necessities is also inadequate. A recent congressional study found that "in many urban areas, rent takes 50 percent or more of income for almost half of poor families—and rent and utilities are fixed expenditures, while food is a flexible budget item and, thus, the first to give in a pinch."[4] There is evidence to support the suspicion that food needs are often unfulfilled within the poverty budget. In 1963 the Department of Agriculture found that "63 percent of those trying to live on its minimum diet were suffering from malnutrition."[5] In 1974, when the food-stamp program was in full operation, the Senate Select Committee on Nutrition and Human Needs reported that chicken and beef were vanishing from the diets of poor people. The substitute that some of the poor seemed to have turned to was pet food. The Committee reported that "as much as one-third of the pet foods sold in ghetto areas are being used for human consumption. For areas with high proportions of elderly poor, the estimates [are] even higher."[6]

Of course, some of the problem resulted from the fact that many poor families did not have as much income as the poverty standard for their family size. In 1975, the median income deficit for poor families was $1,500 below the poverty level for their family size ($1,395 for white families, $1,805 for black families). Some 7.7 million persons in families and unrelated individuals had incomes that were less than 50 percent of the poverty level for their family size; 7.6 million had incomes that were between 50 and 74 percent of their poverty level; and 10.6 million had incomes that were between 75 to 99 percent of their poverty level.

Interestingly, another agency of the federal government that calculates an absolute standard for public income needs arrives at very different conclusions than those of the SSA. The Bureau of Labor Statistics (BLS) annually calculates budgets that reflect the income needed by families to enjoy a moderate, austere, or modestly luxurious life-style. In 1975 the BLS calculated that a nonfarm family of four would require $15,138 for a moderate life-style. This standard is far out of the reach of the poor (it is almost triple the poverty standard). An austere life-style could have been sustained on $9,588, 74 percent more than the poverty standard. If $9,588 were used as the poverty threshold for a nonfarm family of four in 1975, some 65 million Americans would have been judged poor. This would overestimate destitution, but it would probably not seriously exaggerate economic hardship. The general public's estimate of the financial needs of a family of four are much closer to the BLS's calculations than the official standard developed by SSA. Each year since the 1930s, the Gallup Poll has asked citizens to estimate the minimum budget they believe a nonfarm family of four needs to make ends meet. In 1974 they suggested $7,904; in 1975, $8,732; and in 1976, $9,204.[7]

In addition to being unrealistically low, there are numerous other problems with the government's standards. The major ones are discussed briefly below.

Regional variations There are no regional variations in the index to compensate for higher costs in many urban areas and in some sections of the country. Housing costs in New York, San Francisco, or Boston, for example, are certainly greater than in most cities in the South. Variations in other costs (an obvious one being state and local taxes) are also frequently severe. The Bureau of Labor Statistics calculates cost-of-living variations that could be incorporated into the poverty index. The SSA also calculates some of the variations but does not apply them to its standards.[8]

Rural versus urban The 15 percent reduction for farm families is not supported by empirical evidence. While some persons in rural areas may be able to grow some of their own food and may incur lower housing costs, many necessities in rural areas are more expensive. Food prices are often higher in rural areas because of the lack of large supermarkets and because it costs more to transport products to rural areas. Additionally, rural residents may have to travel considerable distances for needed services and thus may suffer higher transportation costs. An obvious example would be the travel necessary to obtain medical care, which is frequently not available in rural areas.

The food budget Since the food plan is the base of the poverty standard, its calculation is critical. Quite clearly, SSA did not decide to use the economy budget as a base because it was deemed adequate for poor people's needs. It was chosen because it kept the poverty standard low. Wilcox reports that SSA originally designed the economy budget for temporary or emergency use only, but decided to use it permanently because more adequate budgets showed too much poverty.[9] In July 1975, the SSA substituted a "thrifty" food budget for the economy budget. The new budget reflects changes in RDA food standards, in public purchasing habits, and in food manufacturing.[10] The new budget, however, has little bearing on the poverty standard, for it does not provide a more generous allowance for food purchases.[11]

The multiplication rate The assumption that food expenditures account for one-third of poor people's budgets is based on a 1955 study. More recent studies indicate that poor people spend about 28 percent of their income on food.[12] Thus, the food budget should be multiplied by a factor closer to 3.4 rather than 3. This would increase the poverty standard substantially.

Table 2.4 provides some examples based on a 1976 study by the Department of Health, Education and Welfare. The figures show that the poverty standard would be substantially affected by changing the food budget to make it more realistic, and/or by changing the food-budget ratio. All the figures in Table 2.4 are based on a multiplier of 3.4 rather than 3. Notice that with this multiplier, 39.9 million persons would have been judged poor in 1974 using the thrifty food budget (the threshold would be $6,360 for an urban family of four). If the food budget were based on only 80 percent of the low-cost plan and a multiplier of 3.4 were used, 41.4 million persons would have been counted poor (the threshold would be $6,494 for an urban family of four). Using the more realistic low-cost budget and a 3.4 multiplier, the poverty threshold would be raised to $8,118 for a family of four and would have yielded a staggering poverty count of 55.4 million. As you may have already observed in Table 2.4, changing the multiplication factor alone increases the number of poor by 15.6 million persons. Changing both the budget and the multiplication factor increases the number of poor by 31.1 million persons.

Pretax income The poverty standard reflects gross, not net, income. An urban family of four with an income of $5,600 in 1975 would not be considered poor by the poverty standard, but their net (or take-home) pay would be considerably less than the poverty standard after deductions for taxes, Social Security, retirement, and insurance.

Median-income ratio Another indication that the poverty standard has been kept unrealistically low is its slipping relationship to United States median-income levels. Median income has increased much faster than the poverty threshold. In 1959 the poverty standard was 54 percent of median income. By 1975 the poverty standard was only 40 percent of median income, and it dropped to 39 percent in 1976. For some family sizes, there is an even greater disparity. For example, in 1974, the poverty standard for a four-person family was only 34 percent of the median income for all four-person families.[13]

TABLE 2.4

Size of the poor population under current and revised poverty cutoffs, 1974 (in millions)

	United States population	Using official poverty cutoffs	The poor Using revised poverty cutoffs*				
			80% of low-cost plan condensed family size	Thrifty plan	80% of low-cost plan	Low-cost plan
Persons	209.3	24.3	39.2	39.9	41.4	55.4
Families	55.7	5.1	8.8	8.7	9.0	12.8
Unrelated individuals	18.9	4.8	8.4	8.2	8.4	9.2
Children ages 5–17	49.8	7.5	10.4	11.1	11.6	15.4

Source: U.S. Department of Health, Education and Welfare, *The Measure of Poverty* (Washington, D.C.: Government Printing Office, 1976), p. 77.

* The poverty level for a nonfarm family of four would be $6,494 under the 80 percent condensed family budget; $6,366 under the thrifty budget; $6,494 under the 80 percent of low-cost budget; $8,118 under the low-cost budget.

In-kind benefits and assets While cash-income security payments (e.g., Social Security and Unemployment Compensation) and cash-assistance benefits (e.g., AFDC, SSI, and general assistance) are included in SSA's measures of income, neither assets nor in-kind benefits such as food stamps and Medicaid are included (these programs are explained in Chapters 5 and 6). Since some families (especially elderly ones) may have low incomes but assets they can draw on, the failure to include assets distorts the poverty calculations. Admittedly, some possessions might be difficult to evaluate, but others are easily identified and noncontroversial. While it might be arguable whether a four-year-old car is an asset or a liability, bank deposits, stocks, and bonds should obviously be taken into consideration.[14]

The failure to include in-kind benefits is even more severe. In-kind benefits such as food stamps are quite expensive ($5.7 billion in 1976), go to a large number of people (between seventeen and nineteen million per year recently), and definitely improve the life of recipients. A recent study by Smeeding concluded that if the poverty figures were adjusted for underreporting of income by the poor, taxes paid by the poor, and receipt of in-kind benefits, the number of persons below the poverty line would have been 8.7 percent of all persons in 1968 (rather than 13 percent), 8.0 in 1970 (rather than 13 percent), and 5.4 in 1974 (rather than 12 percent). This would drop the poverty count down to some seventeen million in 1968 and 1970, and some eleven million in 1972.[15]

A study by the Congressional Budget Office reached similar conclusions for fiscal year 1976 (see Table 2.5). Before any transfer income, 20,237 households (25.5 percent of all households) were below the poverty threshold. Social-insurance payments (Social Security) reduced the number of poor households to 11,179. Adding cash assistance reduced poor households to 9,073. In-kind aid reduced the number to 5,336, and adjustments for taxes paid raised the number slightly to 5,445 households. This would leave 6.9 percent of all households, or about 14,157 million persons, in poverty.

Consumer price index The 1969 decision of SSA to base increases in the poverty standard on changes in the consumer price index rather than on actual increases in food prices seems quite illogical. In the 1970s the cost of food has increased about twice as fast as the overall prices reflected by the CPI. Thus, the poverty standard has been kept artificially low by this decision. There is, in fact, empirical evidence that poor people's costs are much different than those of middle- and upper-income citizens. It would be much more accurate to adjust the poverty standard according to actual changes in poor people's costs.[16]

TABLE 2.5
Households below the poverty level under alternative income definitions: fiscal year 1976

Households in poverty	Pretax/ pretransfer income	Pretax/ post-social- insurance income	Pretax/ post-money- transfer income	Pretax/ post-in-kind- transfer income		Posttax/ post-total- transfer income
				I*	II	
Number in thousands	20,237	11,179	9,073	7,406	5,336	5,445
Percent of all families	25.5	14.1	11.4	9.3	6.7	6.9

Source: Congressional Budget Office, *Poverty Status of Families Under Alternative Definitions of Income* (Washington, D.C.: Government Printing Office, 1977), p. xv.
* Excludes Medicare and Medicaid payments.

In sum, the defects in the SSA measures run in both directions. Some of the households counted among the poor have incomes in excess of SSA standards. But there are also millions of people who, although they earn more than the poverty standard, constitute the uncounted poor, because the poverty standard is set unrealistically low. The obvious question is: Do the various defects in the SSA standard offset one another and thereby yield a fairly accurate image of American poverty? This seems doubtful, but the government has not attempted to conduct this type of analysis.

An educated guess would be that, with all its flaws, the SSA standard underestimates poverty. When adjustments for in-kind benefits and taxes are made, they reduce the number of poor by about ten to fifteen million.* Yet, adjustments in food budgets and the multiplication factor show that the poverty standards underestimate the poor by anywhere from fifteen to thirty-one million (see Table 2.3). Since most in-kind benefits go to persons in the lowest income quintile (see Chapters 5 and 6), those persons not counted in the poverty estimates because of the unrealistically low thresholds are unlikely to be receiving in-kind aid. They are, however, more likely to be paying significant taxes. Thus, a much improved measure that considered in-kind benefits, taxes paid, unreporting of income, and raised the food budget and multiplication factor would probably show anywhere from five to twenty million additional poor.

RELATIVE STANDARDS

Some have argued that absolute standards of poverty should be replaced by a relative standard. A relative standard defines poverty not in terms of the basic resources required for subsistence but in terms of the ability to enjoy a life-style that is at least close to the modal standard of living in a society. Peter Townsend describes the spirit of a relative standard: "Individuals, families and groups in the population can be said to be in poverty when they lack the resources to obtain the types of diets, participate in activities, and have the living conditions and amenities which are customary, or are at least widely encouraged or approved, in the societies to which they belong."[17]

---

* A serious flaw in studies that make adjustments for in-kind benefits is that they assume the value of the benefit is worth its actual cost to the government. Often this is not the case. For example, the value of medical care rendered to a poor person by a Medicaid mill may be much less than its cost—in fact, the care may be absolutely worthless or even harmful. See Michael Harrington, "Hiding the Other America," *The New Republic*, February 26, 1977, pp. 15–17.

The most obvious way to formulate a relative definition would be to peg it to median income. The poor might be defined as those who earn less than 50 percent of the median income for their family size. For example, in 1974 the median income for four-person families was $14,747. Any four-person family with a median income of less than $7,373, then, would be considered poor. This calculation would raise the poverty level for a four-person family in 1974 by some 46 percent, and increase the poverty count significantly.

Economist Lester Thurow suggests a variation of the relative approach. Thurow suggests adopting the notion of a poverty band rather than a poverty line.

> No one can logically define and defend any precise dollar figure as the poverty line or as equally valid for all uses. This would be true if there were no problems in defining and calculating a comprehensive income measure . . . . There should be recognition that there is a band over which definite poverty shades into economic sufficient. . . .[18]

Like the Townsend standard, this definition would require a more flexible poverty line that would take into account the fact that a certain amount of income is necessary to maintain a family at or close to the median level in society. Once a family (or individual) slipped below this level, it would enter the poverty band, and any further significant slippage would thrust the family into poverty. This kind of standard would indicate not only how many persons live in poverty, but also how many live close to destitution and definitely in economic hardship.

Relative standards have both advantages and disadvantages. The most obvious disadvantage is that median income tends to be highest for couples with one to three children. As the number of children increases, median family income declines. Measuring poverty by some proportion of the median income of large families would suggest that poor families with large numbers of children need less income than do average-sized families. Similar inequities would result for single individuals or single-parent families. The poverty-band idea also would create an obvious problem. Assistance programs have to be oriented toward persons with specific needs. To keep the programs from being wasteful, the needs of poor families frequently have to be defined rather carefully.

While relative standards have drawbacks, they also provide valuable insights. The major attraction of the relative standard is that it would more clearly delineate the overall distribution of wealth in America. A recent study by the Department of Health, Education and Welfare revealed that if the poverty line were based on 50 percent of median family income, it would show that about 19 percent of all families were poor during every year back to 1959.[19] This indicates little change in the distribution of income, although in-kind benefits are not taken into consideration.* A relative standard also draws attention to the fact that millions of Americans live just above the absolute poverty line for their family size. In 1974, for example, 34.6 million Americans lived below 125 percent of the poverty level for their family size. Forty-five million persons lived below 150 percent of the poverty level for their family size, and 69.4 million persons lived below 200 percent of the poverty level for their family size. In 1975, 37.2 million Americans lived below 125 percent of the poverty level for their family size, as did 35.5 million persons in 1976.[20]

THE DISTRIBUTION OF INCOME

The large number of individuals who earn very low incomes indicates either a shortage of total income in American society or severe maldistribution of the income that is available. The evidence clearly indicates that the problem is maldistribution. If in 1976 the total income earned in America was equally divided among every man, woman, and child, each person would have received $6,441.[21] For a four-person family this would be an income of $25,764. However, because of the actual distribution of income, the median income for families in 1975 was $14,960 and millions of families received very low incomes. For example, in 1976, 18.2 percent of all families earned less than $7,000, 22 percent received less than $8,000, and 30 percent earned less than $10,000. Among unrelated individuals, 47 percent earned less than $5,000 and 75 percent earned less than $10,000 (see Table 2.6).

Income has always been severely maldistributed in America. As Table 2.7 shows, since 1947 the poorest 20 percent of American families have received some 5 percent of before-tax income yearly, while the richest 20 percent have consistently received over 40 percent of all before-tax income. If the fourth and fifth richest groups are combined, this top 40 percent have consistently received an average of almost 66 percent of all before-tax income. Indeed, the richest 20 percent have consistently received more income than the combined bottom 60 percent.

---

* In considering the distribution of income, in-kind benefits would have to be calculated for all income groups if an accurate picture is to be developed (see Chapter 3).

TABLE 2.6

Families and unrelated individuals by total money income in 1976

Total money income	% of families*	% of unrelated individuals†
Under $2,000	2.0%	12.4%
2,000 to 2,999	1.9	14.7
3,000 to 3,999	3.1	11.9
4,000 to 4,999	3.4	8.2
5,000 to 5,999	3.9	7.2
6,000 to 6,999	3.9	6.2
7,000 to 7,999	3.9	5.5
8,000 to 8,999	4.1	4.9
9,000 to 9,999	3.8	4.3
10,000 to 10,999	4.2	4.6
11,000 to 11,999	3.9	2.9
12,000 to 12,999	4.1	3.0
13,000 to 13,999	4.1	2.0
14,000 to 14,999	3.9	2.0
15,000 to 15,999	4.4	1.8
16,000 to 16,999	3.8	1.4
17,000 to 17,999	4.0	1.1
18,000 to 19,999	6.9	1.7
20,000 to 24,999	12.9	2.1
25,000 to 49,999	15.9	1.7
50,000 and over	1.9	0.3
Median income	$14,958	$5,375
Mean income	$16,870	$7,236

Source: U.S. Bureau of the Census, "Money Income and Poverty Status of Families and Persons in the United States: 1976 (Advance Report)," *Current Population Reports,* Series P-60, no. 107, September 1977, p. 2.
* Based on a total of 56,710,000 families.
† Based on a total of 21,459,000 unrelated individuals.

In actuality, income maldistribution is considerably more severe than the figures in Table 2.7 indicate. The figures are based on data that include welfare payments for the poor, but do not include such items as realized and unrealized capital gains, which go primarily to wealthy individuals. In a recent study, Peckman and Okner adjusted the data for wage supplements, capital gains, the value of the services of owner-occupied homes, and indirect business taxes. These adjustments reduced the income of the poorest 20 percent by 0.6 percentage points and increased that of the wealthiest fifth by 5.3 percentage points.[22]

TABLE 2.7

Distribution of before-tax income

	Income rankings					
Year	Lowest fifth	Second fifth	Middle fifth	Fourth fifth	Highest fifth	Highest five percent
1947	5.1	11.8	16.7	23.2	43.3	17.5
1948	5.0	12.1	17.2	23.2	42.5	17.1
1949	4.5	11.9	17.3	23.5	42.8	16.9
1950	4.5	11.9	17.4	23.6	42.7	17.3
1951	4.9	12.5	17.6	23.3	41.8	16.9
1952	4.9	12.2	17.1	23.5	42.2	17.7
1953	4.7	12.4	17.8	24.0	41.0	15.8
1954	4.5	12.0	17.6	24.0	41.9	16.4
1955	4.8	12.2	17.7	23.4	41.8	16.8
1956	4.9	12.4	17.9	23.6	41.1	16.4
1957	5.0	12.6	18.1	23.7	40.5	15.8
1958	5.0	12.5	18.0	23.9	40.6	15.4
1959	4.9	12.3	17.9	23.8	41.1	15.9
1960	4.8	12.2	17.8	24.0	41.3	15.9
1961	4.7	11.9	17.5	23.8	42.2	16.6
1962	5.0	12.1	17.6	24.0	41.3	15.7
1963	5.0	12.1	17.7	24.0	41.2	15.8
1964	5.1	12.0	17.7	24.0	41.2	15.9
1965	5.2	12.2	17.8	23.9	40.9	15.5
1966	5.6	12.4	17.8	23.8	40.5	15.6
1967	5.5	12.4	17.9	23.9	40.4	15.2
1968	5.6	12.4	17.7	23.7	40.5	15.6
1969	5.6	12.4	17.7	23.7	40.6	15.6
1970	5.4	12.2	17.6	23.8	40.9	15.6
1971	5.5	12.0	17.6	23.8	41.1	15.7
1972	5.4	11.9	17.5	23.9	41.4	15.9
1973	5.5	11.9	17.5	24.0	41.1	15.5
1974	5.4	12.0	17.6	24.1	41.0	15.3
1975	5.4	11.8	17.6	24.1	41.0	15.5

Source: U.S. Bureau of the Census, "Money Income in 1974 of Families and Persons in the United States," *Current Population Reports,* Series P-60, no. 101, table 22, p. 37.

In two other studies, similar findings were reported. Peckman adjusted the figures for nonreporting and underreporting of income (see Table 2.8). While many people assume that low-income earners tend to have jobs that

TABLE 2.8

Distribution of before-tax income adjusted for nonreporting and underreporting of income

Rank	Before adjustment		After adjustment	
	Income range (dollars)	Percent of income received	Income range (dollars)	Percent of income received
Lowest fifth	2,760	4.1	3,070	3.2
Second fifth	2,760–5,380	10.9	3,070–5,890	10.5
Middle fifth	5,380–7,850	17.5	5,890–8,620	17.0
Fourth fifth	7,850–10,980	24.9	8,620–12,260	23.9
Highest fifth	10,980 and over	42.7	12,260 and over	45.8
Top 5 percent	17,840 and over	15.8	19,920 and over	19.1
Top 1 percent	33,330 and over	4.8	44,560 and over	6.8

Source: Joseph A. Pechman, "Distribution of Federal and State Income Taxes by Income Classes," Presidential Address, American Finance Association Annual Meeting, New Orleans, Louisiana, December 28, 1971, p. 6.

TABLE 2.9

Distribution of money income compared to total income

Rank	Money income		Total income*	
	Money income range (dollars)	Percent of income received	Total income range (dollars)	Percent of income received
Lowest fifth	3,150	3.7	3,800	3.0
Second fifth	3,150–6,100	11.1	3,800–8,200	9.5
Middle fifth	6,100–8,800	16.5	8,200–12,100	16.5
Fourth fifth	8,800–12,500	26.2	12,100–17,500	23.0
Highest fifth	12,500 and over	42.5	17,500 and over	48.0
Top 5 percent	over 19,700	16.8	over 29,700	22.0
Top 1 percent	over 32,000	4.9	over 60,000	9.3

Source: Roger A. Herriot and Herman P. Miller, "Who Paid the Taxes in 1968?" U.S. Bureau of the Census Paper prepared for the National Industrial Conference Board meeting in New York, March 18, 1971, p. 3.
* Total income includes before-tax money income as published by the Bureau of the Census: $76 billion in underreported money income; $67 billion of imputed income; $18 billion in realized capital gains; $27 billion in retained corporate earnings; $74 billion in indirect taxes (taxes either shifted back on wages or dividends or forward onto consumers) less transfer payments.

allow them to hide income, the data show that controlling for nonreporting and underreporting of income reduced the distribution to the poorest fifth by 0.9 percent and raised the richest fifth by 3.1 percent. Herriot and Miller made an adjustment between money income and total income and found an even greater discrepancy between the rich and the poor (see Table 2.9). The poorest fifth received only 3 percent of total income, while the richest fifth received 48 percent. The richest 7 percent alone received three times as much income as the poorest fifth of the population.

It should be noted that, in recent years, cash-assistance payments to the poor have increased, but the poor have not received a larger share of before-tax income. As Peckman notes, it would seem that "increases in government transfer payments [are] needed to prevent a gradual erosion of [the poor's] income shares."[23] Additionally, during the last fifteen years, the effective rate of taxation for the top 15 percent of income groups has declined.[24] This means that, in recent years, after-tax income has been even more heavily skewed in favor of top-income earners.

Wealth is more severely maldistributed than income. A very small percentage of the total population controls the great majority of wealth in America. One-half of one percent of families own 22 percent of all wealth in America.[25] As Table 2.10 shows, one percent of all families own 33 percent of total wealth and 67 percent of all corporate stock.[26] The top 5 percent control 53 percent of total wealth and 83 percent of all corporate stock. The wealthiest 20 percent of the population own most wealth (77 percent) and almost completely own the corporate wealth in America (97 percent). The other 80 percent of all families own only 23 percent of wealth and 3 percent of corporate stock. Indeed, within this 80 percent, 25 percent of the families have virtually no wealth at all and 61 percent control only 7 percent of all wealth.[27] These figures indicate that opportunity is far less equal in American society than most would like to believe.

TABLE 2.10

Distribution of wealth in America

	Top 1%	Top 5%	Top 20%	Remaining 80%
Total wealth	33%	53%	77%	23%
Corporate stock	62%	86%	97%	3%

Source: Data from Edward C. Budd, ed., *Inequality and Poverty* (New York: Norton, 1967), p. xxii.

CONCLUSIONS

The absolute method used by the federal government to measure the extent of American poverty by year is extremely flawed. All things considered, it probably severely underestimates poverty. But while the standard is unrealistically low, it still shows large numbers of American poor. In 1976, after cash assistance to the poor, there were still some twenty-five million people identified as poor.

Relative measures of poverty are best thought of as a complement to absolute standards. Both absolute and relative measures provide important insights. Relative measures more clearly reveal the number of persons who cannot live close to the modal standards in a society. Simple relative measures of American poverty show large numbers of poor and severe maldistribution of income and wealth. A small proportion of the American population is extremely wealthy, while millions have little or no wealth. In later chapters (especially Chapters 3 and 7), we show how these conditions relate to American poverty.

NOTES

1. Mollie Orshansky, "Children of the Poor," *Social Security Bulletin* 25 (1963): 2–21.

2. See Clair Wilcox, *Toward Social Welfare* (Homewood, Ill.: Irvin-Dorsey, 1969), p. 27.

3. Mollie Orshansky, "Counting the Poor: Another Look at the Poverty Profile," *Social Security Bulletin* 27 (1965): 3–29.

4. "Hunger—1973," Prepared by the Staff of the Select Committee on Nutrition and Human Needs, United States Senate (Washington, D.C.: Government Printing Office, 1973), p. 1.

5. Cited in Frederick J. Perella, Jr., *Poverty in American Democracy: A Study of Power* (Washington, D.C.: United States Catholic Conference, 1974), p. 23.

6. U.S. Congress, Senate, Select Committee on Nutrition and Human Needs, *National Nutrition Policy Study. Report and Recommendations,* Vol. VIII, June 1974, p. 20.

7. "Family of Four Need $177 Weekly," *The Houston Post,* 25 March 1976, C3.

8. U.S. Department of Health, Education and Welfare, *The Measure of Poverty* (Washington, D.C.: Government Printing Office, 1976), p. 26.

9. Wilcox, *Toward Social Welfare,* p. 27.

10. See Betty Peterkin, *The Measure of Poverty: Technical Paper XII, Food Plans for Poverty Measurement* (Washington, D.C.: U.S. Department of Health, Education and Welfare, 1976), pp. 33–61.

11. Ibid., pp. 37–41.

12. See Herman P. Miller, *Rich Man, Poor Man* (New York: Crowell, 1971), p. 120.

13. Peterkin, *The Measure of Poverty,* p. 72.

14. See Burton Weisbrod and W. Lee Hansen, "An Income–Net Worth Approach to Measuring Economic Welfare," *American Economic Review* 58 (December 1968): 1315–1329.

15. Timothy M. Smeeding, "Measuring the Economic Welfare of Low Income Households and the Anti-Poverty Effectiveness of Cash and Non-Cash Transfer Program," Ph.D. dissertation, University of Wisconsin–Madison, 1975.

16. Peterkin, *The Measure of Poverty,* p. 104.

17. Peter Townsend, "Poverty as Relative Deprivation: Resources and Style of Living," in Dorothy Wedderburn, ed., *Poverty, Inequality and Class Structure* (London: Cambridge University Press, 1974), p. 15.

18. Lester Thurow, *Poverty and Discrimination* (Washington, D.C.: The Brookings Institution, 1969), p. 21.

19. Peterkin, *The Measure of Poverty,* p. xxiv.

20. Ibid., p. 109; U.S. Bureau of the Census, "Characteristics of the Population Below the Poverty Level: 1975," *Current Population Reports,* Series P-60, no. 106, June 1977, p. 18; and U.S. Bureau of the Census, "Money Income and Poverty Status of Families and Persons in the United States: 1976 (Advance Report)," *Current Population Reports,* no. 107, September 1977, p. 24.

21. Congressional Budget Office, *Poverty Status of Families Under Alternative Definitions of Income,* February 1977, p. 2.

22. Joseph A. Pechman and Benjamin Okner, *Who Bears the Tax Burden?* (Washington, D.C.: Brookings Institution, 1964), p. 46.

23. Joseph A. Pechman, "The Rich, the Poor, and the Taxes They Pay," *Public Interest,* Fall 1969, p. 25.

24. Michael Harrington, *Socialism* (New York: Bantam, 1973), p. 373.

25. Herman P. Miller, "Inequality, Poverty, and Taxes," *Dissent* 22 (Winter 1975): 44.

26. See also Frank Ackerman, Howard Birnbaum, James Wetzler, and Andrew Zimbalist, "Income Distribution in the United States," *Review of Radical Political Economics,* Summer 1971, pp. 23, 25; and Lester C. Thurow, *Generating Inequality: Mechanism of Distribution in the U.S. Economy* (New York: Basic Books, 1975).

27. Harrington, *Socialism,* p. 373.

3

THE CAUSES OF POVERTY

Numerous factors contribute to poverty in America, but some are far more important than others. In this chapter, the four major causes of poverty are examined. Poverty is shown to result primarily from capitalism, elite rule, racism and sexism, and geographic isolation. We examine each of these factors, illuminate the conditions created by each, and analyze their interactions to show how they create conditions that force some Americans into poverty. We begin with a discussion of the American economic system and its underlying philosophy.

CAPITALISM

Capitalism can be defined as "an economic system in which one class of individuals ('capitalists') own the means of production ('capital' goods, such as factories and machinery), hire another class of individuals who own nothing productive but their power to labor ('workers'), and engage in production and sales in order to make private profit."[1] Capitalism is so engrained in the American fabric that many Americans equate it with Americanism. Capitalism is even confused with democracy. Many Americans tend to believe that, without capitalism, a political system could not be a democracy.

But, of course, democracy and capitalism refer to two different things. Capitalism describes the economic system; democracy describes the relationship between the rulers and the ruled in a political system, and usually embodies such principles as majority rule and minority rights, political representation, and free elections. Many countries have socialist rather than capitalist economic systems, but are democracies. The most obvious examples are England, Sweden, Denmark, and Norway. It is no accident, of course, that Americans equate capitalism with democracy. It is to the advantage of the owners of the means of production to forge the two in the public's mind. For analytical purposes, however, it is important to remember that capitalism and democracy are separate concepts and are not immutably linked.

In the sections that follow, we discuss capitalism in terms of four components. As each component is analyzed, we reflect on its implications for poverty. It will be noted that capitalism as it has evolved in American society differs considerably from its pure theoretical form.

Private Enterprise

In a capitalist economy the means of production are privately owned. Those individuals who own the means of production receive all profits for their private use. Making a profit is the essential function of industry. Conversely, in a socialist economic system, the major means of production are state owned (that is, owned by all the people), profits are returned to the public treasury, and profit is only one of the reasons for production. An important alternative to profit might be to provide goods or services needed by some sector of the public. In a capitalist economy, the best profits might be obtained by catering to the needs of the wealthy and the middle class, ignoring the unprofitable needs of lower-income or poor groups.

One corollary of the private-enterprise doctrine is the sanctity of private property. Citizens are taught at an early age in the United States that personal property is essential to individual dignity and liberty. It is beneficial to those who own the means of production for citizens to equate their right to ownership of property with the right of big business to own and do as it wishes with its property. This serves the dual function of convincing citizens to accept the legitimacy and privilege of great wealth and providing business with a defense against regulation by government of the way it uses its property. Historically, business has fought any type of regulation of its use of property, including child-labor laws, fire safety codes, work safety conditions, the minimum wage, and, of course, unionism.

Free Enterprise

In a capitalist economy the market is, theoretically at least, open to anyone who wants to enter it for the purpose of offering a product or service for sale or profit. Quite obviously, the necessity of possessing the resources required to go into business keeps some persons from being "capitalists," as does the problem of competing with large industries.

Under free enterprise, the price of goods and services should reflect the availability and public demand for them. If a product or service is abundant and demand low, the price should decline, just as it should rise if there is scarcity and high demand. This is known as the law of supply and demand. A number of things can interfere with this law, but the most obvious is monopoly or oligopoly. If one or even a few firms can dominate a market, competition will be effectively eliminated and the firms can set prices at a profitable level without worrying about offering a better product and/or price. Throughout American history, the economy has often been plagued by conditions that have limited or even stifled competition. Currently, certain conditions have nullified competition in many areas of the economy (see Chapter 7).

Materialism-Individualism

Under capitalism it is understood that individuals work not for the collective good but for their own self-interest. Because people work for their own self-interest, it is assumed they will be more highly motivated than they would be if working for the collective good alone. Personal greed, in other words, is considered functional. Proponents of capitalism argue that, with everyone trying to maximize his or her own self-interest, people achieve their greatest potential and thus contribute most successfully to the larger society. Cumulatively, individual interests are considered to be consistent with overall social interests.

Theoretically, the market should not favor anyone except those who offer the best product or service at the most competitive price. Thus, a natural selection process takes place. Those who compete most successfully in the market survive and reap the most profits, while those who fail to compete successfully are soon forced from the market (their unprofitable businesses fail). In this form of Social Darwinism, the fittest survive. Because profits go to those who are the most successful in the market, wealth (or accumulated profits) indicate who is the most worthy. Wealth, even if inherited, indicates success and accomplishment warranting public veneration.

Three very important corollaries of materialism-individualism have an impact on poverty. The first involves the notion of greed as a motivator. Capitalism argues that people cannot be motivated by concern for the collective interests of society and must instead be motivated primarily by self-interest. While greed may, indeed, motivate people, it can also cause them to do things that are quite harmful or even dishonest. For example, a capitalist may gain an edge on the competition by paying workers extremely low wages, by ignoring unsafe working conditions, or by polluting the environment. These actions are likely to keep some persons poor and cause others to be too unhealthy or maimed to earn a living.

The second corollary involves the virtue of self-reliance. Under pure capitalism, economic insecurity is deemed necessary to force people to be self-reliant; thus, welfare programs have no place in a capitalistic economy. The assumption is that anyone who does not prosper in the system fails not because of problems with the economic, social, or political infrastructure, but because he or she lacks self-reliance. The economic system in particular is considered to be infallible for those who really try to succeed. Failure, then, becomes tantamount to moral weakness, even sin. This applies equally to the aged, mothers of small children, those temporarily ill, the handicapped, those with limited skills, and sometimes even to children.

A third corollary is closely aligned with the above two. Capitalists believe that the economic system rewards individuals equitably. According to this notion, if people receive very low wages, it is because they deserve very low wages. Either they possess limited skills or they fail to work hard enough or with enough imagination—consequently, they are worth only a limited wage. Conversely, those who earn high incomes do so because of their superior abilities and contributions.

There are, of course, a number of factors that can interfere with equitable economic rewards for labor. Most obviously, racial, sexual, or ethnic discrimination can deny some persons their just opportunities and/or compensations. Similarly, inheritance of great wealth or maldistribution of wealth can confer on some persons very considerable advantages in the market. Some groups may also be better represented in the political system and consequently more likely to receive favorable treatment at the hands of government.

Perhaps more fundamentally, economist Lester C. Thurow challenges the whole theory that the compensation one receives for labor is generally consistent with one's skills (see Chapter 7).[2] Thurow argues that there are just so many good-paying jobs in our society. The ability to perform most of these jobs after some training, he argues, is fairly common among the population. However, given a pool of labor to draw from, industry naturally chooses to train those individuals with the "best" educations and backgrounds. It is quite naturally assumed that those with "good" backgrounds and "desirable" characteristics will be the easiest to train and the most compatible to work with. Once the good-paying jobs are taken, those individuals left in the labor pool have no choice but to accept low-paying jobs, if they can be obtained, or simply be unemployed. Thurow's argument, then, is that it is not one's skills that determine compensation, but the characteristics of the job market (the number of good jobs and the employee selection process).

Laissez Faire

A last fundamental tenet of capitalism is that the government should not interfere in the market. Government interference supposedly upsets the market balance, interrupting the natural processes of survival and destruction necessary for the market to be viable and self-adjusting. Pure capitalists believe that, in an unregulated market, competition would be keen enough to force entrepreneurs to offer good-quality products and services to the public. While some economists still believe that laissez-faire is the proper way for the market to regulate and adjust itself, this is essentially a minority position. It should be understood that laissez-faire has never been anything but a myth in America. From colonial times, businesses successfully sought aid, assistance, and regulation of markets from the federal and state governments. Businesses have always sought to use the government to protect and further profits, falling back on laissez-faire defenses only when governments seek to regulate them in ways they find objectionable.

In recent years, businesses such as Lockheed and Penn Central have even turned to the government as the banker of last resort to save them from bankruptcy. The government eventually bailed these and other businesses out. Even though such actions are an obvious violation of capitalist theory, the government could not afford to regard the situation so simplistically—many factors had to be considered. What, for example, would have happened to all the workers employed by these industries had they gone bankrupt? The workers would, of course, have been the innocent victims, and to have so many persons thrown out of the job market during a period of already high unemployment would have had a very negative impact on the overall economy. In a complex society, considerations may be too involved to permit many of the simple assumptions of capitalism.

ENGELHARDT

'I Can't Stop Now, Kid—There's This Company
I've Got To Beef Up . . .'

Engelhardt in the *St. Louis Post-Dispatch*.

Additionally, since the New Deal, both Republican and Democratic administrations have used monetary, interest, and credit policies in their attempts to avoid violent cycles of recession, depression, and prosperity and keep the economy on an even keel. It has become rather widely accepted that, without government intervention, capitalism creates a quite unstable economy. Despite the considerable involvement of the government in the economy, there is still much opposition to more fundamental government intervention, such as economic planning, and the issue of government participation in the economy is far from resolved.

Economist Dale Tussing suggests a number of important corollaries of laissez-faire capitalist philosophy.[3] First, in an economic system that operates on the myth that everyone must survive without assistance from the government, aid to the poor is naturally illegitimate. Because aid to the poor is considered illegitimate, there will always be a gap between the needs of the poor and assistance. The aid that is given will generally not be generous enough to actually stop the cycle of poverty. Mostly, aid will institutionalize poverty, keeping the poor in a state of destitution. Because the poor are considered irresponsible and unworthy, aid will be primarily in the form of goods (e.g., food stamps) and services (e.g., Medicaid) rather than cash.

Tussing also points out that a society that does not accept the legitimacy of welfare will have more welfare programs than will a society that accepts the principle of welfare.[4] This paradox results from the fact that a society that does not accept welfare will fail to develop a comprehensive program for dealing with poverty. Instead, every need of the poor will spark a separate political struggle, often resulting ultimately in some type of legislation designed to deal with the problem. As the struggles over poverty multiply, a crazy quilt of piecemeal, frequently overlapping, sometimes contradictory, and generally inadequate welfare programs will be created.

Of course, the major reason that welfare programs are considered illegitimate is that the government is not willing to accept responsibility for the welfare of all citizens. Indeed, capitalism assumes that some people will be barred from the job market for certain periods of time, and that other people will be rewarded at a very low level for their labor. While welfare support has expanded considerably in recent years, this philosophy still prevails in America. The low minimum wage ($2.30 an hour in 1977) and the acceptance of certain levels of unemployment are the result. The level of unemployment considered "acceptable" has varied between 3 percent and 8 percent since World War II. Most presidents since that period have viewed 3 to 5 percent unemployment as acceptable, but President Ford, eager to curb inflation, was willing to accept 7 to 8 percent unemployment.

Unemployment in the 7 to 8 percent range means that some seven to eight million persons are excluded from the job market. If persons are unemployed for any period of time, they are almost certainly thrust into poverty. Thus, as long as extremely low-paying jobs and unemployment are acceptable within the economy, some people will always be poor. Capitalism, as it presently operates, then, makes some poverty inevitable.

One last corollary suggested by Tussing and several other scholars[5] is that, since welfare programs are considered illegitimate in a strictly laissez-faire economy, any welfare program created by the ruling class for that class must be camouflaged. Because of the need for disguise, many of the most lucrative federal programs to aid middle- and upper-income groups in our society result from income-tax exemptions built into the federal tax code. For example, although middle-income and rich families do not receive a check each year from the federal government to help them buy a home, the same effect is achieved by allowing them to treat all interest and taxes on their homes as tax deductions. The tax deductions help anyone who can afford to purchase a home (including millionaires), but do not aid those too poor to become home owners. Because a tax deduction increases in value as income goes up, those who earn the largest incomes actually receive the most help from the federal government in buying a home. Studies show that, through deductions for interest and taxes, the federal government helps the rich by paying 70 percent of all interest and taxes on their homes, while paying only 19 percent of these expenses for middle-income citizens and providing no help for the poor.[6] Each year the tax-deduction program constitutes the largest federal housing program in the budget (tax exemptions are included in the budget under the title of tax expenditures). In 1976, this program cost $11.3 billion, while housing programs designed to help those too poor to buy a home cost $2.6 billion.

The interesting point is that the tax-deduction system cost over four times as much as the housing program for the poor, but, since it is not in the form of a cash outlay, it is difficult to detect and consequently noncontroversial. The housing program, on the other hand, is very visible and therefore quite controversial.

Other examples of disguised welfare programs for rich and middle-income abound. There are literally dozens of other tax-deduction provisions in the federal tax code that aid wealthy and middle-income groups, but never attract much public attention. Deductions, for example, are allowed for medical costs, interest on life insurance, charitable contributions, and common credit costs. Other deductions are designed to encourage investment, exporting, petroleum exploration and development, equipment replacement, and expansion of employees. In 1976 the federal government estimated that tax expenditures (which do not include all deductions) cost $91,820 billion (about three times the cost of all welfare expenditures). The deductions are so lucrative, in fact, that every year some of the richest individuals and corporations manage to pay little or no federal taxes. For example, between 1972 and 1975, a total of 590 citizens earned incomes in excess of $200,000 but paid no federal taxes. Thousands of other citizens with very high incomes also paid very little in taxes. During this same period, twenty-nine major corporations reported total profits of almost $3 billion, but paid no federal taxes. Sixty-four other corporations paid at rates of 10 percent or less despite profits of almost $11 billion.[7]

Copyright 1978 by Herblock in *The Washington Post*.

Some corporations, such as the major oil companies and the major airlines, are almost total freeloaders, paying little or no taxes. Yet such corporations generally do not think of themselves as welfare recipients, although in many ways they are. Without government aid they could not stay in business. Ironically, the same corporations that lobby for tax exemptions and welcome every other form of federal and state aid continue to verbalize support for laissez-faire capitalism and severely criticize efforts to aid the poor.

Federal welfare programs for the rich and middle-income groups in 1976 also included $5.8 billion in cash subsidies to farmers, shipbuilders, railroads, airlines, and dozens of other businesses. Another $12 billion was spent in credit and in-kind transfers to help these businesses.[8] There are also programs that aid mostly the nonpoor, such as state-supported universities, federal programs to provide low-cost loans to home buyers (FHA loans administered by the Federal Housing Administration), aid to small businesses, and programs to protect and guarantee the savings of the public (Federal Deposit Insurance Corporation). Even middle-income citizens have become so used to all these programs that they fail to appreciate what a large role the government plays in aiding them. Average citizens who receive aid from dozens of programs all their lives continue to think of themselves as being "self-made"—shining examples of self-reliance. But, as Tussing says, "acceptance of welfare depends on its form not its content."[9]

In summary, Tussing suggests three major differences between welfare for the rich and middle class and welfare for the poor under capitalism.[10] First, welfare for the poor is kept low, because aid to the poor is considered tantamount to rewarding sin. Second, aid to the poor is clearly labeled as welfare, while aid to the nonpoor is disguised. Third, welfare for the poor includes intervention into their lives. The family's budget is controlled and the activities of the family members are monitored. Welfare recipients who are judged guilty of behaving sinfully (buying alcohol or engaging in adultery) risk being removed from the welfare roles. Rich and middle-income citizens who engage in sin, of course, do not have to fear losing their tax deductions or having their FHA loan revoked.[11]

ELITE RULE

The realities of political leadership and citizen influence in the United States contribute substantially to poverty. Political leaders in America are generally not drawn from the poor or even from blue-collar or low-income white-collar groups. Rather, the overwhelming majority emerge from the richest 20 percent of American families.[12] One result is that political leaders generally do not share the characteristics of the poor, nor do they adequately understand the needs of the poor. It is also important to note that, because the destitute have very little influence or power in the political system, there are few real pressures on political leaders to be concerned with the poor.

Students of the American political system generally agree that political power in the United States is in the hands of a small number of people, and that those who rule are not generally accountable to the poor.[13] Dye, for example, reaches the following conclusion:

> Great power in America is concentrated in a tiny handful of men. A few thousand individuals out of 200 million Americans decide about war and peace, wages and prices, consumption and investment, employment and production, law and justice, taxes and benefits, education and learning, health and welfare, advertising and communications, life and leisure.[14]

On the basis of empirical investigation, Dye and Pickering concluded that about 5,500 people

> control half of the nation's industrial assets, half of all assets in communications, transportation and utilities, half of all banking assets, and two-thirds of all insurance assets; they control nearly 40 percent of all the assets of private foundations, half of all private university endowments; they control the most prestigious civic and cultural organizations; they occupy key federal government positions in the executive, legislative, and judicial branches; they occupy all the top command positions in the Army, Navy, Air Force and Marines.[15]

To some extent these findings are not very surprising. In any political system, power must be invested in individuals capable of making decisions for the larger society. And, regardless of the underlying political philosophy of a system, power will eventually coalesce in the hands of a few. Lasswell and Lerner make this point: "The discovery that in all large-scale societies the decisions at any given time are typically in the hands of a small number of people confirms a basic fact: Government is always government by the few, whether in the name of the few, the one, or the many."[16] The important point, however, is not how many rule, but the extent to which those with power are held accountable to the public. Great controversy prevails among political scientists over the extent to which the ruling few in America are responsible to their constituents.

Social scientists have developed two basic theories of political power in America: elitism and pluralism. Neither theory maintains that the general public (much less the poor) has any great influence in the political process or any great control over political leaders. Elite theorists, however, are the most pessimistic about the influence the public has in the political system. Elite theory can be summarized as follows:

1. American society is divided into two groups: the few who rule and the many who are ruled. The rulers are influenced very little by the ruled.

2. Those who shape public policies differ substantially from those who are governed. Elites disproportionately are drawn from upper-socioeconomic groups, are better educated, have better skills of communication, have more time to spend on public affairs, and are primarily white, Anglo-Saxon, Protestant males.

3. Elite ranks are not closed. New members can be accepted into the inner circle as long as they have the "right" characteristics and accept the basic legitimacy of elite rule. Talented nonelites can be co-opted into the system to keep down agitation or even revolution. Movement of nonelites into elite ranks, however, must be slow, so that the established elites and their values can be maintained.

4. Elites share a consensus about certain rules of the game. No one can be accepted into elite ranks unless he or she accepts these rules. The key rule that must be accepted is that the elite system is legitimate and must be maintained. Anyone who violates this article of faith is excluded from influence.

5. While there is competition among elites, it takes place over a very narrow range of issues. These issues are not fundamental to the existence of the system. Elites agree on more points than they disagree on.

6. Public policy, the decisions made by elites in the form of legislation, most usually reflects the values of elites, not the demands of the public. Changes in public policies reflect changes in elite values more often than citizen wishes. Unless seriously threatened by public action, an unusual occurrence, policy change will be incremental (step-by-step) in nature. This slow process of change preserves elite positions and prerogatives. On those occasions when the public does become seriously antagonized over a public issue, elites can generally placate them by passing legislation—legislation that is primarily symbolic. Only when elite positions are seriously threatened by public actions (e.g., riots, depressions, or reform movements) will drastic alterations in policy occur.

7. Elitism assumes that the public is largely apathetic, ill-informed, and passive. Generally speaking, elites influence nonelites a great deal more than they are influenced by them. Elites having control over public information and democratic symbols can generally manipulate nonelites to accept their policies and prerogatives. Thus, a largely apathetic and uninformed public has little influence or control over public leaders.[17]

Among those social scientists who agree that elitism provides a fairly accurate description of American democracy, there is considerable disagreement over the desirability of elite rule. Some believe elite rule is the most viable form of government;[18] others feel that it is a complete perversion of the democratic process.[19] Some social scientists, while accepting the fact that few citizens have great power in the system and that the rulers have considerable discretion in their decisions, still maintain that elite rule functions so as to preserve basic democratic principles and, at the same time, provide necessary leadership and direction for the political system. These theorists are called pluralists. Pluralism is by far the most widely accepted theory among social scientists. Pluralist theory can be summarized as follows:

1. While citizens do not directly participate in decision making, decisions are not made by isolated elites acting unilaterally. Elites reach most decisions through a process of bargaining, accommodation, and compromise with other elites.

2. The public's interests are protected by competition between conflicting elites. Competition restrains elite powers and provides some protection for average citizens from elite abuses. Competition most often takes place with and between political, business, and labor elites.

3. Citizens can influence public policies by choosing between competing elites. Additionally, the electoral system, political parties, and interest groups allow citizens to hold elites accountable for their actions.

4. Since elite ranks are open, citizens can also influence elites by becoming one of them or by forming new groups to oppose disliked elites or policies.

5. The elite system is viable because elites are not consolidated. There are different elites for different policy areas—education, agriculture, business. Thus there is no single ruling elite, but instead a complex of elites who have influence over one issue area but may have little influence over other issues.

6. Public policy does not directly represent majority preferences, but it does represent a compromise between those actively interested in a particular policy issue. In the final analysis, the compromise reflects reasonably well the public's preferences.

7. The policy preferences of nonactive citizens are not completely ignored, because these individuals represent potentially powerful groups in
the system and elites prefer to keep them placated and their basic needs
met.

8. Elites are always restrained in their power by certain institutionalized
rules of the game that must be observed. Formal rules are spelled out in
the constitution and public statutes and elites have also formulated a series
of informal rules that govern fair play.[20]

Pluralists, then, argue that democratic values are maintained in our
society by voters choosing between multiple, competing elites who fulfill
public needs by making policy through a process of bargaining, compromise, and accommodation. Democratic principles are protected to the extent that elite ranks are not closed, by citizen mobilization through groups
and parties, and by the fact that democratic rules can be enforced against
abusive elites.

Despite its popularity, pluralism is not an accurate description of political reality in America. In fact, pluralism is best understood as a rational-
ization of elite rule.[21] The comfort pluralists take in such factors as
decision making by elite interaction is unjustified. Decision making by
elite interaction is far from being the equivalent of individual participation
or direct citizen influence over decision making. A central principle of
democracy is that citizens should be able to directly participate in the
decisions that affect their lives. As Bachrach has said: "The central theme
of classical democratic theory is based on the supposition that man's
dignity and indeed his growth and development as a functioning and re-
sponsive individual in a free society, is dependent upon an opportunity to
participate actively in decisions that affect him."[22] This citizen role is
stifled in a system of elite rule.

In response to the second point above, it must be noted that the frag-
mentation of political power between competing elites is not the same as
political equality. Political equality requires that individuals have equal
influence over public policies. While this condition can never be fully
realized in a complex society, it is almost abdicated under elite rule.

As regards point three, when the only choice citizens have in an elec-
tion is between competing elites, they frequently have little real choice at
all. If the elites share basic values, as elite theorists admit they do, to
choose between them may mean very little, since they may not differ
greatly in the policies they support.

Fourth, it means little to say that elite ranks are open if only certain
types of people can realistically compete for political power and if only

those with certain values will be accepted by elites even if they win office. Certainly, political ranks in America are open, but it is much harder for some to acquire the right skills and resources than it is for others. While all adults may be legally eligible for recruitment into elite ranks, a much smaller number are socially or financially eligible. Those who are not socially eligible may overcome obstacles to power, but the barriers are much more severe.

Fifth, the fact that there are multiple elites rather than one consolidated elite is comforting, but it is certainly not a guarantee of citizen influence. Regardless of how many elite interests there are, if elites agree on all the really important values it may make little difference which elite rules. Additionally, many elites do have power over a wide range of issues. For example, elites in the executive branch or in Congress may have substantial influence over a broad range of issues.

Sixth, it is not realistic to suggest that citizens can control elites through groups and political parties, both of which are frequently elite dominated. Also, for citizens to control elites through these mechanisms requires a great deal of citizen interest, knowledge, and mobilization. In the United States, citizen political participation is very low, as is political knowledge.[23] Most citizens fail to vote regularly, and most have little understanding of political issues or familiarity with political leaders.

Seventh, it makes absolutely no sense to talk about inactive groups influencing elites. Groups like blacks, women, and the poor frequently have little success in influencing the system, even when they try very hard.[24] Quite obviously their values do not influence leaders when they are inactive. The objective condition of out-groups such as blacks, women, and the poor serve as the best indication of how influential they are in the political process. As later chapters will show, these groups are seriously deprived compared to average norms.

Finally, the concept of political rules is a two-edged sword. On the one hand, some constitutional and legal rules do provide average citizens with certain protections against overt suppression. But it should be recalled that the constitution did not stifle human slavery, sexual suppression, minority discrimination, and all kinds of other maladies that have been, and continue to be, heaped on the powerless in our society. More importantly, informal rules tend to set the boundaries of legitimate political options in such a way as to severely suppress the most deprived groups. Parenti bears quoting at length on this point:

> The very agenda of legitimate conflict is shaped by widely accepted and unquestioned belief systems and power distributions that

predispose the decision maker to view the claims of certain groups as "reasonable" or "essential" and the claims of other groups as "questionable" or "outrageous." The systemic norms and rules governing political procedures operate with something less than egalitarian effects. To say that the political system is governed by the "rules of the game" is to apply an unfortunate metaphor. In most games the rules apply equally to all competitors, but in political life the symbolic norms, standards, and practices that govern traditional forms of political competition are themselves part of the object of competition. Rules that regulate procedures and priorities in any social system cannot be extricated from the substantive values and interests that led to their construction. Rather than being neutral judgments, they are the embodiment of past political victories and, as such, favor those who have "written" them.[25]

A good example was the reaction of political leaders to demonstrations by welfare recipients for better benefits and treatment during the early 1970s. The "Welfare Rights" movement evoked considerable hostility from many politicians. They could not imagine anyone on welfare talking about having rights. Their feeling was that welfare recipients should be grateful for anything they were given. Thus, the rules of the game, far from protecting the public, can lead to the suppression of their needs. Bachrach and Baratz refer to the ability of powerful groups to limit the political options under consideration as their ability to make nondecisions.[26] Quite obviously, the options that are not considered may be as important as or more important than the ones that are.

In the final analysis, the most direct and insightful way to evaluate the extent to which our political system fairly represents the needs and interests of all citizens and provides them an adequate chance to influence policy is to ask a very simple question: Are political influence and its benefits widely distributed in our society? In other words, are some groups almost always dominant while others are almost always suppressed? Both pluralists and elitists admit that political influence is not widely distributed and that some groups consistently are either unrepresented or underrepresented in our society.

This critique of the public's role in the political system should make the following points quite clear: (1) power in America is centered in the hands of a small number of people; (2) those with power are drawn mostly from upper-socioeconomic groups; and (3) those who rule have considerable discretion about the decisions they make, because neither the general public nor the poor typically have any great influence over them. Normally the poor must depend on either the benevolence or wisdom of decision makers for assistance. Decision makers may decide to attack poverty conditions, for example, not because they empathize with the conditions of the poor, but because they understand that poverty causes social problems such as crime, ill health, and alienation. Generally, of course, this is not the case.

PREJUDICE: RACISM AND SEXISM

America has a long history of racism and sexism. Both racism and sexism have survived so long in the United States because capitalist philosophy always puts the blame for failure on the victim of the system. Culture, IQ, genes, shiftlessness, and immorality—rather than prejudice or discrimination—have been blamed for the poverty of blacks, Spanish-speaking Americans, American Indians, and women. Women, like minorities, have only recently obtained statutory aid in their battle for equality,* and progress has been slowed by inadequate enforcement of some antidiscrimination statutes, inadequate statutory authority in some areas, and a sluggish economy which has made progress difficult (see Chapter 7). Not surprisingly, both minorities and women are disproportionately represented among the poor in America.

While both minorities and women have made some progress toward equality in the last twenty years, the legacy of hundreds of years of suppression is not easily overcome. Minorities were generally accorded only the most inferior education, and women were long excluded from many of the most prestigious universities and from most graduate programs, especially those in medicine, law, and the sciences. Even when minorities were able to obtain good educations, they were still excluded from many positions and were normally passed over for promotion. Even well-educated and capable women were discouraged, until recently, from pursuing professional careers.

The most important civil rights laws for minorities in the twentieth century have been in effect only since the mid-1960s. While these laws have removed many of the barriers to minority progress and have made available many new opportunities, the gains have been slow. For example, in 1964, median black family income was only 50 percent of the median for white families. By 1968 the percentage increased to 60 percent, but by

---

* For minorities we are referring to twentieth-century legislation.

1973 it had fallen back to 58 percent. In 1975 the percentage climbed to 61.5 percent (see Table 4.2, p. 64), but decreased to 59 percent in 1976.[27] At the current rate of progress, it would take a couple of hundred years for black family income to be equal to that of white families.

The situation with women is very similar. In 1976 the median income for women was $8,100, while the median income for men was $13,460. In 1974 women held 63 percent of all jobs that paid between $3,000–4,999, 58 percent of all jobs that paid between $5,000-6,999, but only 5 percent of all jobs which paid in excess of $15,000.[28] Because women are increasingly the heads of families, past and present discrimination against women has thrust many families into poverty.

As subsequent chapters detail, poverty cannot be eradicated without dealing with the problems brought about by racism and sexism.

GEOGRAPHIC ISOLATION

The fact that many Americans live outside the social and economic mainstream of our society contributes substantially to poverty. People isolated in rural areas, especially in the South and in Appalachia, have fewer job opportunities, the worst educational systems, and the poorest health care, because these sections of the country do not fully share in the prosperity and growth of the rest of the country. This creates a dual problem: large numbers of poor people and few funds to deal with them. The South, for example, is the region with the most poor, but it is also the least wealthy region. Thus, welfare payments in the South are generally extremely low.

As Tussing points out, geographic isolation also "breeds differences in culture and dialect, which in turn reinforces isolation."[29] Long-time residents of Appalachia or other rural areas may find it extremely difficult to acculturate successfully to urban areas where their opportunities might be greatly improved. Still, because of limited opportunities and aid in rural areas, many of the rural poor are forced to move to urban areas. Thus, despite the fact that many of the nation's poor still live in rural areas (about 40 percent), many of the urban poor are the products of rural deprivation.

During and after World War II, literally millions of poor blacks migrated to urban areas in the North and South in the hope of making a better life for themselves. The expected opportunities rarely materialized. Today, many of the nation's most desperate poor are urban blacks whose dreams of success in the city (The Promised Land) have long been dashed.

Similarly, Appalachian whites who migrate to the cities frequently end up in what are called "hillbilly ghettoes."[30] The problem of rural poverty, therefore, is closely linked with and contributes substantially to urban poverty.

CONCLUSIONS

This analysis of the causes of poverty enables us to identify the likeliest victims of poverty in America. We would expect minorities, women and female-headed families, those born in lower socioeconomic groups, those with little political influence, and those who have been raised or still live in the most isolated sections of the country to have the greatest chance of being poor. The next chapter demonstrates that these expectations are correct.

NOTES

1. Howard Sherman, *Radical Political Economy* (New York: Basic Books, 1972), p. 31.

2. *Generating Inequality: Mechanisms of Distribution in the U.S. Economy* (New York: Basic Books, 1975).

3. *Poverty in a Dual Economy* (New York: St. Martin's Press, 1975), pp. 69–115. Tussing's theory of poverty is exceptionally enlightening and many of the points raised in this chapter were stimulated by or drawn from this work.

4. Ibid., p. 87.

5. Ibid.

6. See Stanley S. Surrey, *Pathways to Tax Reform* (Cambridge, Mass.: Harvard University Press, 1973), p. 37.

7. See U.S. Congress, *Congressional Record,* Proceedings and Debates of the 94th Cong., 2d sess., Friday, October 1, 1976, 122, no. 151, pt. 3; and Harrell Rodgers, *Crisis in Democracy: A Policy Analysis of American Government* (Reading, Mass.: Addison-Wesley, 1978), Chapter 6.

8. Surrey, *Pathways to Tax Reform,* p. 7; and *Special Analysis, Budget of The United States: Fiscal Year 1978* (Washington, D.C.: Government Printing Office, 1977), p. 21.

9. Tussing, *Poverty in a Dual Economy,* p. 121.

10. Ibid., pp. 88–89.

11. Ibid.

12. Kenneth Prewitt and Alan Stone, *The Ruling Elites: Elite Theory, Power, and American Democracy* (New York: Harper & Row, 1973), p. 137.

13. For examples from various political perspectives, see Robert A. Dahl, *Democracy in the United States: Promise and Performance* (Chicago: Rand McNally, 1973); Thomas R. Dye and L. Harmon Zeigler, *The Irony of Democracy* (North Scituate, Mass.: Duxbury Press, 1975); Michael Parenti, *Democracy for the Few* (New York: St. Martin's Press, 1974); Edward S. Greenberg, *Serving the Few* (New York: Wiley, 1974); Peter Bachrach, *The Theory of Democratic Elitism* (Boston: Little, Brown, 1967).

14. Thomas R. Dye, *Who's Running America?* (Englewood Cliffs, N.J.: Prentice-Hall, 1976), p. 3.

15. Thomas R. Dye and John W. Pickering, "Governmental and Corporate Elites: Convergence and Differentiation," *Journal of Politics*, November 1974, p. 905. In this source Dye and Pickering suggest some 4,000 critical elites. Dye adjusts the figure in *Who's Running America?*.

16. Harold Lasswell and Daniel Lerner, *The Comparative Study of Elites* (Stanford, Cal.: Stanford University Press, 1952), p. 7.

17. This list was summarized from *The Irony of Democracy: An Uncommon Introduction to American Politics*, 4th ed., © 1978 by Wadsworth Pub. Co., Inc., Belmont, Ca. 94002. By permission of the publisher, Duxbury Press, pp. 3–6.

18. Dye and Zeigler, *The Irony of Democracy*, is the best known articulation of this point of view.

19. See Peter Bachrach, *The Theory of Democratic Elitism: A Critique* (Boston: Little, Brown, 1967); G. William Domhoff, *Who Rules America?* (Englewood Cliffs, N.J.: Prentice-Hall, 1967).

20. This list was summarized from Dye and Zeigler, *The Irony of Democracy*, pp. 9–13, by permission; Robert Dahl, *Who Governs?* (New Haven: Yale University Press, 1961); and Nelson Polsby, *Community Power and Political Theory* (New Haven: Yale University Press, 1963).

21. For critiques, see Henry Kariel, *The Decline of American Pluralism* (Stanford, Cal.: Stanford University Press, 1961); Charles McCoy and John Playford, eds., *Apolitical Politics: A Critique of Behavioralism* (New York: Crowell, 1967); Michael Parenti, "Power and Pluralism: A View from the Bottom," *The Journal of Politics* 32 (August 1970): 501–530; Jack L. Walker, "A Critique of the Elite Theory of Democracy," *American Political Science Review* 60 (June 1966); Theodore Lowi, *The End of Liberalism* (New York: Norton, 1969).

22. Bachrach, *The Theory of Democratic Elitism*, p. 98.

23. See Rodgers, *Crisis in Democracy: A Policy Analysis of American Government* (Reading, Mass.: Addison-Wesley, 1978), Chapters 2 and 3.

24. See Parenti, "Power and Pluralism . . . ," pp. 508–530.
25. Ibid., p. 529. By permission of The Southern Political Science Association.
26. Peter Bachrach and Morton S. Baratz, "Decisions and Non-Decisions," *American Political Science Review*, September 1963, pp. 632–642.
27. U.S. Bureau of the Census, "Social and Economic Studies of the Black Population in the United States in 1975," *Current Population Reports*, Series P-23.
28. All figures from special Census study to celebrate 1975 as International Women's Year. See U.S. Bureau of the Census, "A Statistical Portrait of Women in the U.S.," *Current Population Reports*, Series P-23, no. 58, April 1976, pp. 1–7.
29. Tussing, *Poverty in a Dual Economy*, p. 80.
30. See Hal Bruno, "Chicago's Hillbilly Ghetto," in Hanna H. Meissner, ed., *Poverty in the Affluent Society* (New York: Harper & Row, 1973), pp. 102–108.

4

CHARACTERISTICS OF THE POOR

Poverty exists in all regions of America and affects every racial and ethnic group, the young and the old, the employed and the unemployed. Some persons, however, are much more likely to be poor than are others. In this chapter, we analyze the poor to determine which groups have the highest potential of being destitute. Identifying the poor provides insight into the causes of poverty and the reforms necessary to abolish it.*

POVERTY AND RACE

One of the most frequent misconceptions about poverty is that most of the poor are black. In fact, there are almost twice as many poor whites as poor blacks in America. As Table 4.1 shows, 55.8 percent of the poor in

---

* As this book went to press, the most recent complete figures on the American poor were for 1975. Where available, 1976 figures have been used.

TABLE 4.1

Poor by race: 1973–1975

Year and number of poor (in millions)	Race	Number of poor of that race (in millions)	Percent of all poor	Percent of all persons of of that race who are poor
1973 (22,973)	Spanish origin	2,366	10.3%	21.9%
	White	12,776	55.6	8.4
	Black	7,388	32.1	31.4
	Other races	443	1.9	—
1974 (23,370)	Spanish origin	2,575	11.0	23.0
	White	13,161	56.3	8.6
	Black	7,182	30.7	30.3
	Other races	452	2.0	—
1975 (25,877)	Spanish origin	2,991	11.6	26.9
	White	14,779	57.2	9.7
	Black	7,545	29.1	31.3
	Other races	562	2.1	—
1976 (24,975)	Spanish origin	2,783	11.1	24.7
	White	13,930	55.8	9.1
	Black	7,595	30.4	31.1
	Other races	667	2.7	—

Source: Derived from U.S. Bureau of the Census, "Characteristics of the Population Below the Poverty Level," *Current Population Reports,* Series P-60, various years. See especially U.S. Bureau of the Census, "Money Income and Poverty Status of Families and Persons in the United States: 1975 and 1974 Revision (Advance Report)," *Current Population Reports,* Series P-60, no. 103, September 1976, p. 3, and the Advance Report cited in Table 4.2.

1976 were white, 30.4 percent were black, 11.1 percent were of Spanish origin, and 2.7 percent were of other races. The distribution of poverty among the races has changed only modestly in recent years. Still, while the majority of the poor are white, minorities do have a much greater potential of being poor. As Table 4.1 shows, 24.7 percent of all citizens of Spanish origin and 31.1 percent of all blacks were poor in 1976, compared to only 9.1 percent of all whites. There is clearly a hazard involved in being a minority in America.

Whites

The poor whites who make up the majority of the American poor represented some 13,930 million families and unrelated individuals in 1976. The majority of poor whites (about 53 percent) live in metropolitan areas, but only a small percentage (5 percent) live in the poverty pockets of central cities. Most poor whites live outside central cities in low-income suburban neighborhoods. Of those poor whites who do live in the inner city, a majority live in declining ethnic neighborhoods.

About 47 percent of all poor whites live outside metropolitan areas. Like their counterparts in metropolitan areas, poor rural whites generally are low-skill or unskilled workers, many of whom are being placed outside the job market by automation. The rural poor include many residents of Appalachia, small farms, and small towns that are suffering economic depression.

Blacks

The total black population in 1976 was 24,399 million, with 7,595 million families and individuals counted among the poor.[1] While civil rights laws have allowed blacks to make some progress in recent years, blacks are still severely disadvantaged economically compared to whites. In 1975, black median family income was $9,240, compared to $15,540 for white families. Table 4.2 shows the ratio of black to white family income from 1964 to 1976. The figures indicate that blacks made significant strides in closing the income gap between 1964 and 1968, but the rate of progress slowed, halted, and even reversed in later years. In constant dollar terms, black incomes did not move upward from 1970 to 1976.[2] One reason is that the black unemployment rate has consistently been about double the white unemployment rate. During the first quarter of 1975, black unemployment was 13.6 percent; among black teenagers it was 39.8 percent. These same high rates of unemployment continued through 1977.

The black poor are heavily urbanized. About five million, or 66 percent of all black poor, live in metropolitan areas, with 81 percent of all poor urban blacks residing in central cities. Of those poor blacks living in central cities (4,167 million), 64 percent live in poverty pockets. Thirty-two percent of all poor blacks live in rural areas, with 81 percent living in rural poverty pockets.

TABLE 4.2

Changes in black income relative to white income: 1964–1975

	Median family income		
	Blacks	Whites	Black as percent of white
1964	$3,724	$ 6,858	50%
1965	3,886	7,251	50
1966	4,507	7,792	58
1967	4,875	8,234	59
1968	5,360	8,937	60
1969	5,999	9,794	61
1970	6,279	10,236	61
1971	6,440	10,672	60
1972	6,864	11,549	59
1973	7,269	12,595	58
1974	7,800	13,400	58
1975	8,780	14,270	61.5
1976	9,240	15,540	59

Source: U.S. Bureau of the Census, "Social and Economic Status of the Black Population in the United States in 1974," *Current Population Reports,* Series P-23, no. 54, p. 25; "Money, Income and Poverty Studies of Families and Persons in the United States: 1976 (Advance Report)," *Current Population Reports,* Series P-60, no. 107, September 1977, p. 1.

The black poor are generally isolated from the economically healthier sectors of society whether they live in cities or rural areas. The urban core has the nation's highest unemployment, and rural poverty areas have few good jobs and high unemployment among minorities. Those poor blacks in the job market tend to be unskilled workers, such as manual laborers, porters, restaurant helpers, and domestics.

Some 69 percent of poor black families in 1976 were headed by a female. Some 35 percent of all black families in 1976 were headed by a female. The large number of female-headed families among blacks is primarily a result of hundreds of years of racism, which has made it difficult (or impossible) for many black men to support a family, and welfare laws that force males to abandon their families so that needy women and children can obtain public assistance. In 1974, only 56 percent of all black children lived with both of their parents.[3]

Spanish Origin*

In March 1976, there were some 11 million persons of Spanish origin in 2.5 million families in the United States.[4] Most Spanish-origin families live in urban areas, with the majority residing in central cities. Some 2.1 million Spanish-origin families, 84 percent, live in metropolitan areas. The breakdown for Spanish-origin families by type in 1976 was:[5]

		% of total
Mexican American	6.6 million	59.3%
Puerto Rican (mainland)	1.8 million	15.8
Cuban	700,000	6.2
Central or South American	800,000	6.8
Other	1.3 million	12.0

Median family income for Spanish-origin families in 1976 was $10,260, compared to $14,960 for all families and $15,540 for white families. Median income for men of Spanish origin was $6,800, more than twice the median income of Spanish-origin women, at $3,200. Thirty-seven percent of Spanish-origin men had incomes of less than $5,000 in 1975, as did 71 percent of women of Spanish origin.[6]

Generally, citizens of Spanish origin tend to be less well educated than the general public. Only 39 percent of all Spanish-origin persons twenty-five years old and over were high-school graduates in 1975, compared to 64 percent of the general population. About 19 percent of all Spanish-origin citizens had completed less than five years of school, compared to less than 4 percent of the general population.[7]

Some 2,783 million of the American poor are of Spanish origin, constituting some 630,000 families. There are substantial differences in proportions of Spanish-origin families below the poverty level by type of Spanish origin. The largest group of Spanish-origin poor are Mexican Americans. About 1.8 million (27 percent) Mexican Americans are poor. Some 1.3 million of the Mexican-American poor live in Arizona, California, Colorado, New Mexico, and Texas. A large proportion of the Mexican-American poor are migrant workers, many of whom are transients.

---

* Because of the large numbers of illegal aliens among Spanish-origin citizens, and because many Spanish-origin citizens are itinerant, the Spanish-speaking poor are probably seriously undercounted by the U.S. Census Bureau.

Mexican Americans tend to have larger than average families (about 4.9 persons per family), earn considerably less than the median family income ($9,498 in 1975), and are less well-educated than average (only 31 percent of all adults are high school graduates).[8]

The next largest group of Spanish-speaking poor are mainland Puerto Ricans. Thirty-three percent of all mainland Puerto Ricans are poor. The median income for Puerto Rican families in 1975 was only $7,629. Only 28.7 percent of all Puerto Ricans have graduated from high school and, among Puerto Ricans over twenty-five, only 60 percent can read and write English.[9]

Most of the Puerto Rican poor are isolated in ghetto areas of large cities. One million of all mainland Puerto Ricans live in New York City, with 85 percent living in low-income neighborhoods in the Bronx, Brooklyn, and Manhattan. The Puerto Rican poor are generally semiskilled or unskilled workers who are nudged out of the job market during periods of economic slack. Additionally, Puerto Ricans, like blacks, have seen jobs vanish in the city—only to reappear in the suburbs out of their reach. A study of the fifteen largest American metropolitan areas revealed that, between 1960 and 1970, the suburbs gained three million jobs, while central cities lost 836,000 jobs.[10] Additionally, nearly 60 percent of all poor Puerto Rican families are headed by single women who have much lower earning power than men, because of low skills and discrimination in the job market.[11]

Of the remaining Spanish-speaking American poor, the largest group is Cuban Americans. About 14 percent of all Cuban Americans are poor. Poor Cubans generally have the additional stumbling block of a language barrier and hold unskilled jobs. However, of the Spanish-speaking Americans, Cubans have adapted most readily to the United States and have most often prospered. Before migrating to America, many Cubans were prosperous citizens in their homeland. Thus, they have an advantage over other Spanish-speaking peoples who generally came to America in an attempt to alleviate their own poverty. In contrast to other Spanish-speaking groups, 51 percent of all Cuban adults have a high school education. In 1975 median income for Cuban Americans was $11,410.[12]

American Indians and Orientals

Observe on Table 4.1 that some of the poor are simply classified as "other races." This, unfortunately, is the classification used by the Census Bureau for American Indians and Americans of Oriental ancestry. There are no specific statistics on the incidence of poverty among the some 2.1 million American Orientals. Clearly, some sections of the United States have large Oriental communities that contain many poor citizens. In the Chinatowns of both New York and San Francisco, block after block of crowded tenements house the poor. Many Oriental poor work steadily, but for extremely low wages. The major barriers for many Orientals are language and job discrimination. One's poverty is particularly acute when no one knows you exist.

Among American Indians, who number only about 810,070, the incidence of poverty is estimated to be about 45 to 50 percent. A little less than 50 percent of all Indians live on reservations, but almost 90 percent of all reservation Indians are estimated to be poor.[13] Along with Puerto Rican Americans, Indians are thought to be among America's poorest citizens. Median family income in 1974 was estimated to be just over $7,000.

POVERTY AND AGE

For the most part, the majority of all the poor in America cannot personally do much to alleviate their condition, because they are children or the aged (see Table 4.3). In 1976, some 54.3 percent of all the poor were either sixty-five or older or under eighteen years of age. Poor children alone numbered 10.3 million and constituted 41 percent of all poor Americans. One American child in six was poor. Similarly, one aged person in six was poor. The elderly poor numbered 3.3 million and counted for 13.3 percent of all poor Americans. The percentage of the total population who are sixty-five or older is growing rapidly. In 1970, Americans sixty-five or older numbered 20.1 million—one in ten persons. In 1975 the elderly population numbered 22.3 million, almost one in nine persons. By year 2000, the elderly are expected to number 30.6 million—one in eight persons. Without improvement in retirement benefits or public policies, poverty among the aged can be expected to increase substantially.

Poverty among the aged is probably severely underestimated by the Social Security Administration standards. In 1976 the poverty standard for a single, aged individual was $2,720; for an aged couple, it was only $3,417. Needless to say, these levels are extremely low. In 1975 a report by the National Council on the Aging showed that 23 percent of all the aged have annual incomes below $3,000.[14] This would include 5.1 million aged persons. Additionally, millions of other elderly persons would be judged poor if they did not live with relatives.

TABLE 4.3

Children and aged poor: 1969–1975

Year	Under 18 years—number below poverty level (in millions)	Poverty rate	Percent of all poor	65 years and over—number below poverty level (in millions)	Poverty rate	Percent of all poor
1976	10.3	16.0%	41.0%	3.3	15.0%	13.3%
1975	10.9	16.3	42.0	3.3	15.3	12.7
1974	10.0	14.8	42.7	3.1	14.6	13.2
1973	9.4	13.7	40.9	3.3	16.3	14.3
1971	10.3	14.5	40.2	4.3	21.6	12.9
1969	9.5	13.5	39.1	4.8	25.7	17.7

Source: U.S. Bureau of the Census, "Characteristics of the Population Below the Poverty Level," *Current Population Reports*, Series P-60, various years.

Almost 90 percent of all persons sixty-five and over are white, and over 59 percent are women.[15] Only about one-third of the elderly poor are couples. Most aged poor are single persons, mostly widows (about 70 percent). Two-thirds of all the elderly live in urban areas. Many of the aged own their homes or have an equity in a home, but many of the elderly poor live in rented rooms, decaying hotels, or apartment houses. While most aged citizens are white, aged minorities have a much higher poverty rate. Only 14 percent of all elderly whites were poor in 1975, as compared to 36 percent of all aged blacks.[16]

Poverty among old people aggravates all the usual problems of retirement. It adds to the financial strain, makes good health a commodity that must be purchased, and reinforces the loneliness, feelings of rejection, and immobility of old age.

The thought of children being poor, deprived, even hungry is difficult for most Americans to accept. It is a sad fact, however, that, during the 1970s, over 40 percent of all the poor have been children. Poverty among children is particularly regretful, not only because it punishes the innocent, but also because it contributes substantially to the continuation of poverty. As noted in Chapter 1, a child who grows up in poverty may be seriously handicapped by that experience. Crowded, unsanitary housing contributes to health problems, and malnutrition and lead-paint poisoning can cause permanent brain damage. Further, poor neighborhoods generally have inferior schools. Frequently, school teachers and officials either believe the poor are not worth teaching or feel so overwhelmed by crowded classrooms and inadequate facilities that they essentially give up. Children in poor neighborhoods are also exposed to criminal role models and may begin to see crime as more glamorous, and even more dignified and profitable, than the kinds of jobs most of the poor have.

POVERTY AND THE SEX OF THE FAMILY HEAD

Poverty is much more prevalent among families headed by women. Because of past and present discrimination in education and the job market, women are generally less capable of earning an income adequate to support a family. In 1976, for example, the median income for men who worked year round was $13,460, while for comparable women the median income was $8,100.[17] However, in 1975, median income for male-headed families was $12,965; for female-headed families, it was only $5,797.[18] In 1975 women college graduates had average incomes lower than those of men with only a high school education.[19] While women continue to make progress in the job market, over half of all working women are employed in clerical, operative, and service positions. The lower earning power of female heads contributes very substantially to poverty. As Table 4.4 shows, 9.4 percent of all families were poor in 1976. But while only 5.6 percent of all male-headed families were poor, a formidable 33.0 percent of all female-headed families were poor.

TABLE 4.4

Percent of families below poverty level, by sex and race of family head: 1976

	Number in millions		Poverty rate
All families: total	5,311		9.4%
Male head	2,768	52%	5.6
Female head	2,543	48%	33.0
White families: total	3,560		7.1
Male head	2,182	61%	4.9
Female head	1,379	39%	25.2
Black families: total	1,617		27.9
Male head	495	31%	13.5
Female head	1,122	69%	52.2

Source: U.S. Bureau of the Census, "Money Income and Poverty Status of Families and Persons in the United States: 1976 (Advance Report)," *Current Population Reports,* Series P-60, no. 107, September 1977, p. 20.

As the number of children in the family increases, the incidence of poverty becomes more frequent.[20] With four children, 21 percent of all families and 64.3 percent of all female-headed families were poor in 1975. When the number of children increased to six, 42.2 percent of all families were poor, while 87.9 percent of all female-headed families were poor.

While poverty among female-headed families is severe for all races, it is even more severe for minority females. As Table 4.4 indicates, among poverty families, 52 percent are headed by males and 48 percent are headed by females. Thirty-nine percent of all poor white families are headed by females, while 69 percent of poor black families are headed by females. Because of double discrimination (race and sex), black females have traditionally had an earning potential lower than that of white females. In recent years, the median income of black women with year-round, full-time jobs has increasingly approached that of their white counterparts. By 1974 the ratio of black to white earnings was 92 percent, up from 75 percent in 1967.[21]

The inability of many female family heads to earn an adequate living has serious implications for poverty eradication, because the number of female-headed families is increasing quite rapidly. Between 1960 and 1975, female-headed families increased 73 percent. In 1975, female-headed families numbered over 7.2 million and constituted 13 percent of all families. The number of children in female-headed families grew from 4.2 million in 1960 to 6.9 million in 1970 to 10.5 million in 1975.[22]

As Table 4.5 shows, the proportion of all poor families headed by a female increased from 23 percent in 1959 to 47.2 percent in 1976. Between 1959 and 1975, poor female-headed families increased by 38 percent, while poor male-headed families decreased by more than 100 percent. With increases in divorce, separation, and single parenting, the number of female-headed families is likely to continue to rise.

While both the incidence of poverty among female-headed families and the increase in such families are significant, these findings should not obscure one very important point: 52 percent of all poverty families are headed by males, 79 percent of whom are white males. Thus, while poverty is severe among minorities and female-headed families, the majority of the poor are white and living in male-headed families. And, while a slight majority of the poor children were living in female-headed families in 1975, there were almost as many poor children in male-headed families.

POVERTY AND EDUCATION

As one might expect, most heads of poor families are not well educated. In 1975, almost 42 percent of all poor heads had eight or fewer years of education and only 23.7 percent spent at least four years in high school (see Table 4.6). Male heads of poor families are generally less well educated than are female heads. Among black male heads, 61.6 percent have eight or fewer (51 percent have fewer) years of education. Only 15.9 percent of all black male heads and 19.8 percent of all white male heads have at least four years of high school. Only 10.2 percent of all poor heads attended college for some period of time. Minority heads, both male and female, rarely have attended college.

TABLE 4.5

Increases in female-headed poor families: 1959–1976

Year	All poor families (number in millions)	Male head (number in millions)	% male head	Female head (number in millions)	% female head
1959	8.3	6.4	77.0%	1.9	23.0%
1969	5.0	3.2	63.5	1.8	36.5
1971	5.3	3.2	60.4	2.1	39.6
1972	5.1	2.9	57.5	2.2	42.5
1973	4.8	2.6	54.6	2.2	45.4
1974	4.9	2.6	52.8	2.3	47.2
1975	5.4	3.0	55.4	2.4	44.6
1976	5.3	2.8	52.8	2.5	47.2

Source: U.S. Bureau of the Census, "Characteristics of the Population Below the Poverty Level," *Current Population Reports*, Series P-60, various years.

TABLE 4.6

Educational attainment of head of families with income below poverty level, by sex and race: 1975

Educational attainment*	All families	Male head	Female head	White male head	Black male head	White female head	Black female head
Elementary: total	41.8%	48.8%	32.4%	46.8%	61.6%	32.6%	31.8%
Less than 8 years	28.1	33.8	20.4	30.7	51.0	19.8	21.1
8 years	13.7	14.9	12.0	16.1	10.6	12.9	10.7
High school: total	48.0	38.5	60.8	39.1	33.9	58.5	64.4
1–3 years	24.3	18.9	31.6	19.3	18.0	26.2	38.9
4 years	23.7	19.6	29.2	19.8	15.9	32.3	25.5
College: total	10.2	12.8	6.8	14.2	4.5	8.9	3.6

Source: U.S. Bureau of the Census, "Money Income and Poverty Status of Families and Persons in the United States: 1975 and 1974 Revisions (Advance Report)," *Current Population Reports*, Series P-60, no. 103, September 1976, pp. 37–39.

* Based on head of family aged twenty-five years or older (4.6 million).

POVERTY AND WORK EXPERIENCE

A slight majority of all poor heads were employed at some time during 1975 (see Table 4.7). Almost 20 percent of all poor heads worked 50 to 52 weeks during 1975, but were unable to earn their way out of poverty. The overwhelming majority of these year-round workers were employed full-time. Among male-headed families, 28 percent worked year round without being able to escape poverty. Another 30.7 percent of all the poor worked from 1 to 49 weeks. Of this group, 35 percent worked 27 to 49 weeks, and 65 percent worked from 1 to 26 weeks. The majority of those employed 1 to 49 weeks worked full-time, especially those who worked from 27 to 49 weeks. Forty-nine percent of all poor heads were not in the job market. Most of those outside the job market are women with dependent children, disabled persons, and the elderly.

Male family heads, especially whites, were much more likely to be in the job market than were either white or black female family heads. Slightly over 61 percent of all male-headed families were in the job market as opposed to only 36.5 percent of all female heads. White male heads were slightly more likely (62.7 compared to 53.4 percent) to be employed than were black male heads. There was very little difference in work participation between black and white female-headed families (36.2 compared to 37.2 percent). Black female heads, however, more often worked year round than did white female heads.

POVERTY AND RESIDENCE

Some 61 percent of all poor Americans live in metropolitan areas. As noted, poor blacks are more likely to live in metropolitan areas than are poor whites (66 percent compared to 53 percent) and they are much more likely to live in central-city poverty areas (see Table 4.8). If present trends continue, poor blacks will increasingly become the major residents of the central-city core. In 1910, 73 percent of all blacks lived in rural areas. However, to escape rural poverty and discrimination, blacks in large numbers migrated to urban areas. By 1970, 81 percent of all blacks lived in urban areas, 58 percent in central cities.[23] By 1975 the twelve largest American cities contained one-third of all black Americans and two-thirds of the black population living outside the South.[24]

As blacks have migrated to the city, whites have moved to the suburbs in increasing numbers. In the early 1970s, whites were leaving the central

TABLE 4.7

Work experience of heads of poverty families in 1975, by race and sex

	Head worked last year	Worked 50–52 wks	Worked 1–49 wks	Head did not work last year	Head in armed forces
All Races	50.4%	19.6%	30.7%	49.1%	.5%
White	53.4	21.5	31.9	45.8	.7
Black	41.9	14.9	27.0	58.0	.1
Male-headed	61.5	28.0	33.4	37.5	.9
White male-headed	62.7	29.2	33.4	36.1	.2
Black male-headed	53.4	22.2	31.2	46.3	.3
Female-headed	36.5	9.2	27.3	63.5	—
White female-headed	37.2	7.9	29.2	62.8	—
Black female-headed	36.2	11.1	24.9	63.8	—

Source: U.S. Bureau of the Census, "Money Income and Poverty Status of Families and Persons in the United States: 1975 and 1974 Revisions (Advance Report)," *Current Population Reports*, Series P-60, no. 103, September, 1976, pp. 37–39.

TABLE 4.8

Residential distribution of the poor, 1976

	All races (in millions)	White— including Spanish origin (in millions)	Poverty rate— white	Black (in millions)	Poverty rate— black
Entire United States	24,975	16,713	9.1%	7,595	31.1%
Nonfarm	23,716	15,734	8.9	7,361	30.8
Farm	1,259	979	13.3	234	49.9
Inside metropolitan areas	15,229	9,659	7.9	5,149	28.6
Inside central city	9,482	5,068	11.3	4,167	31.0
In poverty area	4,306	1,554	31.3	2,654	40.8
Outside central city	5,747	4,591	5.9	982	21.5
In poverty area	996	489	15.1	455	39.4
Outside metropolitan areas	9,746	7,054	11.4	2,447	38.2
In poverty area	5,224	3,055	16.0	1,973	43.2

Source: U.S. Bureau of the Census, "Money Income and Poverty Status of Families and Persons in the United States: 1976 (Advance Report)," *Current Population Reports*, Series P-60, no. 107, September 1977, p. 25.

"I Don't Understand It — Why Can't They Behave
As If They Had Good Educations, Good Housing
And Good Jobs?"

From *The Herblock Gallery* (Simon & Schuster, 1968).

city at the rate of 900,000 a year.[25] By 1970 only 40 percent of all whites living in urban areas lived in central cities. As whites and other middle- and upper-income citizens have fled the central city, the tax base of the city has been steadily eroded. With a smaller and smaller base of middle-income citizens and businesses to tax, the cities have had to reduce services while increasing the tax rate on those who have not been able to move to suburbia. Reduced services often contribute to the deterioration of the city and often handicap the poor. Underfunded schools provide poor education, financially stricken hospitals provide poor health care, inferior housing breeds tensions and spreads and aggravates disease, inadequate transportation makes it difficult to obtain a job, reduced police forces encourage crime, and a shortage of recreational opportunities encourages delinquency and vandalism.

Thirty-nine percent of all the poor live in rural areas, including 42 percent of all white poor and 32 percent of all black poor. In 1975, 42 percent of all blacks who lived outside metropolitan areas were poor, compared to only 12.6 percent of white rural residents. While farm residence is actually very small, 50.1 percent of all blacks who lived on farms in 1975 were poor.

The 9.5 million poor Americans who live in rural areas are primarily the victims of the disappearance of the family farm and corporate channeling of rural-earned profits to urban areas. Wealth in rural areas generally results from the development of land and natural resources. As farming, mining, and timber processing have become more and more the preserve of large corporations, automation has cut down on the need for labor and profits are banked in those urban areas where corporations have their headquarters. Rather than small farmers spending their money in their own community, corporations such as Tenneco often buy needed machinery and supplies outside the community and circulate elsewhere any profits they earn. The economic impact of such actions on rural areas has been severe.

Movement of corporations into rural businesses has often put small entrepreneurs out of business. Farm helpers, or sharecroppers, have often lost their jobs as a result of the decline of the family farm; frequently, they are unable to relocate. Other areas of the country, such as Appalachia, have been stripped of their natural resources and abandoned in a scarred and depleted condition. Those Appalachians who once depended on the mines for work often have little inclination to leave their homes to locate new opportunities, and often have few skills to offer in the job market.

As in central cities, economic deprivation in rural areas sets off a cycle of debilitating conditions. Medical services are much less plentiful in rural areas, housing often deteriorates, prices are generally high because of low demand and a lack of competition, and services such as education suffer from inadequate funding. The cycle of poverty is thus perpetuated.

Regional Distribution of the Poor

The highest concentration of poverty is in the South. The South contains 33 percent of the American population and 41 percent of all the American poor. Thirty-five percent of all poor whites live in the South, as do 57 percent of all poor blacks (see Table 4.9). Some 11 percent of all the whites who live in the South are poor, compared to 33.1 percent of all blacks who live in the South. While the South is clearly the poorest region in America with 15.2 percent of all citizens living in poverty, 10.2 percent of all citizens in the North, 9.9 percent in the north central states, and 10.5 percent in the West are poor. Black poverty is severe in every region in America, averaging 29.5 percent. Thus, while the South needs more aid than do other regions, poverty is clearly severe in all regions and only nationwide reforms can alleviate the problem.

TABLE 4.9

Regional distribution of the poor

	Number in millions			Poverty rate		
	All races	White	Black	All races	White	Black
Northeast	4,949	3,637	1,229	10.2%	8.3%	29.5%
North Central	5,657	4,091	1,480	9.9	7.9	29.7
South	10,354	5,914	4,336	15.2	10.8	33.1
West	4,015	3,071	550	10.5	9.0	25.8

Source: U.S. Bureau of the Census, "Money Income and Poverty Status of Families and Persons in the United States: 1976 (Advance Report)," *Current Population Reports,* Series P-60, no. 107, September 1977, p. 25.

CONCLUSIONS

Those with the highest probability of being poor in America are minorities (especially minorities who live in the central-city core and rural areas), children (especially those in female-headed families), the aged, members of families headed by a poorly educated person (especially if the head is a minority). Groups that have been subjected to discrimination and exploitation throughout American history, such as minorities and women, are—not surprisingly—disproportionately represented among the poor. Also disproportionately represented are persons who generally cannot through their own efforts deal with their poverty—children, the aged, and female family heads with small children and/or large numbers of children. These findings provide some insights into the way reforms would have to be tailored to deal with poverty.

Quite obviously, all discrimination against women and minorities must be ended and the legacy of past discrimination dealt with. Many other poor persons could escape poverty if the job market were substantially expanded and improved. Many women with small children would need child-care assistance to get into the market, as well as job training. Those persons who cannot earn a living can be removed from poverty only by adequate public assistance.

In the next two chapters we analyze how the government has responded to the poor, and in Chapter 8 we examine welfare reforms in more detail.

NOTES

1. U.S. Bureau of the Census, "The Social and Economic Status of the Black Population in the United States 1975," *Current Population Reports,* Series P-23, no. 54 (Washington, D.C.: U.S. Government Printing Office), p. 1.

2. Ibid., p. 2.

3. Ibid., p. 4.

4. U.S. Bureau of the Census, "Persons of Spanish Origin in the United States: March 1976 (Advance Report)," *Current Population Reports,* Series P-20, no. 302 (Washington, D.C.: U.S. Government Printing Office), p. 1.

5. Ibid., p. 3.

6. Ibid., pp. 1–6.

7. Ibid., p. 1.

8. The U.S. Commission on Civil Rights, *Puerto Ricans in the Continental United States: An Uncertain Future* (Washington, D.C.: U.S. Government Printing Office, 1976), p. 9.

9. Ibid., p. 35.

10. Ibid., p. 57.

11. Ibid., p. 56.

12. Ibid., p. 9.

13. Mariellen Procopio and Fredrick J. Perella, Jr., *Poverty Profile 1975* (Washington, D.C.: Campaign for Human Development, 1975), p. 50.

14. Louis Harris Associates, *The Myth and Reality of Aging in America* (Washington, D.C.: The Council on the Aging, 1975), p. 131.

15. U.S. Bureau of the Census, "Demographic Aspects of Aging," *Current Population Reports* (Washington, D.C.: U.S. Government Printing Office , 1975), p. 3.

16. Ibid., pp. 54–55.

17. U.S. Bureau of the Census, "Money Income and Poverty Status of Families and Persons in the United States: 1975 and 1974 Revisions (Advance Report)" *Current Population Reports,* Series P-60, no. 103 (Washington, D.C.: U.S. Government Printing Office, 1976).

18. The U.S. Commission on Civil Rights, *Puerto Ricans in the Continental United States: An Uncertain Future,* p. 56.

19. U.S. Bureau of the Census, "A Statistical Portrait of Women in the U.S.," *Current Population Reports,* Series P-23, no. 58 (Washington, D.C.: U.S. Government Printing Office, 1976), p. 45.

20. See Mollie Orshansky and Judith S. Bretz, "Born to Be Poor: Birth-place and Number of Brothers and Sisters as Factors in Adult Poverty," *Social Security Bulletin*, January 1976, pp. 21–37.

21. U.S. Bureau of the Census, "A Statistical Portrait of Women in the U.S.," p. 61.

22. Ibid., p. 15.

23. U.S. Bureau of the Census, *Statistical Abstract of the United States 1971* (Washington, D.C.: U.S. Government Printing Office, 1971), Table 14, p. 11.

24. Heinz Kohler, *Economics and Urban Problems* (Lexington, Mass.: D.C. Heath, 1973), p. 80.

25. Ibid., p. 77.

5
PROGRAMS IN AID OF THE POOR

Federal, state, and local governments administer hundreds of programs to provide services and aid to the public. Examples would include everything from food stamps and hot-lunch programs to secondary and higher education, police and fire protection, health-care programs, and pension plans for local, state, and federal employees. Broadly defined, these services are called social welfare programs. Between 1965 and 1976, social welfare expenditures at all levels of government increased from $77.2 billion to $331.4 billion.[1]

Social welfare programs are of three basic types:

1. Social insurance programs such as Social Security, Medicare, and unemployment compensation. Social insurance programs are based on employee and/or employer contributions and benefits are wage related.

2. Cash-assistance programs such as Aid to Families with Dependent Children (AFDC) and Supplemental Security Income (SSI).

3. In-kind programs such as food stamps and Medicaid, which provide a noncash service.

Table 5.1 shows how public-oriented social welfare expenditures are disbursed to various income quintiles. The government also provides cash and in-kind benefits to businesses, but they are not considered here. Table 5.1 indicates that, in fiscal 1976, 31.9 percent of all social insurance expenditures went to the poorest 20 percent of citizens. Over 60 percent of all cash assistance went to the least affluent quintile, as did 53 percent of all in-kind benefits.[2] If the second lowest quintile is added in, some 70 to 80 percent of all public-oriented cash and in-kind social welfare expenditures go to the poorest 40 percent of all citizens.

In this and the next chapter, we analyze some of the major social welfare programs designed for the public. Our focus is on how the programs work, their strengths and weaknesses as antipoverty techniques, and their

TABLE 5.1

Distribution of federal, state, and local benefits: fiscal year 1976

Quintiles[a]	Social insurance[b]	Cash assistance[b]	In-kind transfers[b]
Low 20%	31.9%	61.7%	53.2%
Second 20%	28.4	20.6	26.3
Third 20%	16.2	9.4	10.5
Fourth 20%	12.0	5.0	5.4
High 20%	11.5	3.9	4.4
	100.0%[c]	100.0%	100.0%
Total dollars in billions	$124.0	$18.0	$41.0

Source: Congressional Budget Office, *Poverty Status of Families Under Alternative Definitions of Income* (Washington, D.C.: Government Printing Office, 1977), p. 5.
[a]The upper limits of each quintile are as follows: low 20% ($1,812), second 20% ($7,871), third 20% ($13,994), and fourth 20% ($21,682).
[b]Social insurance includes Social Security and Railroad Retirement, government pensions, unemployment insurance, worker compensation, veteran's compensation. Cash assistance includes veteran's pensions, Supplemental Security Income, Aid to Families with Dependent Children. In-kind transfers include food stamps, child nutrition, housing assistance, Medicare, and Medicaid.
[c]Components may not add to totals because of rounding.

impact on the poor and on poverty in general. Later chapters suggest alterations and alternatives to these programs.

OVERVIEW

Table 5.2 shows the major social welfare programs in operation in the mid-1970s, the basis of eligibility, source of funding, form of aid, and expenditures and beneficiaries in fiscal years 1975, 1976, and 1977. The major social insurance programs in 1975 cost $95.5 billion (74 percent of all social welfare expenditures) and $110.2 billion (75 percent of all social welfare expenditures) in 1976. Cash-assistance expenditures in 1975 totaled $15.2 billion (12 percent of expenditures) and $16.2 billion in 1976 (11 percent of expenditures). In-kind programs cost $17.7 billion in 1975 (14 percent of expenditures) and $21.0 billion in 1976 (14 percent of all expenditures).

The rapid growth of social welfare programs in the 1970s is dramatically evidenced by an examination of individual programs. Between 1970 and 1976 the cost of AFDC increased from $4.8 billion to $9.7 billion. Food-stamp costs increased from $577 million in 1970 to $5.7 billion in 1976. SSI, a new federal program in 1973, cost $4.6 billion in its first year, and $6.5 billion in 1976. Between 1972 and 1976 Medicaid increased in cost from $3.3 billion to $14.7 billion.[3] These very substantial increases indicate a growing dependency on antipoverty programs, a dependency brought about to a large extent by the severity of economic conditions during the 1970s. However, as we detail in Chapter 7, at the same time the welfare programs were being increased in size, other decisions were being made by the federal government which seriously increased poverty (e.g., acceptance of high unemployment, high interest rates, a high tax rate on middle-income citizens).

While social welfare expenditures account for an increasingly large share of the total federal budget, welfare programs designed primarily to deal with the needs of poor citizens do not constitute a very large share of the total. For example, in 1976, cash-assistance expenditures by the federal government (not counting state contributions) constituted about 3 percent of the total federal budget. In-kind federal expenditures for food stamps and Medicaid accounted for another 4 percent. The broadly oriented social insurance programs such as Social Security, Medicare, and unemployment compensation accounted for 31.5 percent of the total federal budget.

"What Are We Willing To Spend To
Save Some Territory At Home?"

From *The Herblock Gallery* (Simon & Schuster, 1968).

THE IMPACT OF AID PROGRAMS ON POVERTY

Given the amount of money spent on social welfare expenditures, an obvious question is: How many of the poor receive aid and how many are removed from poverty by that aid? The best estimates are that, in 1975, only about 60 percent of the nonaged poor received any type of assistance, with only about 35 percent receiving any type of cash aid.[4] The aged poor always qualify for SSI (as long as they meet the asset and other categorical requirements) and/or Social Security, Medicaid (in forty-nine states) and food stamps (in forty-five states). In five states—California, New York, Nevada, Wisconsin, and Massachusetts—SSI recipients are not eligible for food stamps, because these states have opted to cash out the value of food stamps and add it to the state supplement to SSI.

The number of persons removed from poverty by social welfare expenditures has increased over the years. In 1965, 33 percent of the pretransfer poor were moved over the poverty line by cash welfare.[5] Plotnick

TABLE 5.2

Selected programs

Program	Basis of eligibility	Source of income	Form of aid	Fiscal 1975		Fiscal 1976		Fiscal 1977	
				Expenditures (billions)	Beneficiaries (monthly average in millions)	Expenditures (billions)	Beneficiaries (monthly average in millions)	Expenditures (billions)	Beneficiaries (monthly average in millions)
Social insurance programs									
Old Age Survivors and Dependent Insurance (OASDI)	Age, disability, or death of parent or spouse; individual earnings	Federal payroll taxes on employers and employees	Cash	63.7	30.9	72.6	33.0	81.9	33.3
Unemployment compensation	Unemployment	State and federal payroll tax on employers	Cash	17.0	16.0	19.8	17.5	14.8	11.0
Medicare	Age or disability	Federal payroll tax on employers and employees	Subsidized health insurance	14.8	24.7	17.8	26.0	21.2	25.2

Cash assistance programs								
Aid to Families with Dependent Children (AFDC)	Certain families with children; income	Federal–state local revenues	Cash and services	9.2	11.1	9.7	11.4	10.3	11.4
Supplemental Security Income (SSI)	Age or disability; income	Federal–state revenues	Cash	5.9	4.0	6.1	4.3	6.3	4.4
In-kind programs									
Medicaid	Persons eligible for AFDC or SSI and medically indigent	Federal–state local revenues	Subsidized health service	12.7	8.4	15.1	9.2	17.2	10.4
Food stamps	Income	Federal revenues	Vouchers	4.7	17.1	5.7	18.5	5.0	17

Source: *Social Security Bulletin*, February 1978, p. 61. Some of the 1977 figures are tentative.

and Skidmore found that, in 1972, 17.6 million households, including 39.5 million persons, were poor before they received cash welfare assistance or Social Security. Cash welfare and Social Security reduced the number of poor to about 23 million persons. Thus, 44 percent of the pretransfer poor were moved over the poverty line by cash welfare and Social Security in 1972.[6]

These figures, however, are deceptive for two reasons. First, as noted in Chapter 2, the federal government does not attempt to calculate in-kind benefits in poor persons' income. If in-kind benefits were included, many of those counted as poor would be pushed over the artificially low poverty threshold. One study concluded that if income were adjusted for underreporting of cash assistance, taxes paid, and in-kind benefits, only 7 percent of all households, or 5.2 percent of all persons, would have been counted as poor in 1972 (more detailed figures are provided in Chapter 2).[7]

Second, some programs are much more likely than others to remove recipients from poverty, and some persons are much more likely to qualify for the kind of aid that will remove them from poverty. For example, Social Security benefits are generally much better than cash-assistance benefits, and they go primarily to people (the aged) who can qualify for at least one aid program and generally more. Not surprisingly, Social Security removes more people from poverty than does any other program.

> In both 1965 and 1972, the overwhelming majority of pretransfer poor households that escaped poverty were dependent upon Social Security to do so. And the fraction of households kept from poverty by this program rose sharply from 21 percent in 1965 to 30 percent in 1972. . . . This impact has been mostly concentrated among the elderly—36 percent of the pretransfer poor aged households were made nonpoor by Social Security in 1965, 51 percent of them in 1972.[8]

Welfare programs for the nonaged are not nearly as effective at reducing or preventing poverty. It has been calculated that only 3 percent of the pretransfer poor were made nonpoor by cash welfare in 1965. Even after substantial funding increases, the proportion increased only to 6 percent in 1972.[9]

Thus, some poor persons are much more likely to be removed from poverty than are others. Plotnick and Skidmore calculated the following probabilities that selected groups would be removed from poverty by cash welfare in 1972:[10]

1. Elderly white couple   87%
2. Elderly black couple   70%
3. Widow (white)   48%
4. Widow (black)   ·   34%
5. Widower (white)   67%
6. Female family head (white)   29%
7. Female family head (black)   25%
8. Male family head (black)   13%
9. Male family head (white)   29%

Table 5.3 provides estimates for 1976 based on social insurance programs, cash assistance, in-kind programs, and tax policies. The study shows that 21 percent of the population was below the poverty line before receipt of any benefits, but cash transfers (from social insurance and cash

TABLE 5.3

Estimated impact of public programs on the poverty population in fiscal year 1976

	Number of persons (millions)	Percentage poor		
		Before programs	After cash transfer	After all programs
Age groups				
Persons under 25 years	95.8	20.4%	14.6%	8.1%
Persons 25–64 years	98.3	14.1	8.1	5.3
Persons 65 years and older	22.9	54.1	12.8	4.6
All persons	217.0	21.1	11.4	6.5
Poverty-prone groups				
Mothers with children	19.0	58.4	41.8	14.0
Families with aged head	27.2	53.7	13.5	5.6
Nonwhite units	27.6	40.8	27.6	13.0
Units in South	71.4	26.5	16.6	11.0
Single persons	21.6	47.8	25.0	17.0

Source: Harold Watts and Felicity Skidmore, "An Update of the Poverty Picture Plus a New Look at Relative Tax Burdens," *Focus: Institute for Research on Poverty Newsletter 2*, no. 1 (Fall 1977): 5. Reprinted by permission.

welfare) reduced the poor population to 11.4 percent. When taxes and in-kind transfers are considered, the poverty count is further reduced to 6.5 percent of the total population. Again, however, there are two caveats. First, the impact of the programs is exaggerated considerably because of the artificially low poverty standards in use. Second, some groups are much more likely to be aided than are others.

For example, before taxes and transfers, 27 percent of those defined as poor are aged, but the impact of all programs reduces aged poverty to 7.5 percent of the total. However, while 43 percent of the pretransfer poor are under twenty-five, 55 percent of all the posttransfer poor are under twenty-five. Similarly, 41 percent of all pretransfer poor live in the South, but, because of extremely low benefit levels in this region, 56 percent of all the posttransfer poor live in the South.

GENERAL PROBLEMS WITH AID PROGRAMS

Social welfare expenditures are considerably less effective in reducing and preventing poverty than they should be. There are many reasons for this, the most obvious being that there is no overall program designed to deal with the poor. Instead, a whole series of individual, frequently duplicative, programs have been created in serial installments by various levels of government in response to a particular problem or in response to some of the needs of a particular segment of the total poverty population. Often, benefits are keyed not to need, but to whether an individual fits into the "eligible" category of a particular program.

Each of the major social welfare programs has its own eligibility standards and its own methods of defining income and poverty. Responsibility for administration of the various welfare programs is spread among the federal, state, and local governments in a complex and often dysfunctional way. For example, the Social Security Administration administers Social Security and SSI, the Department of Agriculture administers food stamps, and Health, Education and Welfare administers AFDC and Medicaid. Consider the following data compiled by HEW to show that the income security system is not an integrated system.*

---

* Source: U.S. Congress, House, Hearing before the Subcommittee on Public Assistance and Unemployment Compensation of the Committee on Ways and Means, 95th Cong., May 4, 1977, p. 14.

	AFDC	SSI	Food stamps	Medicaid
Form of benefit	Cash	Cash	Coupons	Services
Benefit reduction rate	67% earned 100% unearned	50% earned 100% unearned	30%	NOTCH
Eligible unit	Family	Individual	Household	Individual or family
Income definition	All programs use a net income definition, but all use a different set of exemptions and deductions.			
Accounting period	1 month	3 months	1–2 months (varies with household)	6 months
Assets test	Varies by state	$1500 market value	$1500 equity value	Varies by state
Policy control	HEW-state	HEW	USDA	HEW-state
Financing	HEW-state	HEW	USDA	HEW-state
Administration	State	HEW	State	State

One result is that the programs lack horizontal equity—persons with the same degree of need do not receive the same degree of aid. This horizontal inequity results from the categorical nature of much welfare aid, from state and local variations in welfare benefit levels, and from variations in the way rules are interpreted by localities or even by individual welfare offices and personnel—even the patience or savvy a particular person manifests in dealing with the welfare bureaucracy can have an effect.

The programs also lack vertical equity—those with the most severe needs do not receive aid before those with less severe needs. In fact, aid often goes to families whose needs are far less severe than those of families who never receive any aid. Additionally, because state welfare guidelines are not pegged to the Social Security Administration poverty guidelines for any of the major assistance programs, some persons who would not be considered poor by the federal standards receive aid, and many persons continue to receive aid after they have received enough assistance to cross the poverty threshold for their family size.

As noted, much of the inequity of current programs results from the fact that they are categorical—that is, they serve only persons with particular characteristics. For example, the major cash-assistance program

(AFDC) is designed only for heads of families with dependent children. In practice, most AFDC aid is limited to female heads of families with dependent children. This means that unrelated individuals, couples without children, and, of course, intact, male-headed, poor families are generally left out. A single man or woman who becomes needy will generally have great difficulty obtaining assistance, even though he or she needs help badly. Particularly hard hit are young, unemployed persons who have never been in the job market and middle-aged, single persons who fall on hard times.

Other than food stamps, a poor person who cannot qualify for AFDC can only seek general assistance from the state—if the state he or she lives in has a general-assistance program. In January 1976, forty-two of the states had a general-assistance program, but with a total of only 1,002,629 recipients. About a third of the states with a general-assistance program provide benefits to only a few hundred families a year. Benefit levels under general assistance are normally very low. In January 1976, the average general-assistance case (family or individual) received $146.53 per month, or $103.67 per recipient.[11] Total state and local expenditures for general assistance in fiscal 1976 were $1.2 billion.

One final reason why aid programs do not do a better job of eliminating poverty is because of severe regional variations in levels of spending. The South, which has the largest number of poor, spends less per recipient than does any other region of the country. In fiscal 1976 the South's total (state and federal) expenditure for each poor resident was $784. The midwestern states averaged $1,589, the western states averaged $1,512, and the Northeast averaged expenditures of $2,425 per recipient, over three times the per-person expenditure in the South. Federal contributions to state welfare expenditures are proportional to state expenditures, with a higher federal contribution in states with low per capita income. The Department of Health, Education and Welfare calculates that in fiscal 1978 the South will receive 37.2 percent of all federal funds spent on AFDC, SSI, and food stamps. The Northeast will receive 22.8 percent of funds, the north central states 22.9 percent, and the West only 17.2 percent. Still, state contributions in the South are so low that federal adjustments cannot compensate for state discrepancies. For example, in the Northeast, state and local governments spent an average of $1,100 per poor resident in 1976. In the South, state and local governments spent less than $200 per poor citizen. State and local spending variations ranged from $1,422 per poor recipient in Massachusetts to $1,345 in Hawaii, to only $62 in Mississippi, $64 in New Mexico, and $72 in Arizona.[12]

Medicaid expenditures, like AFDC expenditures, are particularly severely maldistributed. In recent years, New York state has been responsible for about one-quarter of all Medicaid expenditures. A congressional study found that ". . . the seven states with the highest Medicaid payments provide 57 percent of payments while containing one-quarter of the poverty population, whereas the 25 states at the bottom of the Medicaid ladder contain half of the poverty population but disburse only 19 percent of Medicaid payment."[13] Thus, the most generous states may provide aid beyond that necessary to move a person or family beyond the poverty level, while other states may do little or nothing for many of their poor.

In addition to these general problems, the individual programs have numerous deficiencies. Let's now turn to some of the major programs and examine their strengths and weaknesses as antipoverty techniques.

AID TO FAMILIES WITH DEPENDENT CHILDREN

AFDC is the major cash-assistance program. Prior to 1961 it provided aid only for children whose parents were dead, disabled, or absent. Amendments in 1961 extended benefits to certain poor parents with dependent children. Between 1965 and 1976, the number of families served by AFDC more than tripled. AFDC is administered by the states with all program costs shared among the federal, state, and local government. The federal government pays about 55 percent of costs, the states about 34 percent, and local governments pay about 12 percent. Variations by state, however, are large. The federal contribution is based on state spending with an adjustment for low-per-capita-income states. In high-per-capita states (thirteen in all), the federal share is the minimum 50 percent. In low-per-capita states like Arkansas, South Carolina, and Mississippi, it is 75 percent, 76 percent, and 79 percent, respectively.

Eligibility requirements for AFDC are established by the states with some federal guidelines. However, because of the complexity of AFDC regulations, few AFDC families are treated exactly the same, even within the same state or locality. Twenty-eight states have an AFDC–UF program for unemployed fathers. In states with a UF program, some unemployed fathers with dependent children and some employed fathers who work less than 100 hours a month qualify for AFDC. However, as the figures below show, the standards for male heads are so restrictive that few can qualify. In 1975 and 1976 some 3.5 million families (with 11.3 million recipients) received AFDC benefits. The monthly average for families headed by a male was only 120,000 in 1975 and 147,000 in 1976. At any given time, about 20 percent of all AFDC families include a father, but about two-thirds of these men are incapacitated and a woman is the family head.

Between fiscal years 1974 and 1975 the number of total families served increased yearly, but, as the figures below show, the number of actual persons served declined in 1976:

Total AFDC	1976	1975	1974
Families	3,564,000	3,485,000	3,219,000
Recipients	11,280,000	11,328,000	10,849,000
Children	7,979,000	8,078,000	7,807,000
Unemployed-father segment			
Families	147,000	120,000	90,000
Recipients	644,000	527,000	409,000
Children	368,000	307,000	243,000
Other AFDC			
Families	3,417,000	3,365,000	3,129,000
Recipients	10,636,000	10,801,000	10,440,000
Children	7,611,000	7,771,000	7,564,000

Because of the discrimination against men, 80.1 percent of all AFDC families in 1975 were headed by a woman. Most of these AFDC mothers were poorly educated. In 1975 only 28.3 percent of AFDC mothers had at least a high school diploma. The national average for women aged fifteen to forty-four with children is 71 percent.[14] A slight majority of AFDC recipients are white. The figures below show the racial breakdown from 1961 to 1975.[15]

	1961	1969	1973	1975
White	51.9%	50.5%	48.7%	50.2%
Nonwhite	48.1	49.6	51.3	49.8
Black	43.2	47.5	47.6	44.3
Indian	1.6	1.4	1.1	1.1
Other	3.2	0.7	2.6	4.3

In 1975 most AFDC recipients lived in urban areas: 18.8 percent lived in cities of one million or more; 30.3 percent in cities with a population between 100,000 and 1,000,000; 27.4 percent in urban areas with less than 100,000 population; and only 13.8 percent in rural areas.

Contrary to popular thinking, most families do not remain on the AFDC rolls for five and ten years at a stretch. In 1973, female-headed families averaged twenty months on AFDC, male-headed families averaged only nine months. Generally, about 25 percent of all families leave AFDC rolls within six months, half leave within two years, and three-fifths are terminated within three years. However, because of severe economic conditions in 1974 and 1975, the average AFDC recipient stayed on the rolls for a record thirty-one months.

Additionally, some AFDC families are repeaters. Levitan, Rein, and Marwick found that in both 1961 and 1971 one-third of all AFDC families had received assistance before. Of those who were repeaters, two-thirds had been recipients at least twice before. One-fifth had also been denied aid at some time or another.[16] Many AFDC recipients were also raised in families that received assistance. One study showed that more than 40 percent of mothers and/or fathers on welfare in 1961 had been raised in homes where assistance had been received.[17]

Benefits under AFDC

In January 1976 the average AFDC family received $229.12 per month, or $71.52 per recipient. Variations between states, however, are substantial. Each state determines the cash needs of its poor families. Variations in state estimates of need are wide ranging. For example, in 1976 for a family of four, Texas estimated cash need at $187. North Carolina's estimate was $200, Hawaii's $497, and Wisconsin's $456. Only eighteen states attempt to provide enough aid to compensate for the total gap between a poor family's income and the estimated cash need. Texas, for example, provides only $140.25 to a penniless family of four rather than $187. The figures below show the variations in average family AFDC benefits by state in January 1976.

Alabama	$ 94.42	District of Columbia	$233.52
Alaska	284.34	Florida	124.36
Arizona	134.61	Georgia	96.35
Arkansas	121.88	Hawaii	337.21
California	263.25	Idaho	250.22
Colorado	205.85	Illinois	276.78
Connecticut	265.50	Indiana	171.44
Delaware	194.65	Iowa	273.18

Kansas	217.75	North Dakota	246.29
Kentucky	176.93	Ohio	204.19
Louisiana	121.88	Oklahoma	189.10
Maine	177.21	Oregon	243.77
Maryland	184.62	Pennsylvania	283.10
Massachusetts	268.30	Rhode Island	246.70
Michigan	287.25	South Carolina	88.42
Minnesota	264.75	South Dakota	199.72
Mississippi	48.53	Tennessee	104.20
Missouri	141.16	Texas	106.65
Montana	165.57	Utah	234.77
Nebraska	205.35	Vermont	263.51
Nevada	163.24	Virginia	192.86
New Hampshire	225.25	Washington	254.39
New Jersey	278.79	West Virginia	177.79
New Mexico	139.71	Wisconsin	301.12
New York	367.19	Wyoming	178.19
North Carolina	155.64		

While the figures show that benefits are not terribly high in any of the states, in the least-generous states families are kept in a condition of severe destitution.

In addition to cash benefits, AFDC provides a range of supporting services to recipients. The services include employment assistance, adult basic education, vocational rehabilitation, family planning and counseling, day care, and legal services or aid. The figures below show the percentage of AFDC recipients receiving these benefits in 1975:[18]

Employment assistance	8.6%
Adult basic education	1.4%
Vocational rehabilitation	2.5%
Day care	2.7%
Legal services/aid	3.2%

While some of the services only improve the condition of poor families, most are designed to help poor family heads become self-reliant and to prevent the children of the poor from becoming part of the cycle of poverty.

As of July 1972, AFDC recipients are required to register for the

Work Incentive Program (WIN)* which provides employment services and training. This program was intended to help AFDC heads obtain viable employment, so that they will no longer need welfare. Some poor family heads are exempted from the registration requirement. Those exempted include mothers or other relatives who must care for children under six; persons who are ill, incapacitated, or of advanced age; persons who do not live close to a WIN project; persons needed in the home because a family member is ill or incapacitated; and mothers in AFDC–UF families in which the father is in the WIN program.

About 60 percent of all AFDC mothers are exempt from the WIN program because they have children under six or because there is no WIN project in their community. If, however, a mother with children under six wants to volunteer for the WIN program, she may. If an AFDC head is admitted to a WIN training program, child care is made available during training and for thirty days after the head enters the job market. Because funds for day care have been severely limited (see Chapter 8), many AFDC heads have not been able to enter WIN training programs.

In addition to cash assistance and supportive services, all AFDC recipients are eligible for Medicaid and food stamps. In 1973, 99 percent of all families receiving AFDC benefits participated in the Medicaid program and about 60 percent used food stamps.† In addition, 59 percent of all AFDC families had children who participated in the school lunch program, 13.6 percent lived in public housing, 4.4 percent received Social Security, 0.9 percent received veterans benefits, and 8.9 percent received surplus commodities.[18a] In 1975, 99 percent of AFDC families were using Medicaid, and food-stamp participation increased to 75 percent. By 1975 almost all food commodities went to institutions.

Altogether, about 75 percent of AFDC families received benefits from two or more programs in 1975. Between 10 and 25 percent of AFDC households receive benefits from five or more programs. A small number of families receive benefits from ten to twelve programs.[19] Ironically,

---

* Because the initials of this program (WIP) have an unpleasant connotation, the program is known as WIN. The federal government pays 90 percent of the cost of the WIN program in each state.

†Food-stamp participation is rather low, considering the fact that all AFDC families are eligible. Many AFDC heads do not participate because of the complexity of the food-stamp eligibility provisions and because they may live with someone (such as a parent) who is not eligible for food stamps. Unless everyone in a household is eligible for food stamps, no one can receive them. The purchase price of the stamps also discouraged some families, but this requirement was changed in late 1977.

some families who receive benefits from five or more programs remain below the poverty level.[20]

While eligibility for multiple programs helps many of the poor, as we shall see, multiple and overlapping programs also create some serious problems.

Problems with the AFDC Program

As the major cash-assistance program in the United States, AFDC is extremely flawed. The deficiencies of AFDC cause major problems for the poor and contribute considerably to the continuation of the cycle of poverty. Three major problems with AFDC are examined in this section.

Family disintegration The AFDC program contributes to the breakup of many poor families. Since relatively few male-headed families can obtain AFDC benefits, many unemployed men are, in effect, forced to abandon their wives and children, so that their families will be eligible for assistance. Additionally, even some employed, low-income male heads choose to desert their families when they realize AFDC, Medicaid, and food-stamp benefits exceed the value of their income. In 1972 a congressional study concluded that a man with a wife and two children working at a $2.00-an-hour job could increase his family's annual income by an average of $2,158 by abandoning them.[21] In twenty-eight states, AFDC benefits alone exceed the net income from a minimum-wage job. These twenty-eight states contained 61 percent of all AFDC recipients in 1974.[22]

In 1974, median AFDC and food-stamp benefits were $4,116. In thirteen states AFDC and food-stamp benefits for a family of four totaled between $3,900 and $4,500; in fourteen states they totaled from $4,500 to $5,000; and in three states they exceeded $5,000.[23] When taxes and work-related expenses are considered, it would require earnings of $7,425 to match benefits of $4,116.

Discrimination against men by AFDC regulations may also discourage some women from marrying the fathers of their children. One study found that women on welfare were about half as likely as all women heading families with children to remarry within four years.[24] Still, the effect of AFDC rules on illegitimacy rates would seem to be rather small. Between 1940 and 1968 the illegitimacy rate for society as a whole tripled—from one in twenty-five births to one in ten.[25] Yet, even with enormous increases in the AFDC rolls, the proportion of illegitimate children in AFDC families rose only from 25 percent in 1961 to about 33 percent in the 1970s.[26]

There is also no evidence to support the often-stated belief that AFDC mothers have additional children to increase their benefits.[27] While an additional child up to a total of four or five children normally does increase benefits, the increase is far too small to offset the additional costs of a child. Most AFDC families are average size. In 1975, the average number of children in AFDC families was 2.4. The only way most women could benefit from having a child would be for a childless woman to have at least one child. This would make her eligible for AFDC. But, again, there is no evidence to indicate that women have children for this reason.[28]

In sum, it is clear that AFDC creates some of the effects it was ostensibly designed to eliminate. Rather than keep families together, it frequently destroys families and makes it impossible for poor people to create a family. The discrimination against males is designed to make them seek employment. But an unemployed male is automatically assumed to be a shirker, with no consideration given to current rates of unemployment or other economic or personal factors that may keep some men out of the job market or in very poor-paying jobs.

Work disincentives Ironically, perhaps, AFDC can discourage both male and female heads from working. AFDC, food-stamp, and unemployment-insurance recipients must register for job training programs and accept available employment—or forfeit benefits.* As noted, about 60 percent of all AFDC mothers are exempt from this requirement. Another 7 to 10 percent of all AFDC mothers are exempt because of ill health or advanced age. Thus, only about 30 percent of all AFDC mothers could potentially work, unless some of those with children under six sought employment.

The work registration and training program under AFDC (WIN) has been a modest success at best. The program has been stymied by a minuscule number of job training slots, the extremely low skills of many AFDC mothers, the lack of adequate child-care facilities, and the high rate of national unemployment. In a slack job market, AFDC mothers are among the least likely persons to obtain any kind of job that pays a livable wage. The major problem, however, is the job market. The job training programs are limited in value if there are no jobs for the poor to be trained for.

---

* Under AFDC, only the head's proportion of benefits is denied if work or work training is refused. Food-stamp rules require termination of benefits of the whole family.

Despite the WIN program, some increases in child-care facilities, and some work incentives, the percentage of working female heads receiving AFDC increased only slightly between 1965 and 1975. Most studies show an increase of only one to two percent, although more AFDC mothers are working full time and more are in the job market. As the figures below show, in any given month in 1975 about 16 percent of all AFDC mothers were employed. Only about 10 percent were employed full time. However, over a one-year period, 25 to 30 percent of all AFDC mothers worked at some time. Most working AFDC mothers have seasonal or intermittent employment.[29]

AFDC Mothers	1961	1969	1973	1975
Total in labor force	19%	20%	28%	26%
Employed full time	5	8	10	10
Employed part time	9	6	6	6
Unemployed	5	6	12	10

It is difficult to estimate the proportion of all AFDC mothers who could work if jobs were available and if child-care facilities were more numerous. Most studies estimate that, in a tight labor market, some 60 to 75 percent of AFDC mothers could obtain a decent paying job if child-care facilities were available.[30] Currently, there are funds to provide day care for only about 112,000 AFDC families (see Chapter 8). Between four and seven million children would have to be cared for to allow all potentially employable AFDC mothers to join the work force.

The AFDC rules were amended in 1969 to provide an incentive for recipient heads to work. Before 1969, AFDC payments were reduced one dollar for every dollar an employed recipient earned. This was a 100 percent tax and an obvious disincentive to employment. Since 1969, an AFDC recipient may exempt the first $30 of earnings, one-third of all additional earnings, and all job-related costs.* These new provisions lower the official tax rate to 67 percent, but the effective rate may be somewhat lower. Consider the following example.[31] The monthly earnings of an AFDC mother working full time in Los Angeles at $2.50 an hour would

---

* All earnings of a child who is a full-time student or a part-time student working part time are also exempt.

be $433.00. Under the disregard provisions, the following calculations would be made:

Monthly earnings	$433.00
Less payroll deductions	− 54.00
Leaving a net take-home pay of	$379.00
Less work-related expenses	− 212.00
Standard allowance for food and incidentals ($25)	
Transportation, including car maintenance ($80)	
Child care for two children ($107)	
The statutory disregard	− 30.00
Plus one-third of gross wage: 1/3 × ($433 − 30)	− 134.00
Net pay	+$ 3.00

This particular family in Los Angeles would be eligible for $221 in cash AFDC benefits, a $24 food-stamp bonus, and $57 worth of aid under Medicaid. The total value of earnings and assistance would be $735 monthly. The monthly gain from working would be $167, with a monthly cash and in-kind income of $469.

In 1972 an executive-office study showed that the typical AFDC family could earn as much as $3,200 per year and still receive $3,336 in AFDC and food-stamp benefits.[32] This would be an effective tax rate on welfare benefits of 27 percent. If the typical AFDC family earned as much as $4,000, benefits would drop to $2,905, an effective tax rate of 54 percent.[33]

A Government Accounting Office (GAO) study found that, in Los Angeles, a typical AFDC mother with three children could earn $579 monthly before losing any benefits and up to $1,074 monthly before losing all benefits. In Denver the base was $107 monthly, with a cutoff point of $750 a month.[34] Of course, in each state it would be different.

As generous as these provisions are, several factors continue to create work disincentives. First, the disregard provisions are allowed only for those who are unemployed when they apply for AFDC. This encourages working heads to quit their jobs in order to obtain the income exemption. Some persons quit, obtain AFDC benefits, and then do not find or seek work again. Second, in the twenty-eight states with an AFDC–UF program, no man who works more than 100 hours a month can receive benefits, even if his earnings are very small. If a man only earns the minimum wage, he might be better off not working if he can qualify for AFDC–UF.

Finally, even with the disregard provisions approved in 1969, each state has some cutoff point beyond which even one dollar in earnings may cause the loss of all in-kind benefits (this is known as a notch). In some states this cutoff point is set low enough to discourage or limit employment. Because the cutoff point may keep some of the working poor from receiving Medicaid services when ill, some workers quit their jobs to qualify for medical aid.

Extreme variations in benefit levels One of the worst deficiencies of AFDC is the lack of a national minimum for benefits. While in some states benefits may be adequate, and when combined with employment income and in-kind benefits may even be fairly generous, in many states AFDC benefits are low enough to keep even those families that can qualify for aid on the brink of starvation.*

For example, in January 1976, a penniless family of four in Mississippi could receive $60 in AFDC benefits. For $13, this family could have purchased $162 worth of food stamps. But after buying the food stamps, the family would have but $47 for shelter, clothing, and all other necessities. Clearly, the cash benefits from AFDC are much too low. It is not at all surprising that such families were sometimes willing to sell their food stamps to dishonest merchants or even brokers who deal in black-market food stamps for fifty cents on the dollar.[35] Since there is no automatic adjustment for benefit levels, these paltry benefits do not even increase with inflation. Given the high level of inflation during the 1970s, poor families have found AFDC benefits to be of less and less value.

In summary, the AFDC program has severe deficiencies: it excludes millions of needy persons; it causes family disintegration; it often discourages work; and benefit variations are extreme to the point of providing highly deficient aid to many of the poor. One result of these deficiencies is that persons in some states receive considerable benefits, others receive modest aid, and another very large group receives little or no aid. Some of the working poor have to pay taxes to support superior services for other poor persons who do not work.

---

* During recent periods of high unemployment and high inflation, some states actually responded by lowering AFDC benefits. For example, until 1969 Texas was paying AFDC benefits of $102 per month to a woman with one child. In 1969 the benefit for a two-person family was lowered to $86.25. In 1978 the benefits were still $86.25.

FOOD STAMPS

At the urging of President Kennedy, the food-stamp program was revived in 1961 (it was previously in operation during 1939–1942) on a pilot basis, primarily to sell surplus food. In 1971 the program was given uniform national standards and transformed into an income guarantee for needy persons in participating counties. In 1974 the program was extended to all counties. Participation in the program increased from 400,000 persons in 1965 to 4.3 million in 1970 to 12.9 million in 1974. In April 1975, program participation reached an all-time high of 19.2 million recipients. By late 1976 the number of recipients had declined to 17.2 million and, by fall of 1977, had declined to 16.7 million recipients. In September 1977, the program was fundamentally altered by Congress.

The food-stamp program is designed to help needy persons obtain enough food for a nutritionally adequate diet. Until September 1977, persons who qualified for the program could purchase stamps redeemable for food at certified retail or wholesale markets for some proportion of the stamps' value. The amount that the family paid for the stamps depended on their income and family size. The neediest families could obtain the stamps free. However, most families paid between 20 and 30 percent of their net income for the stamps. As the size of the family increased, the family qualified for more stamps. The difference between the purchase price of the stamps and their redeemable value was referred to as the food-stamp bonus and represented the in-kind benefit.

Table 5.4 provides some examples of the way the purchase plan operated. Notice that a one-person household was eligible for $50 worth of stamps if net monthly income was below $245. If the household had a net income of less than $20, the $50 worth of stamps were free. As income increased, the cost of the stamps also increased. Between $210 and the cutoff point of $245, the stamps cost $40. Similarly, a three-person household with a net monthly income of less than $433 was eligible for $130 worth of stamps with the cost varying by income. A four-person household was eligible for $166 worth of stamps if net monthly income was below $533. If a family had liquid assets of $1,500 or more, it was ineligible for food stamps. For households with a member aged sixty or more, the asset limitation was $3,000.

In September 1977, Congress reformed the food-stamp program in several important ways. First, recipients are no longer required to purchase the stamps. Rather than the recipient having to buy a block of stamps to

TABLE 5.4

Food-stamp benefits and costs to recipients, July 1, 1976

One-person household Allotment: $50		Three-person household Allotment: $130		Four-person household Allotment: $166	
Monthly net income	Cash required	Monthly net income	Cash required	Monthly net income	Cash required
$ 0 – 19.99	$ 0.00	$ 0 – 19.99	$ 0.00	$ 0 – 19.99	$ 0.00
20 – 29.99	1.00	20 – 29.99	0.00	20 – 29.99	0.00
30 – 39.99	4.00	30 – 39.99	4.00	30 – 39.99	4.00
40 – 49.99	6.00	40 – 49.99	7.00	40 – 49.99	7.00
50 – 59.99	8.00	50 – 59.99	10.00	50 – 59.99	10.00
60 – 69.99	10.00	60 – 69.99	13.00	60 – 69.99	13.00
70 – 79.99	12.00	70 – 79.99	16.00	70 – 79.99	16.00
80 – 89.99	14.00	80 – 89.99	19.00	80 – 89.99	19.00
90 – 99.99	16.00	90 – 99.99	21.00	90 – 99.99	22.00
100 – 109.99	18.00	100 – 109.99	24.00	100 – 109.99	25.00
110 – 119.99	21.00	110 – 119.99	27.00	110 – 119.99	28.00

Monthly income	Purchase
120 – 129.99	24.00
130 – 139.99	27.00
140 – 149.99	30.00
150 – 169.99	33.00
170 – 189.99	38.00
190 – 209.99	38.00
210 – and up	40.00
Cutoff: $245.00	

Monthly income	Purchase
120 – 129.99	30.00
130 – 139.99	33.00
140 – 149.99	36.00
150 – 169.99	40.00
170 – 189.99	46.00
190 – 209.99	52.00
210 – 229.99	58.00
230 – 249.99	64.00
250 – 269.99	70.00
270 – 289.99	76.00
290 – 309.99	82.00
310 – 329.99	88.00
330 – 359.99	94.00
360 – 389.99	102.00
390 – 419.99	111.00
420 – and up	112.00
Cutoff: $433.00	

Monthly income	Purchase
120 – 129.99	31.00
130 – 139.99	34.00
140 – 149.99	37.00
150 – 169.99	41.00
170 – 189.99	47.00
190 – 209.99	53.00
210 – 229.99	59.00
230 – 249.99	65.00
250 – 269.99	71.00
270 – 289.99	77.00
290 – 309.99	83.00
310 – 329.99	89.00
330 – 359.99	95.00
360 – 389.99	104.00
390 – 419.99	113.00
420 – 449.99	122.00
450 – 479.99	131.00
480 – 509.99	140.00
510 – and up	142.00
Cutoff: $553.00	

Source: Food Stamp Charts, Department of Agriculture, 1976.

obtain a bonus number of stamps, eligible recipients simply receive the bonus stamps. Although recipients do not receive more stamps, they do not have to tie up a considerable share of their total income in stamps to obtain the bonus. Second, only those families and individuals who have net incomes below the poverty line are now eligible for the stamps. Previously, some families who were not counted among the poor could obtain the stamps. Third, a rather complicated deduction system used to calculate net income was replaced by a much simpler one. Presently, each household receives a standard deduction of $60. A working family can also deduct 20 percent of earned income to compensate for taxes, other mandatory deductions from salary, and work-related expenses. Last, certain deductions for excess shelter costs and child care can be claimed.[36]

Additionally, asset limits were set at $1,750 for a family, or $3,000 for a multimember household including a person sixty or over. Asset definitions were made more strict. Mobile homes and campers used for recreation, boats, and expensive cars are now counted as assets.* Work registration requirements under the law were strengthened, and fourteen "workfare" pilot projects were established, in which recipients are required to accept public-service jobs to pay for their food stamps. The general spirit of the reforms was to make the stamps more difficult to obtain and to limit them to the neediest persons.

Because the food-stamp program is national in scope and because the stamp bonus varies with income, some of the inequities of the AFDC program are overcome. Families that receive low AFDC cash benefits can obtain more stamps than can families living in states that pay higher AFDC benefits. Still, as noted earlier, even if a family can obtain enough stamps to cover basic food needs, they still will be in jeopardy if they do not have enough cash income to cover housing, transportation, clothing, and other essentials.

Unlike AFDC, the food-stamp allotment does increase with changes in the cost of living. The stamp bonus is based on the current market cost of the foods that meet the Department of Agriculture's nutritional standards and are reflected in their thrifty food plan. If increases are warranted by market changes, adjustments are made in July and January of each year. Table 5.5 shows the increases in food costs between 1971 and 1976, and

---

* Quite obviously neither alcoholic beverages or tobacco products can be purchased with food stamps. Prepared hot foods are also ineligible for purchase with the stamps. There are a few nonfood products that can be purchased with the stamps. For example, vegetable seeds can be purchased if they are sold in the food section of a grocery store, and American Indians may purchase some fishing gear with the stamps.

TABLE 5.5

Food price changes, CPI changes, food-stamp allotment, food-stamp income eligibility, and poverty levels (1971 first half to 1976 first half)

Calendar year: half	Percentage change from preceding period at compound annual rate		Food-stamp allotment	Family of four			Official poverty threshold	
	Food	All items	Monthly	Food-stamp net income eligibility level			Annual	Annual
				Monthly	Annual			
71: I	3.2%	4.0%	$108	$360	$4,320		$4,137	4,137
71: II	3.8	3.6	108	360	4,320		4,137	
72: I	4.2	3.0	108	360	4,320		4,275	4,275
72: II	4.7	3.6	112	373	4,476		4,275	
73: I	16.2	5.9	112	373	4,476		4,540	4,540
73: II	20.7	9.2	116	387	4,644		4,540	
74: I	14.7	10.6	142	473	5,676		5,050	5,050
74: II	9.2	12.9	150	500	6,000		5,050	
75: I	8.0	8.3	154	513	6,156		5,500	5,500
75: II	7.9	7.3	162	540	6,480		5,500	
76: I	1.2	4.9	166	553	6,636		5,815 (est.)	5,815
76: II	—	—	166	553	6,636		5,815	

Source: U.S. Congress, Congressional Budget Office, *The Food Stamp Program: Income or Food Supplementation* (Washington, D.C.: U.S. Government Printing Office, January 1977), p. 13.

the corresponding increases in the monthly food-stamp allotment and income allowables for a family of four. Notice the rather phenomenal increases in food prices between 1973 and 1975.

Recipient Characteristics

Despite the frequent charges that the food-stamp rolls are replete with middle-income families, the evidence shows that food-stamp recipients are actually the poorest of the poor. This was true even before the reforms of 1977. In September 1975, the average monthly gross income of food-stamp households was only $298—this represents $3,576 on an annual basis, or 23 percent of the mean family income of all American families in 1975.[37] The gross income of 78 percent of all food-stamp households in 1975 fell below the Social Security Administration's poverty threshold, and 90 percent fell below 125 percent of the poverty threshold.[38] Eighty-six percent of all food-stamp bonuses went to families below the poverty level.[39]

Recipients of food stamps are overwhelmingly the elderly, the blind, the disabled, welfare mothers and their children, unemployed workers, and low-income working families. Still, many of the poorest families do not receive food stamps. In 1975, of all the four-person families trying to live on $3,000 or less a year, only 58 percent received food stamps. In fact, only about 55 percent of all families (or 5.9 million out of 10.4 million potentially eligible families) who could have qualified for food stamps in 1975 actually utilized them.[40] The purchasing requirements prior to 1977 were one major reason why many households did not obtain the stamps. The reforms of 1977 were expected to increase participation in the program by some 3 million of the poorest families. Some 1.3 million other families would be eliminated from the program.

Table 5.6 lists some of the other characteristics of food-stamp recipients. In September 1975, the average family size was 3.3 persons. Most recipients lived in metropolitan areas, with 44.8 percent living in central cities. Almost 39 percent of all recipients lived in the South; only 15.2 percent lived in the West. Sixty-four percent of all family heads were female, and 17.2 percent were elderly. The vast majority of all food-stamp recipients were white (62.7 percent). In July 1975, 2.8 million white households received food stamps, as did 1.6 million black families, and 423,780 Spanish-origin families. This would constitute one in every twenty-five white households, one in five black households, and one in seven Spanish-origin households.[41] Only 28.8 percent of all family heads were employed, compared to 68.3 percent of all family heads nationally.

TABLE 5.6

Comparison of food-stamp recipients and total United States households

	Food stamp recipients: July–Sept. 1975— percent distribution[a]	Total United States households: March 1975— percent distribution[b]
Household		
One	24.0%	19.6%
Two	20.5	30.6
Three	17.1	17.4
Four	14.5	15.6
Over four	23.9	16.8
Region census		
Northeast	24.4	22.5
North Central	21.7	26.7
South	38.6	32.7
West	15.2	18.0
Residence		
Nonfarm	98.2	96.2
Metropolitan	64.7	68.6
Inside central cities	44.8	31.4
Outside central cities	19.9	37.2
Nonmetropolitan	33.5	31.4
Farm	1.8	3.8
Family type		
Male head	35.6	86.4
Female head	64.3	13.6
Age of head of household		
Over 65	17.2	20.1
Under 65	82.8	79.9
Race		
White	62.7	88.5
Nonwhite	37.3	11.5
Employment status of head[c]		
Employed	28.8	68.3
Unemployed	12.5	4.9
Not in labor force	58.6	26.8

Source: U.S. Congress, Congressional Budget Office, *The Food Stamp Program: Income or Food Supplementation* (Washington, D.C.: U.S. Government Printing Office, January 1977), p. 25.
[a] Distributions developed from CBO tabulations from USDA September 1975, Food Stamp Survey tape. Race, region, employment status, and residence distribution source: "Characteristics of Households Purchasing Food Stamps," *Current Population Reports*, Series P-23, no. 61, July 1976.
[b] Data based on household information for March 1975, source: "Household Money Income in 1974 and Selected Social and Economic Characteristics of Households," *Current Population Reports*, Series P-60, no. 100, August 1975. Region data based on family data, source "Money Income and Poverty Status of Families and Persons," *Current Population Reports*, Series P-60, no. 103, September 1976.
[c] Employment status refers to employment during week prior to interview.

Benefits of Food Stamps

There is no solid evidence as yet on the nutritional impact of food stamps. There is evidence to indicate that poor families in the food-stamp program are able to purchase more food than comparable nonparticipating families, but there have been no studies to determine whether these increased expenditures measurably improve the diet of the poor. Even in the absence of studies, it would seem safe to conclude that the program has done a great deal to help poor households obtain an adequate diet. A 1975 study concluded that for every one dollar of food-stamp bonus, forty-three cents is freed for nonfood purchases.[42] The same study found that food-stamp households spent approximately $27 per week on food, as compared to expenditures of $17.63 for comparable poor families not in the program.[43] This is an increase of $9.37 per week in food purchases for stamp families.

Besides helping poor families purchase more food, the stamp program increases consumer purchasing power and aids agricultural and other related retail industries. A White House study showed that every one dollar in food-stamp expenditures creates another six dollars in business.[44] Another study found that the GNP increased $311 million in 1972 and $427 million in 1974 because of the food-stamp program, and added between 56,000 and 77,000 new jobs to the economy.[45]

Additionally, along with unemployment insurance, other welfare, and a tax cut in 1975, the food-stamp program helped to cushion the whole economy from the impact of inflation between 1973 and 1976.

SOCIAL SECURITY (OASDI)

The Old Age, Survivors and Dependent Insurance (OASDI) program is the largest of all the social welfare programs. The basic Social Security program was passed in 1935 and has been amended several times to expand its coverage. By 1976 (see Table 5.7) Social Security served 31.9 million persons and cost $72.6 billion. Nine out of every ten workers are currently covered by the program.

Social Security is generally thought of as a compulsory retirement system which workers and their employers pay for during their employed years. In actuality, the Social Security program is broader and more complex than this. Social Security includes benefits for survivors and dependents of those covered by Social Security, disabled workers and dependents, and Medicare. Notice on Table 5.7 that, in 1975, 27.6 million

TABLE 5.7

Beneficiaries and cash benefits in the Old Age, Survivors, and Disability Insurance program (OASDI), selected years, 1950–1976

Beneficiary or benefit	1950	1960	1965	1970	1974	1975	1976
Number of beneficiaries (millions)[a]:							
Total	3.5	14.8	20.9	26.2	30.9	31.9	
Retired workers, dependents, and survivors	3.5	14.2	19.1	23.6	26.9	27.6	
Retired workers only	1.8	8.1	11.1	13.3	16.0	16.5	
Disabled workers and dependents	—	.7	1.7	2.7	3.9	4.3	
Annual cash benefits (billions of dollars)	1.0	11.3	18.3	31.9	58.5	63.7	72.6
Average monthly benefits (dollars):							
All retired workers[a]	44	74	84	118	188	206	218.00
Maximum to men retiring at age 65[b]	45	119	132	190	305[c]	342[c]	387.30
Maximum to women retiring at age 65[b]	45	119	136	196	316[c]	360[c]	403.10
Maximum to persons retiring at age 65[b]	10	33	44	64	94[c]	101[c]	107.90

Source: Department of Health, Education, and Welfare.
[a] As of December of each year.
[b] Assumes retirement at beginning of year.
[c] As of June.

Social Security recipients were retired workers, dependents, and survivors and 4.3 million were disabled workers and dependents.

Funds to support OASDI are obtained by a tax shared by the employee and employer on some proportion of a worker's salary. In 1977 the tax rate was 11.7 percent, shared equally (5.85 percent each) by employees and employers. Of the employer and employee tax of 5.85 percent, 4.375 percent is for OASDI, 0.575 percent is for disability insurance, and 0.9 percent is for Medicare. In 1977 an employee would pay 5.85 percent of his/her salary up to a ceiling of $16,500. The employer matches the employee's contribution. Once the maximum is paid, no additional taxes are collected. In 1977 an employee earning $16,500 or more would pay $965.25 (5.85 percent) to Social Security, and that amount would be matched by the employer. The self-employed pay 7.9 percent of their income up to the ceiling. Congress has the power to change both the tax rate and the ceiling whenever it is considered necessary. In recent years the ceiling has been changed yearly (in 1976 it was $15,300). Once a year, Social Security and Supplemental Security Income (SSI) benefits are adjusted to account for change in the Consumer Price Index (CPI).

Because of the tax ceiling, Social Security is actually a highly regressive tax which is disproportionately paid for by lower income and poor workers. The figures below show the effects of the ceiling.[46] As income increases, a worker pays a lower and lower percentage of his or her income into Social Security. Those at the lowest income levels pay a very high proportion of their total income to Social Security. Many economists believe that employers actually pass the total cost of Social Security on to their employees by paying them less to make up for their contribution. If so, poor people pay an extremely heavy burden for Social Security. Milton Friedman, a noted conservative economist, has called Social Security "the poor man's welfare payment to the middle class."[47]

Adjusted money income levels	Social Security tax rate (1968)
Under 2,000	7.6%
2,000 – 4,000	6.5
4,000 – 6,000	6.7
6,000 – 8,000	6.8
8,000 – 10,000	6.2
10,000 – 15,000	5.8
15,000 – 25,000	4.6
25,000 – 50,000	2.5
50,000 – and over	1.0

Table 5.7 shows how benefit levels have changed over the years. In 1976 the maximum benefit for a man retiring at sixty-five was $387.30. For a woman retiring at sixty-five the maximum was $403.10. The minimum payment was $107.90. Social Security payments to millions of recipients are extremely small. In 1976 the average payment to retirees was only $218. Retirees can supplement their benefits through part-time jobs. In 1977 a retiree could earn $3,000 in wages without any reduction in benefits at the rate of one dollar for every two earned.* Benefits are reduced only for earned wages. A recipient can earn without penalty any amount in the form of interest, dividends, or royalties.

Most persons think of Social Security as a program that collects money from them during their working years, invests this money, and then pays the worker back with interest during retirement at a rate proportional to contributions to the program. In actuality, the relationship between retirement benefits and contributions is rather tenuous. Studies show that most persons receive considerably more in return from Social Security than they ever contributed. For example, Tussing found that "Social Security payments have amounted to, on the average, well over four times the amount paid in by each taxpayer (counting employer and employee shares and interest). . . ."[48] Benefits have been more substantial than contributions and interest because Social Security is actually financed by a tax on the current generation of workers to support ex-workers. Thus, Social Security is not actually a prepaid program. It is in reality a welfare program in which each generation of beneficiaries is aided during their old age by the current generation of workers.[49] In recent years, as births have declined, longevity has increased, and recession and inflation have raged, Social Security benefits have had to be increased, placing a larger and larger burden on the current generation of workers.†

While Social Security can be thought of as a welfare program for the aged paid for by each generation of workers, most of the benefits go to the nonpoor. In fiscal 1976, about 40 percent of Social Security benefits went to persons whose income would have been below the poverty level without Social Security payments.[50]

Still, without Social Security or some other type of guaranteed-income program for the poor aged, poverty would increase very substantially. Currently only about 32 percent of all persons over sixty-five are still in the job market. At the turn of the century, some two-thirds of all

---

* In 1977 Congress decided to phase out limitations on earnings.

†In the fall of 1977, a bill passed Congress which substantially increased the tax rate and benefits over a ten-year period.

persons aged sixty-five were still in the job market. A recent study by the University of Michigan concluded that the average elderly couple has liquid assets (stocks, bonds, cash, etc.) of only $2,400. Twenty percent of the aged have no liquid assets.[51] Another study found that only 12 percent of all retired persons receive private pensions, and those persons are generally those who had had better jobs and had earned higher salaries before retirement.[52]

SUPPLEMENTAL SECURITY INCOME (SSI)

The SSI program commenced on January 1, 1974. The program is designed to provide assistance to needy persons aged sixty-five or older and disabled or blind persons, regardless of their age. Unlike Social Security, a person need never have worked or been the spouse or dependent of a worker to receive SSI benefits. The program constitutes the first guaranteed-minimum-income program in the United States. SSI replaced more than 1,000 state and local public-assistance programs. Still, all but two states supplement SSI payments.

State supplements to SSI can be administered by the state or federal government. In fiscal 1976 the federal government administered state supplements in twenty-six states and the District of Columbia. Some states, such as Mississippi, Ohio, Tennessee, and Wyoming, add less than one percent to the federal payment; but three states (California, Massachusetts, and Wisconsin) more than match the federal payment. Twenty other states administer their own supplements, and in two states administration is shared by the state and federal authorities. Only Texas and West Virginia do not supplement SSI benefits in some way.

Benefits under SSI are fairly modest. One person with a monthly income of $20 or less in June 1977 could receive a maximum stipend of $167.80. A couple may receive a maximum of $251.80. To be eligible for SSI, a single person cannot have liquid assets worth more than $1,500. A couple cannot have liquid assets in excess of $2,250. SSI was designed to supplement inadequate Social Security payments and to replace many poor-paying state and local programs for the aged, blind, and disabled.

SSI funds are not drawn from Social Security assets, but instead are drawn entirely from the federal treasury. For some 72 percent of all aged recipients and some 20 to 30 percent of all blind or disabled recipients, SSI benefits are a supplement to Social Security. For example, a needy, aged person who received the minimum Social Security benefit of $107.90 would probably be able to receive a supplement of $59.90 ($167.80 − $107.90) from SSI. Similarly, SSI payments may supplement Social Security disability payments. SSI recipients are also eligible for food stamps in all but five states, which have cashed out their value, and for Medicaid in the forty-nine states that have a program.

CONCLUSIONS

This analysis should have made one fact quite clear: There is no overall design or unity to the maze of programs that administer to the American poor. Each major program was developed separately to deal with a particular clientele, often with little or no coordination or even, in some cases, concern for other programs. The multiplicity of rules and regulations surrounding each program makes the programs difficult to administer and often renders them worthless to those who need them most. It is difficult to argue with the assessment that "no one setting out to design a national welfare system from scratch would produce the jumble of federal, state and joint programs that has developed over the years." [53]

The major inequities of the programs—extreme regional and even interstate benefit variations, discrimination against intact, male-headed families, and work disincentives—do a great deal to aggravate the conditions of the poor and ultimately maintain rather than relieve poverty.

NOTES

1. Alfred M. Skolnik and Sophie R. Dales, "Social Welfare Expenditures, 1950–76," *Social Security Bulletin,* January 1977, p. 7.

2. See also the estimates in Robert D. Plotnick and Felicity Skidmore, *Progress Against Poverty: A Review of the 1964–74 Decade* (New York: Academic Press, 1975), pp. 55–59.

3. Skolnik and Dales, "Social Welfare Expenditures 1950–76," pp. 5–7.

4. U.S. Congress, Joint Economic Committee, Subcommittee on Fiscal Policy, *Income Security for Americans: Recommendations of the Public Welfare Study* (Washington, D.C.: Government Printing Office, 1974), p. 57.

5. Plotnick and Skidmore, *Progress Against Poverty,* p. 159.

6. Ibid., p. 51.

7. Ibid., pp. 85, 180–181.

8. Ibid., p. 145.

9. Ibid., p. 148.

10. Ibid., p. 162.

11. *Social Security Bulletin,* January 1976, p. 76.

12. Joel Havemann and Linda E. Demkovich, "Making Some Sense Out of the Welfare 'Mess,' " *National Journal,* January 8, 1977, p. 44.

13. Ibid., p. 54.

14. *Economic Report of the President* (Washington, D.C.: Government Printing Office, 1976), p. 100.

15. Sar A. Levitan, Garth L. Mangum, and Ray Marshall, *Human Resources and Labor Markets* (New York: Harper & Row, 1976), p. 328.

16. Sar Levitan, Martin Rein, and David Marwick, *Work and Welfare Go Together* (Baltimore: The Johns Hopkins University Press, 1972), p. 50.

17. Hanna H. Meissner, ed., *Poverty in the Affluent Society* (New York: Harper & Row, 1973), p. 61.

18. Personal correspondence from Harold F. Wienberg, Associate Administrator for Information Systems, Social and Rehabilitation Service, Department of Health, Education and Welfare, May 19, 1977.

18a. Ibid.

19. U.S. Congress, Joint Economic Committee, Subcommittee on Fiscal Policy, *Welfare Alternatives* (Washington, D.C.: U.S. Government Printing Office, August 1976), p. 7.

20. Ibid.

21. U.S. Congress, Joint Economic Committee, Subcommittee on Fiscal Policy, *Income Security for Americans: Recommendations of the Public Welfare Study,* p. 3.

22. U.S. Congress, Joint Economic Committee, Subcommittee on Fiscal Policy, *Public Welfare and Work Incentives in Theory and Practice* (Washington, D.C.: U.S. Government Printing Office, April 1974), p. 13.

23. *Income Security for Americans: Recommendations of the Public Welfare Study,* pp. 7 and 8.

24. *Economic Report of the President,* 1976, p. 98.

25. Levitan, Rein, Marwick, *Work and Welfare Go Together,* p. 9.

26. U.S. Congress, Joint Economic Committee, Subcommittee on Fiscal Policy, *Welfare Alternatives,* p. 14.

27. Ibid., pp. 14–15.

28. *Income Security for Americans: Recommendations of the Public Welfare Study,* p. 80.

29. Levitan, Mangum, and Marshall, *Human Resources and Labor Markets,* p. 326.

30. *Income Security for Americans: Recommendations of the Public Welfare Study*, p. 72.

31. Levitan, Rein, Marwick, *Work and Welfare Go Together*, p. 80.

32. *Economic Report of the President*, 1976, p. 99.

33. Ibid.

34. Cited by Levitan, Rein, Marwick, *Work and Welfare Go Together*, pp. 15–16.

35. *Income Security for Americans: Recommendations of the Public Welfare Study*, p. 60.

36. For a more detailed description of the reforms, see *The Congressional Quarterly* 35, no. 39 (September 24, 1977): 2017–2021.

37. Ibid., p. xv.

38. Ibid.

39. Ibid.

40. Ibid.

41. U.S. Congress, Congressional Budget Office, *The Food Stamp Program: Income or Food Supplementation?* (Washington, D.C.: Government Printing Office, 1977), p. 51.

42. *The Food Stamp Program: Income or Food Supplementation?*, p. xiv.

43. Ibid., p. 37.

44. *The Congressional Quarterly* 34, no. 39: 2587.

45. *The Food Stamp Program: Income or Food Supplementation?*, p. 40.

46. The figures are taken from Roger A. Herriot and Herman P. Miller, "Who Paid the Taxes in 1968?" U.S. Bureau of the Census, Paper prepared for the National Industrial Conference Board Meeting in New York, March 18, 1971, Table 7.

47. Milton Friedman, "The Poor Man's Welfare Payment to the Middle Class," *The Washington Monthly*, May 1972.

48. A. Dale Tussing, *Poverty in a Dual Economy* (New York: St. Martin's Press, 1975), pp. 123–124.

49. *Income Security for Americans: Recommendation of the Public Welfare Study*, p. 11.

50. See the estimates in Plotnick and Skidmore, *Progress Against Poverty*, pp. 56–57.

51. Cited in Bradley R. Schiller, *The Economics of Poverty and Discrimination* (Englewood Cliffs, N.J.: Prentice-Hill, 1976), p. 80.

52. Ibid., p. 82.

53. Havemann and Demkovich, "Making Some Sense out of the Welfare 'Mess,'" p. 46.

6
HEALTH, HEALTH PROGRAMS, AND HEALTH REFORM

Poverty frequently causes illness, and illness can cause poverty. The poor may not be able to maintain a balanced diet, and they are likely to live in poorly heated, unventilated, cramped, or unsanitary housing—conditions that cause sickness and encourage the spread of disease. The psychological strain of poverty can also cause illness. Equally critical, the poor may not be able to afford medical assistance or may have to use badly needed funds to obtain medical care.

Untreated illness in America is especially deplorable, because the United States has the most expensive and sophisticated medical facilities in the world. But, as we shall see, millions of Americans, including many who are not poor, are either not served by these facilities or receive inadequate care.

MEDICAL-CARE COST

Medical care in America is extremely expensive, with costs increasing at a phenomenal rate. Health care cost $118.5 billion in 1975, an increase in excess of 1000 percent over the 1950 cost of $10.4 billion. Estimates are that medical care will cost $158.7 billion in 1978, rising to $233.5 billion in 1980.[1] Currently, medical-care costs are increasing at a rate more than double that of all goods and services, as measured by the Consumer Price Index.[2] Between 1973 and 1975, federal Medicare and Medicaid expenditures increased 40 percent, accounting for more than 80 percent of HEW's health budget.[3]

There are many reasons for spiraling increases in medical costs. Generally high inflation has increased medical costs along with everything else in recent years. Excessive profits for the drug industry have also played a role,[4] as has the tendency of hospitals to install and constantly update all kinds of excessively expensive and frequently underutilized (even unused) equipment, such as hyperbaric chambers, defibrellators, computer terminals, and open-heart-surgery facilities.[5] The single most important factor, however, is that hospitals and doctors have an obvious incentive to increase their prices as often as possible and there is no way to discourage them from doing so. Hospitals are generally reimbursed for all reasonable costs associated with patient care. Similarly, doctors determine the number of tests and services a patient needs; the more services performed, the higher doctors' salaries. Thus the process is inherently inflationary.*

Despite private insurance and federal, state, and local public-health programs, the public must pay a large percentage of the high costs of health care in out-of-pocket costs. The percentage of all costs paid by the public has decreased some, but the overall costs are still burdensome for many families. In fiscal year 1950 the public paid 68 percent of all health costs, private insurance paid only 8.5 percent, and public programs paid 20.2 percent.[7] Table 6.1 shows projections by the Congressional Budget

---

* The process can also be dangerous. Surgeons, for example, make money only by doing surgery and the more surgery they do, the more money they make. The result is a great deal of unnecessary surgery. A House subcommittee calculated that, in 1974, surgeons performed 2.38 million unnecessary operations, causing the needless deaths of 11,900 persons, and inflicting unjustified costs of four billion dollars on the public.[6] Estimates for other years are very similar. In Britain and Sweden, where surgeons are paid a set salary rather than by operation, the rate of surgery is about half the rate in America. Statistics indicate that the British are at least as healthy as Americans, and the Swedish are much healthier.

TABLE 6.1

Fiscal year 1978 estimate of health expenditures (in billions of dollars)

Source of payment	Totals	Long-term hospital care	Psychiatric hospital care	Short-term inpatient care	Out-patient care	Physician services	Dental	Other professional services	Eye-glasses	Nursing-home care	Drugs
Consumer out-of-pocket	$ 49.2 (31.0%)	$0.2	$0.8	$ 5.1	$1.4	$10.6	$ 8.6	$2.3	$2.9	$ 9.6	$7.6
Private insurance	46.0 (29.0%)	0.2	1.4	25.9	1.4	13.8	1.3	0.4	0.02	0.1	1.2
Federal program[a]	43.9 (28.0%)	0.8	2.1	25.5	2.6	6.7	0.4	0.5	0.07	4.6	0.6
State & local gov't programs[b]	18.4 (11.6%)	0.7	4.2	4.3	2.8	2.0	0.3	0.2	0.05	3.4	0.5
Philanthropy	1.2 (0.7%)	0.02	0.06	0.5	0.4	0.02	0.0	0.07	0.0	0.08	0.0
	$158.7	$2.0	$8.7	$61.3	$8.7	$33.1	$10.6	$3.5	$3.1	$17.9	$9.9

Source: Congressional Budget Office, *Catastrophic Health Insurance* (Washington, D.C.: Government Printing Office, 1977), pp. 12–13.
[a] Medicare, Medicaid, Department of Defense, Veterans Administration, Categorical health program and Workmen's Compensation.
[b] Medicaid, other state and local programs, Workmen's Compensation.

office for 1978. With total expenditures of $158.7 billion, the public would pay 31 percent of all costs ($49.2 billion), private insurance would pay 29 percent ($46 billion), federal programs would pay 28 percent ($43.9 billion), state and local governments would pay 11.6 percent ($18.4 billion), and philanthropy would account for 0.7 percent ($1.2 billion).

Medical services such as dental care, eyeglasses, nursing-home care, drugs, and physician fees tend to be paid for by the public. Hospital care is primarily paid for by government programs (52 percent), and private insurance (38 percent). The public directly pays only about 9 percent of all hospital costs.[8]

MEDICAL–CARE COVERAGE

As the $49.2 billion in projected out-of-pocket costs for the public in 1978 indicates, there are many problems with medical-care coverage. A recent study by the Congressional Budget office noted the following:[9]

- *Coverage is uneven.* An estimated 18 million persons are totally without protection under either private insurance or public programs.

- *Certain services are excluded from coverage.* Both public and private insurance plans fail to include certain types of services or insure them very inadequately.

- *Some insurance plans do not adequately cover high expenses.* An estimated 37 million persons are covered under insurance plans that do not adequately cover high expenses or long hospital stays.

- *Tax subsidies do not effectively assist lower-income families.* Tax subsidies are effective in mitigating the impact of high out-of-pocket expenses for middle-income families when insurance is inadequate, but they provide only marginal assistance to lower-income families.

In actuality, projections for 1978 show that some 26 million persons will have no insurance coverage, but 8 million of these people will be covered by public programs. Figures for 1975 show that about half of all private insurance policies limit total benefits to $10,000 or less in a lifetime, and two-thirds limit hospitalization to sixty days or less.[10] Most private policies, of course, exclude preventive care, dental care, eyeglasses, ambulatory care, medical devices, and mental-health care. Many policies also exclude coverage for office and home doctor visits, prescribed drugs, and private and visiting nurse service. As Davis points out, private insurance tends to emphasize "excessive coverage for short hospital stays, insufficient coverage for large medical expenses, and insufficient coverage for lower-cost alternatives to hospitalization [e.g., outpatient treatment centers]."[11]

While most families are financially vulnerable if catastrophic illness strikes, families with higher income are more likely to have insurance and to have adequate coverage. As Table 6.2 shows, only some 16 percent of families with income of $5,000 or less have insurance. Some 60 percent of lower-middle- to upper-income families ($10,000 to $29,999) have coverage, as do some 70 percent of those earning $30,000 and over. However, only 36.7 million persons have unlimited medical coverage.

Catastrophic medical expenses are generally defined as expenses that equal or exceed 10 to 15 percent of yearly family income.[12] A federal study has estimated that 6.9 million families will have out-of-pocket medical expenses in excess of 15 percent of their income in 1978.[13] Most of these families (4.1 million) will be in the lower-income category.

The effects of the high cost of medical care and inadequate coverage are fairly obvious. Some citizens cannot afford medical care (or at least adequate care), others must seriously deplete or even completely deplete their resources to obtain aid, and others can only accept charity care. There have been dozens of congressional investigations of these problems in recent years. Congressional hearings have catalogued reams of case studies pathetically related by citizens who come to Washington to testify about the financial burden that crushed them when death or illness touched their families.[14] Many told of having to mortgage or sell their homes and most of their possessions to obtain or pay for medical care. Others had to declare bankruptcy.

Other citizens told of being hounded mercilessly by collection agencies hired by hospitals and doctors. Some testified to losing their jobs over collection-agency harrassment, and some told of being turned away from hospitals where they sought emergency care for family members when they could not prove they could pay. In some instances, the refusal led to death of the ill or injured person.

HEALTH IN AMERICA

Statistics on the health of Americans are fairly disturbing. The data indicate that Americans are not as healthy as the citizens of many other advanced countries. Some American health problems are particularly

TABLE 6.2
Private major medical coverage (by family income—fiscal year 1978 projections)

Family income	Number of persons with coverage (in millions)	Percent of persons at income level with coverage	Persons with maximum payment limits on coverage (in millions)	Persons with unlimited coverage (in millions)
$ 5,000	6.6	15.6%	3.6	3.0
5,000– 9,999	31.8	44.6	19.7	12.1
10,000–19,999	54.8	61.3	36.8	18.0
20,000–29,999	7.2	56.7	4.6	2.6
30,000 and over	3.0	69.8	2.0	1.0
	103.4		66.7	36.7

Source: Congressional Budget Office, *Catastrophic Health Insurance* (Washington, D.C.: Government Printing Office, 1977) p. 20.

surprising, given the sophistication of the American medical system. For example, the United States ranks twentieth in infant mortality—i.e., in nineteen other countries children have a better chance of surviving their first year of life.[15] America ranks twelfth in maternal mortality. Comparatively speaking, life expectancy in the United States is below the norm of several other countries. Women live longer in six other countries; men live longer in eighteen other countries. In 1971 Anderson reported that, in twelve other nations, the population had fewer ulcers, less diabetes, less cirrhosis of the liver, less hypertension without heart involvement, and less heart disease.[16]

Health statistics for minority Americans are particularly grim. While mortality rates for white infants in the United States compare unfavorably with those of about a half-dozen countries, black-infant mortality is 3.2 times that of whites.[17] Black-infant mortality in much of the South and North is comparable to countries such as Equador. Birch and Gussow point out some implications of such high infant-mortality rates:

> A high infant mortality rate signals the existence of circumstances hostile to life, of an environment in which there are high rates of illness, faulty nutrition, poor conditions for birth, and mothers in poor condition. . . . A high rate of death, in any population, indirectly suggests survival with increased risk of damage in the survivors. To know which are the killing conditions of life is to suspect which are the maiming ones; for in life as on a battlefield, not all the casualties die. Those children who have come through birth and infancy alive have not necessarily come through unscathed, and it is reasonable to anticipate that the condition of the survivors will surely reflect the relative hostility of the environments to which they have been exposed.[18]

Indeed, available studies support these conclusions. A 1971 study reported that "in the city slums there is three times as much heart disease, five times as much mental disease, four times as much high blood pressure, and four times as many deaths before age thirty-five than there is nationwide."[19] The life expectancy of blacks is 10 percent less than that of whites. Studies show that about 50 percent of all children living in slums have untreated medical problems, and almost all need dental care.[20]

In 1976 the Office of Child Health Affairs (OCHA) reported a study that showed that poor children:

- suffer 23 percent more hearing impairment;
- do not grow as tall as other children;

- are more likely to have low hemoglobin values during their years of growth;
- suffer a higher incidence of impetigo, gastrointestinal diseases, parasitic diseases, and urinary tract infections, and those in urban areas are more often the victims of lead-paint poisoning and insect and rodent bites.[21]

The Early and Periodic Screening, Diagnosis and Treatment (EPSDT) program established as part of Medicaid in 1973 verifies these findings. In August 1976, HEW reported that among poor children examined under the program:

- 50 percent are found to be inadequately immunized;
- 25 percent are found to have severe dental problems;
- 10 percent have vision problems;
- 12 percent have low hemoglobin;
- 8 percent suffer from upper-respiratory problems;
- 9 percent in urban areas have elevated blood lead levels;
- 3 percent have hearing problems.[22]

The cyclical effect created by medical neglect, ill health, and poverty is often devastating. Consider the following:

The poor woman giving birth is likely to be entering the hospital for the first time since becoming pregnant.

She is likely to be anemic and undernourished.

She is likely to have a difficult time at birth with a very high chance of giving birth prematurely.

The baby will probably be traumatized by birth and require intensive pediatric attention.

On being dismissed from the hospital, the baby will go home to an environment which is often unsanitary, overcrowded, and inadequately heated.

The infant may be fed milk from unwashed nipples or dirty bottles and she may be kept on a diet of diluted milk for economic reasons for longer than is healthy.

She may suffer from a series of infectious diseases and chronic illnesses associated with poverty.

She may seem listless, apathetic, and unresponsive.

She may be called a "poor learner," a slow developer, or become one of the thousands of cases simply called "failure to thrive."

She may be emotionally, socially, and intellectually unprepared for school.

She may fail in school and drop out.

She may become one of the nation's unemployed teenagers, where the rate of unemployment is as high as 50 percent.

She may unintentionally become pregnant.

And she may become the poor woman giving birth who is likely to be entering the hospital for the first time since becoming pregnant.[23]

As late as 1975, Davis reported that, every year, thousands of Americans needlessly die or are permanently disabled by curable or preventable diseases because they cannot obtain medical care. Davis reported the following grim facts:

1. Every year many American children become blind or suffer a permanent hearing loss from conditions that simple medical examinations could detect and that adequate care could have reversed.

2. The poor, particularly in rural areas and among minority groups, have high rates of mortality from curable diseases of early infancy, infectious disease, and respiratory ailments.

3. Only 20 to 25 percent of the elderly with known debilitating conditions received influenza vaccine during 1972.

4. Almost 2 million children under the age of fourteen have never been vaccinated against the dread diseases of diphtheria, tetanus, and whooping cough; 40 percent of all children between the ages of one and four are not protected against polio; and 40 percent of children under the age of thirteen have not received rubella vaccine.[24]

MEDICAID AND MEDICARE

The Medicare and Medicaid programs were designed to deal with some of America's most severe medical problems. Both programs were enacted as part of the Social Security Amendments of 1965. The name similarity of these two programs causes them to often be confused. They are, however, very different programs. Medicare is a federal program with uniform benefits available to almost all elderly persons who participated in the Social

Security program, be they rich or poor. Medicare also covers persons who become disabled if they have been entitled to Social Security disability payments for at least two consecutive years, and those with end-stage renal (kidney) disease.

Medicaid is an assistance program for the needy which is funded out of the public treasury. It is a state-federal program, with varying benefits available to recipients of AFDC, SSI, and, in some states, other medically needy persons. In twenty-one states, only AFDC and SSI recipients are eligible. In twenty-eight states, as well as the District of Columbia, Guam, Puerto Rico, and the Virgin Islands, it covers AFDC and SSI recipients and some other low-income people. Arizona is the only state that does not participate in the Medicaid program (see Table 6.3).

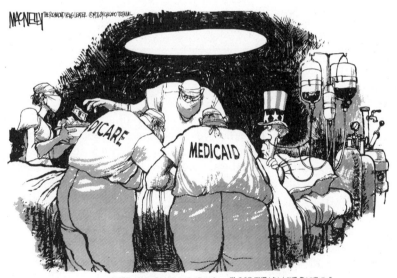

" THERE! I THINK WE GOT IT ALL....CLOSE THE WALLET, DOCTOR."

McNelly in *The Richmond News Leader.*

The cost of the Medicare and Medicaid programs is substantial and has increased significantly in recent years. Medicare cost $14.8 billion in 1975 and served an average of 24.7 million persons per month. The 1975 cost of Medicare was literally double that of 1970. In 1976 the cost of Medicare rose to $17.8 billion. Medicaid cost $12.7 billion in 1975 and served an average of 8.4 million persons per month. In 1976 Medicaid cost $15.1 billion and served an average of 9.2 million persons per month.

TABLE 6.3

Medicaid recipients by basis of eligibility, fiscal years 1975-1976 (in thousands)

	Fiscal year 1975		Fiscal year 1976		% of change
Basis of eligibility	Number	Percent	Number	Percent	1975-1976
Total	23,519	100.0%	24,377	100.0%	+ 3.6%
Aged 65 and over	3,878	16.5	3,900	16.0	+ 0.6
Blindness	120	0.5	117	0.5	− 2.5
Permanent and total disability	2,507	10.7	2,763	11.3	+10.2
Dependent children under 21	10,231	43.5	10,571	43.4	+ 3.3
Adults in families with dependent children	4,908	20.9	5,069	20.8	+ 3.3
Other needy recipients	1,875	8.0	1,958	8.0	+ 4.4

Source: U.S. Department of Health, Education and Welfare, *Medicaid Statistics, Fiscal Year 1976,* No. (SRS) 77-03154, March 1977, p. 3.

Benefits under Medicare

There are two parts to Medicare: Basic Medical Insurance (MI) paid for through Social Security deductions, and Supplementary Medical Insurance (SMI) that recipients can opt to purchase. Medical Insurance helps recipients pay for inpatient hospital care, posthospital extended care, and posthospital home health care. If a recipient is hospitalized, Medicare pays all expenses beyond the first $124 incurred during the first sixty days. If the recipient must stay in the hospital more than sixty days, the patient pays $31 a day from day sixty-one to day ninety. After ninety days of hospitalization, Medicare benefits normally end. However, all recipients have a lifetime reserve of sixty days of hospital care which can be used at their discretion. During these sixty days the patient pays $62 a day and Medicare pays the excess. While the sixty reserve days can be used only once, the basic Medicare coverage is renewable as long as there are sixty days between hospital trips.

Supplemental Medical Insurance pays for some physician cost, for some home health-care service, and for some outpatient hospital service and therapy. For the twelve-month period beginning July 1977, recipients must pay $7.70 per month for this extra insurance coverage.

If recipients opt for this coverage, they pay the first $60 of any physician costs in a year, and Medicare pays 80 percent of all reasonable fees in excess of $60.

Medicaid Benefits

Medicaid benefits are designed for persons who are too destitute to pay for medical services. As a consequence, the program does not simply assist with medical expenses, as does Medicare, but instead assumes all the costs of certain basic medical services. Under the Medicaid program, the federal government has established certain basic medical services for AFDC and SSI recipients. If a state will pay for these services for AFDC and SSI recipients, the federal government will make a contribution to their costs. The minimum required services are:

1. inpatient hospital services, other than services in an institution for tuberculosis or mental diseases;
2. outpatient hospital services;
3. physicians' services;
4. other laboratory and X-ray services;
5. home health services;
6. skilled nursing-facility services; early and periodic screening, diagnosis, and treatment of physical and mental defects in eligible people under twenty-one; and family-planning services and supplies.

Additionally, if the state wants to expand the list of basic services and include needy persons who do not receive AFDC or SSI, the federal government will also pay a proportion of these costs. The optional services are:

1. private-duty nursing services;
2. clinic services;
3. dental services;
4. physical therapy and related services;
5. prescribed drugs, dentures, prosthetic devices, eyeglasses;
6. other diagnostic screening, preventive, and rehabilitative services;
7. inpatient hospital services, skilled nursing-facility services, and intermediate care-facility services for individuals aged sixty-five or over in institutions for tuberculosis or mental diseases;
8. intermediate care-facility services;
9. inpatient psychiatric hospital services for individuals under twenty-one;

10. any other remedial care or medical care recognized under state law and specified by the Secretary of Health, Education and Welfare;

11. remedial care recognized under state law, furnished by licensed practitioners (e.g., chiropractors).

As a matter of practice, all states with Medicaid programs pay for some medical services beyond the basics required by the federal government. Illinois, Minnesota, and New York provide all seventeen of the services that the federal government supplements. However, Mississippi pays for only six extra services, Florida for five, and Wyoming for just three.[25]

Because each state can decide how extensive its Medicaid program will be (as long as the basic services are provided), the benefits included under the program vary considerably by state, and the percentage of all poor persons covered may also vary considerably. For example, in 1976 the Massachusetts Medicaid program covered 90 percent of all persons living below the poverty level in that state; Illinois' program covered 70 percent; Alaska's program covered only 4 percent; North Dakota's covered only 12 percent; and South Dakota's program covered only 13 percent.[26]

Variations in services provided and the costs of medical care create substantial differences in the cost of Medicaid per recipient by state. In the first quarter of 1976, the average monthly Medicaid payment per recipient varied from $846 in Alaska to $265 in Minnesota to $66 in Mississippi to a low of $64 in Missouri.

Like AFDC, the federal government pays from 50 to 78 percent of a state's Medicaid costs, depending on the per capita income of the state. In 1976 the federal government paid 78 percent of Mississippi's Medicaid costs, because that state had the lowest per capita income in the nation.

Medicaid's services are much broader than those supplemented by Medicare. Medicaid pays for inpatient hospital care, outpatient hospital services, laboratory and X-ray services, skilled nursing-facility service, physician services, screening, diagnosis, and treatment of children under twenty-one, home health-care services, and family-planning services. In many states Medicaid pays for dental care, prescribed drugs, eyeglasses, clinical services, intermediate-care-facility services, and other diagnostic, screening, preventive, and rehabilitative services (see Table 6.4).

Some persons may receive both Medicare and Medicaid. If a Medicare recipient is sufficiently needy, Medicaid may pay the $7.70 premium for SMI, the $60 deductable for physician fees, the 20 percent of physician fees in excess of $60 not covered by Medicare, and all costs not covered by Medicare for hospital or home-care expenses.

TABLE 6.4

Payments under Medicaid (in millions) by type of service, fiscal year 1971–1976

Fiscal year	Total[a]	Total vendor payments	Inpatient hospital services	Skilled nursing services	Intermediate-care-facility services	Physician's services	Prescribed drugs	Dental services	Outpatient hospital services	Clinic services	Other[b]
1971	6,148	5,939	2,288	1,674	—	717	473	181	d	d	605
1972	7,859	7,375	2,944	1,778	405[c]	804	549	186	d	d	710
1973	9,262	8,810	3,113	1,849	1,162	955	612	211	247	242	417
1974	10,503	10,149	3,399	2,027	1,601	1,086	707	265	291	290	482
1975	12,733	12,354	3,915	2,472	2,203	1,236	827	341	348	392	621
1976	14,704	14,245	4,518	2,599	2,781	1,387	960	387	523	347	744

Source: Department of Health, Education and Welfare, *Medicaid Statistics, Fiscal Year 1976*, No. (SRS) 77-03154, March 1977, p. 6.
[a] Includes per capita and premium payments and payments for screening services.
[b] Includes laboratory, radiological, other practitioners; home health, and family planning.
[c] Beginning January 1972, payments to intermediate care facilities were defined as medical assistance under Title XIX.
[d] Included in other care.

Problems with Medicare

The basic problem with Medicare is that it does not cover a majority of the medical costs of its recipients. Quite obviously, a person struck with catastrophic illness would, after 150 days, exhaust his or her hospital benefits. However, a five-year study (1966–1971) indicated that, while this is a problem for some recipients (about 3 percent), most Medicare beneficiaries never exhaust their hospital coverage.[27] The more serious problem for most recipients is that they have to share certain of the costs under MI and SMI and they must make large expenditures for noncovered services. For example, a person hospitalized for ninety days would incur a personal debt of $1,054 plus 20 percent of all physician costs if covered by SMI, and 100 percent of physician costs if they did not subscribe to SMI. A person who spent 150 days in the hospital (using all sixty reserve days), would incur a debt of $4,774 plus some proportion of physician fees, depending on whether they had SMI coverage.

Because of these kinds of expenses, Medicare pays for only about 42 percent of the health costs of the aged.[28] About 20 percent of the aged receive Medicaid benefits to supplement Medicare. When Medicare, Medicaid, and private insurance are combined, they pay 71 percent of the health expenses of the aged.[29]

Another problem with Medicare is that it provides little help for those who must enter a nursing home. By 1978 it is estimated that 1.3 million persons will be residents of nursing homes at a cost of about $14.7 billion. Some 50 percent of all costs (or about $8 billion) will be paid directly by the consumer, with Medicaid paying for the other 50 percent.[30] Cost per recipient is very high. By 1978 it is estimated that 90 percent of all nursing-home residents will incur charges in excess of $5,000.[31]

Lack of adequate aid for nursing homes has also caused a lack of regulation of many of these facilities. In recent years nursing homes have become big business. By 1975 there were 23,000 nursing homes with 1.2 million beds.[32] According to the U.S. Senate Subcommittee on Long Term Care, in 1972, 106 publicly held corporations controlled nearly 20 percent of all nursing homes and accounted for a third of all profits.[33]

Rapid growth and high profits in the nursing-home industry have resulted in many substandard facilities, many of which provide poor to outright dangerous care. Estimates of the percentage of nursing homes with life-threatening conditions vary from 30 to 80 percent. The Senate Subcommittee on Long Term Care estimates that at least 50 percent are substandard.[34] Nursing homes have been charged with unsanitary conditions, poor food, inadequate control and administration of drugs, and negligence leading to death or injury. Testimony before the Senate Subcommittee on Long Term Care charged that 20 to 40 percent of all medication administered in nursing homes is given in error.[35]

Problems with Medicaid

The most immediate problem with Medicaid is that it does not provide benefits to all poor persons. The Congressional Budget Office estimated that, in 1975, eight to ten million persons with incomes below the poverty level were not eligible for the program.[36] A 1976 study estimated that in the South only 24 percent of all poor children receive Medicaid services.[37] The primary groups of poor people excluded from the program are single persons and families without children. Coverage is further flawed because many poor people live in states that provide fairly modest Medicaid benefits. Many doctors, particularly in the South, also refuse to see Medicaid patients. Only 41 percent of all dentists will see Medicaid patients.[38]

A whole series of problems have surrounded Medicaid's EPSDT program. Since 1967, all Medicaid states have been required to provide early and periodic screening and treatment for all children under twenty-one years of age of parents who are eligible for Medicaid. Two recent studies found that only about three million of the about thirteen million eligible children have been screened, and even fewer have been treated for any diseases or illnesses found.[39] In September 1976, a House subcommittee charged that failure of the states to carry out the program "has caused unnecessary crippling, retardation, or even death of thousands of children."[40] The subcommittee estimated that about five million of the unscreened children would have been found to be in need of medical care: one million with perceptual deficiencies such as hearing defects; 650,000 with eye defects, 777,000 with learning disabilities; and 435,000 with iron deficiency anemia.

Both Medicare and Medicaid programs have been plagued by fraud. The problems have not been caused so much by recipients as by individual physicians, medical laboratories, dentists, and pharmacies. A congressional investigation concluded that 10 percent of all Medicare funds are disbursed to doctors and laboratories for services never performed. The committee estimated that physicians alone were receiving $300 million a year for services they had billed for but not actually rendered.[41]

Fraud in the Medicaid program is probably worse. In many cities, clinics designed only to serve Medicaid beneficiaries have sprung up. Most of these clinics seem to be in the business only to make as much money as possible. Many are simply small storefronts where Medicaid patients are subjected to as many tests as possible, with little concern for the results of the tests or the maladies of patients. Investigators found numerous instances in which laboratories made kickbacks to the physician who referred the work, as well as evidence that lab-test results are often ignored.[42] Many Medicaid physicians and labs receive in excess of $100,000 a year.

As part of a congressional investigation, former Senator Frank Moss (D.-Utah) and a number of investigators visited over 100 Medicaid clinics, produced a Medicaid card, and complained only of a cold. Although Moss and the investigators had been certified as healthy by a private physician, they were subjected to over 100 X-rays, given all kinds of drugs, put through hundreds of unnecessary tests, and shuttled from one doctor to another. In one instance an investigator turned in a soap-cleaner solution as a urine sample and the lab test reported it to be normal.[43] This type of fraud severely reduces the benefits of the medical program to poor people who need honest and competent medical care.

One last problem is the frequently demeaning nature of charity health care. Medicaid medicine is most often dispensed by Medicaid mills and through hospital emergency rooms. The doctor's attitude toward and treatment of the Medicaid patient is often impersonal and hurried—and, at worst, hostile, condescending, and careless. The shortcomings of this type of medical care are rather apparent. A short case study perhaps makes the point most forcefully. What follows is an excerpt from a description published by the Children's Defense Fund of an actual incident involving a twelve-year-old Boston youth from a poor family. The boy awoke one morning coughing and vomiting violently.

> First we called the police . . . and they said they couldn't send nobody around to our house unless we could prove it was an emergency. McKay [an older brother] said I should get on the phone and cough for 'em. He wasn't joking neither.
>
> So we went down to the corner and waited for the bus and, man, it was so cold out that we might as well have frozen together. And I kept up this gagging and choking. So maybe after half an hour the bus comes and we get on. Then we had to transfer to another bus.
>
> We arrived [at the hospital emergency room] real early too, and this waiting room . . . was crowded with people.
>
> Now here's the truth: We must have got there by eight o'clock, and we didn't talk to no one, no one, man, until eleven, or maybe even later. An then it was this woman who took our names and stuff like that, you know.

Then they brought this guy in on a table with wheels, and they said he died. The man died there after doctors saw him.

So then, like at twelve, the woman calls our name and . . . tells my mother that we don't have the right kind of insurance to get medical help. McKay has to go home and get something that proves she can come to the hospital.

Now it's like one, one-thirty, and I ain't seen no one. Finally they get all the stuff straightened out on the paper.

They thought it would be better for my mother to say she was on welfare than to say she had a job. She didn't care. She just wanted me to see the doctor, 'cause I wasn't getting any better.

Finally they call my name and I see this doctor. He tells me to take off my shirt and lie on a table, one of those tables like that other guy died on, only this one had a clean sheet. And it's cold in this little hall they got me in, too. Then the doctor goes out and he don't come back.

And I'm lying there with my shirt off, freezing, so finally . . . I get dressed.

Now . . . McKay goes home . . . but he asked someone before he left how come no one's helping me, and the woman tells him it's her job to choose which people who come into the room look the sickest. And since I didn't look that sick she kept me waiting.

You ain't going to believe that nobody came until six-thirty. Then this other doctor comes. And he's looking so tired . . . he looks like he should see a doctor himself. Then he asks if I'm hungry. I say I ought to be, haven't eaten since last night.

So he gives me this great hard candy and he tells me where he buys it and pats my face. Nice guy.

Then he leaves and I hear him tell another man: "There's a boy in there who is very sick. We got to find him a bed." And I started to cry.

When nobody came back I . . . went to get my mother, but she was gone.

Then, like at about ten o'clock in the night, a nurse came . . . to say a policeman's outside waiting to take me home. She says I should be in the hospital and they've been waiting for a bed to open up, whatever that means, but since they had no room they were sending me home.

But before I left she took some blood from me.

"You going to drink it?" I asked her. She didn't laugh. "Too late for that nonsense," she said. "I been here all day lady," I told her. "Me too," she said.

Anyway, the cop took me home and had to carry me into the house.

Three and a half months later, Wilson Diver finally got into a hospital. Medical tests indicated tuberculosis, possible leukemia, and malnutrition.[44]

Any attempt to reform the medical-care field in America will have to address one broad problem that transcends the Medicare and Medicaid programs. The problem is simply that, in the United States, there really is no medical system. There are instead 350,000 physicians and 7,000 hospitals, mostly working on a private entrepreneurial basis. Consequently, medical care and its geographical distribution cannot be planned. Responding to a profit motive, doctors concentrate in certain geographic locations, avoid others, and leave millions without adequate medical care regardless of ability to pay. In 1976 the Commission on Physicians for the Future disclosed that 45 million Americans live in areas where there are too few doctors to treat them. It is estimated that, in Appalachia, there is only one doctor for every 7,000 inhabitants. In slum areas such as Brooklyn's Bedford-Stuyvesant, there is only one doctor for every 100,000 persons.[45] In wealthy Beverly Hills, on the other hand, there is one doctor for every eighty residents.

Physician maldistribution is a manifestation of the fact that there is no internal or external organization to evaluate medical care periodically to help it adjust to changing public needs. Of course, there is also no organization to coordinate the various aspects of the medical field. The results include overtraining of doctors for some fields (such as surgery) and undertraining for other fields (such as family medicine); and, of course, severe equipment and facility duplication between hospitals only a stone's throw apart. Any reform of American health care needs to either establish or provide incentives for national planning.

REFORMING AMERICAN HEALTH CARE

There are numerous options for reforming American health care. Medicare and Medicaid could be redesigned to cover a larger clientele and a larger percentage of health-care costs; more nonpoor citizens could be encouraged to obtain private health insurance through such incentives as tax credits for premiums; the federal government could finance catastrophic health insurance.

At this writing, numerous bills that rely on one or more of these options are before Congress.[46] None of these proposals, however, would deal with the most severe problems plaguing American health care. Genuine and viable reform would have to: (1) ensure that all persons have access to medical care; (2) eliminate the financial hardship of medical bills; (3) limit the rise in health-care costs; (4) provide quality control over health care; and (5) encourage medical-service planning. These five goals are critical.

Only some form of national health system (socialized medicine) or national health insurance could meet all these goals. At present, the United States is the only major industrialized nation in the world, except South Africa, that does not have a national health system or national health insurance.[47] Pressures for reform are growing. As early as 1969, the national Governor's Conference, with thirty Republican members, endorsed national health insurance. There is currently little support in the United States for a national health system (socialized medicine) and little chance that such a system will be instituted in the immediate future. Support for national health insurance, however, is substantial and growing. A national insurance program would leave medicine in the hands of doctors and the medical establishment, would not undermine the ability of M.D.'s to earn a good living, would not deny patients the right to choose their own physician, or deny physicians the right to choose their patients. National health insurance would simply guarantee payment to doctors and hospitals under one comprehensive medical-insurance plan.

There is no question that the United States could afford such a plan. In 1975 Americans spent $118.5 billion on health care, an expenditure that equaled 8.3 percent of our gross national product. Other nations spent smaller proportions of their gross national product to provide comprehensive, universal health care. Canada, for example, spends 7.3 percent of its gross national product for comprehensive national health insurance. We are, in other words, already spending sums sufficient to provide a national health program; we are just not getting as much for our money because of the waste and excess profits our system allows.

A recent federal study reached two revealing conclusions. First, that even without national health insurance, total U.S. health spending will rise almost 40 percent to $223.5 billion by 1980. Second, national health insurance, while considerably more comprehensive than other proposals, would cost the same or only slightly more than other options. Estimates are that national health insurance would cost about $248.3 billion in 1980, about the same as proposals supported by the American Medical Association and the American Hospital Association. A bill proposed by the private-health-insurance industry would cost an estimated $243.5 billion. A catastrophic health-insurance bill supported by Senators Long and Ribicoff would cost an estimated $233.5 billion.[48]

The Health Security Bill

The major national-health-insurance proposal presently before Congress was introduced by Senator Edward M. Kennedy (D.-Mass.) and Congressman James Corman (D.-California). The Kennedy-Corman proposal is entitled the health security bill. Its six major provisions are outlined below.

Comprehensive benefits Almost all medical services, rather than only selected services, would be covered if the bill were enacted. All physician's fees, hospital care, home health services, optometry and podiatry services, and medical devices and appliances would be covered. Additionally, at the outset, the dental care of all children up to age fifteen would be paid and dental service would be extended over the first five years of the program. With some limitations, psychiatric services, drugs, and nursing-home care would also be covered. Medicare would no longer be needed and Medicaid would exist only to supplement a few services for poor families (such as dental care for poor adults). One obvious advantage of comprehensive coverage is that citizens would have to pay for health care only once, rather than the four times citizens pay now (out-of-pocket payments for uncovered services, health-insurance premiums, payroll taxes for Social Security, and income taxes). Comprehensive benefits would also allow citizens to seek care for all their needs rather than just those covered; hopefully, this would refocus health care on prevention rather than acute care. Experience in other countries and with prepaid plans in the United States does not support the frequent claim that comprehensive benefits would lead to unnecessary or excessive trips to the doctor.

Last, comprehensive benefits would also lead to a better planned and delivered medical system. Since medicine now chases dollars, it is organized on the basis of what pays rather than on the basis of what people need. With all needs covered, health-care services would be more logically designed and delivered.

Universal coverage Under the health security bill, everyone would be eligible for health care, regardless of income, age, geographic location, or past history of illness. This approach is considered superior to one that would provide different services to different groups for three reasons. First, a multiple-benefit program inevitably provides less services for the poorest citizens on the ground that they are less worthy of aid. Second, considerable savings result from simply making everyone eligible. Without complex eligibility provisions, no bureaucracy is needed to determine eligibility or to run experience ratings and means tests. Recent studies show that the turnover in the Medicaid program is between 50 and 70 percent a year. This means that record keeping and investigation require about 5 billion unnecessary dollars per year. Under universal coverage, these costs are avoided. Last, universal coverage is important because it establishes health care as a right, not a handout.

Incentives for health-care-delivery reforms   The health security bill would not attempt to scrap the existing system, but it would attempt to stimulate reforms. For example, doctors who opted for fee-for-service practice rather than group practice would not be paid less than doctors in group practice, but they would be burdened with heavier paperwork, which would cut down on their profits. Additionally, in an effort to redistribute the physician population, more money would be allowed for services in underserviced areas than in overserviced areas.

Quality control   To make certain that high quality was maintained in medical services, a Commission on the Quality of Health Care would be established. The commission would develop and enforce national standards for doctors and hospitals. All physicians in the program would be required to enroll in continuing-education programs. Only qualified surgeons would be allowed to perform operations, and elective surgery would be performed only when consultation with appropriate specialists had been held. The commission would also supervise the sale and prescription of all drugs to ensure that patients were not overmedicated or given dangerous drugs.

Cost control   One lesson of the present medical system is that fee-for-service payments for doctors and cost-plus payments for hospitals lead to runaway inflation in medical costs. Rather than attempt to regulate doctors and hospitals, the health security bill would simply provide a medical budget each year. Doctors and hospitals would have to stay within this budget, but they would have the power to alter services and fees under it to obtain maximum efficiency in medical care. The budget would also allocate funds for more M.D.'s and for financial support for students while they attend medical school. These policies would help to control costs and provide incentives for efficiency.

Progressive financing   Under the health security bill medical care would be financed through the federal income tax. Fifty percent of the money for the program would be collected by:

- a 3.5 percent tax on employer payrolls;
- a one percent tax on the first $20,000 a year in wages and nonearned income;
- a 2.5 percent tax on the first $20,000 a year of self-employed income.

The other 50 percent would come from federal general revenues. While taxes would increase some for average citizens (assuming there was no tax reform), citizens would no longer need to pay for private insurance and they would no longer suffer out-of-pocket expenses for medical care. The federal tax, although only minimally progressive, would more equitably spread the burden for the health-care system.

Private insurance companies would not be used under the system because the experience in this and other countries indicates that the administrative costs under private insurance are simply much too high.[49] For example, in 1974, private insurers took $3.6 billion of the $28.4 billion paid in premiums for administrative costs. This represents 12.8 percent of premium income. Both Canada and Australia tried to use private insurers, but both decided that administrative costs were simply too high. Without private insurers, Canada's administrative costs in 1974 were less than 4 percent. Additionally, a recent study by HEW provided more evidence that private administration is too costly. The study showed that states which have allowed Medicaid programs to be administered privately have spent 30 percent more on administrative costs than have those states who administer the programs themselves.[50]

CONCLUSIONS

Substantial reform of the health-care system would do much to aid the poor and even eliminate some poverty in America. At the least, people would not become poor for lack of medical care; fewer children would be born with mental or physical handicaps attributable to inadequate prenatal care; fewer children would be handicapped by untreated preventable or curable diseases and physical defects; and the poor could obtain quality health care, both preventive and acute, without having to barter their personal dignity. Further, the aged, both poor and nonpoor, would be more secure in their retirement years, because they would not have to fear losing their savings in the event of serious illness.

It would be surprising if the health security bill were passed intact. It is highly likely that the bill will be the focus of debate over reform and that any reform will reflect many of the qualities and alternatives stipulated by the bill. The Long-Ribicoff bill mentioned earlier is the only bill currently pending before Congress which is likely to challenge the Kennedy-Corman bill. But Long-Ribicoff is not a viable alternative to the present medical system; it is primarily an attempt to maintain the present system with only Band-Aid changes. The Long-Ribicoff bill would provide catastrophic coverage to those hospitalized sixty days or longer, but would leave the patient to pay 25 percent of all hospital costs and 20 percent of all physician costs. Medicaid would be replaced by comprehensive coverage for those earning less than the poverty level. Citizens above the poverty line would be given some tax incentives to buy private health insurance.

The Long-Ribicoff bill meets none of the conditions of viable reform.[51] It would not ensure medical care for all citizens or eliminate the financial hardships. The plan is completely unresponsive to the need to control medical costs, the need for quality control, and the need for medical planning. Still, because of the power of Russell Long (Dem.-La.) in the Senate, the Long-Ribicoff proposal may become a serious rival to the Kennedy-Corman bill.

NOTES

1. Congressional Budget Office, *Catastrophic Health Insurance* (Washington, D.C.: Government Printing Office, 1977), p. xiv.

2. U.S. Congress, Hearings before the Subcommittee on Health, *Medicare-Medicaid Administrative and Reimbursement Reform,* 94th Cong., 2d sess., July 1976, p. 252.

3. Ibid., p. 30.

4. See Milton Silverman and Phillip R. Lee, *Pills, Profits and Politics* (Berkeley: University of California Press, 1976), p. 30.

5. See David Hapgood, *The Screwing of The Average Man* (New York: Bantam Books, 1974), p. 115.

6. "11,900 Deaths Caused by Unnecessary Surgery, Report Says," *The Houston Post,* 26 January 1976, p. 1.

7. *Catastrophic Health Insurance,* p. 11.

8. Ibid., p. 14.

9. Ibid., p. xv.

10. U.S. Department of Health, Education and Welfare, *Forward Plan for Health* (Washington, D.C.: Government Printing Office, 1976), p. 117.

11. Karen Davis, *National Health Insurance: Benefits, Costs, and Consequences* (Washington, D.C.: The Brookings Institution, 1975), p. 11.

12. See *Catastrophic Health Insurance,* p. 7, note 4.

13. Ibid., p. xiv.

14. See Abraham Ribicoff, *The American Medical Machine* (New York: Saturday Review Press, 1972); and Edward Kennedy, *The American Medical Machine* (New York: Simon and Schuster, 1972).

15. *Forward Plan for Health,* p. 118.

16. Fred Anderson, "The Growing Pains of Medical Care," in Stephen Lewin, ed., *The Nation's Health* (New York: H.W. Wilson, 1971), p. 33.

17. *Forward Plan for Health,* p. 118.

18. Herbert C. Birch and Joan Dye Gussow, *Disadvantaged Children: Health Nutrition and School Failure* (New York: Harcourt, Brace and World, 1970), p. 13.

19. Anderson, "The Growing Pains of Medical Care," p. 33.

20. U.S. Congress, Senate, Hearings before the Subcommittee on Executive Reorganization, *Health Care In America,* 90th Cong., 1st sess., Part 2, June 1968, p. 688.

21. U.S. Department of Health, Education and Welfare, Office of Child Health Affairs, *A Proposal for New Federal Leadership in Maternal and Child Health Care in the United States* (Washington, D.C.: Government Printing Office, November 1976), pp. 9–10, 15.

22. U.S. Department of Health, Education, and Welfare, Health Care Financing Administration, *EPSDT: The Possible Dream* (Washington, D.C.: U.S. Government Printing Office, July 1977), pp. 1–2.

23. Heather Hutchinson, "Hunger and Malnutrition," unpublished paper, University of Houston, 1976, p. 10.

24. Davis, *National Health Insurance,* pp. 9–10.

25. Joel Havemann and Linda Demkovich, "Making Some Sense Out of the Welfare 'Mess,'" *National Journal,* January 8, 1977, p. 51.

26. Ibid.

27. *Catastrophic Health Insurance,* p. 25.

28. Ibid., p. 26.

29. Ibid.

30. Ibid., p. xiv.

31. Ibid., p. 5.

32. U.S. Congress, Senate, Report of the Subcommittee on Long-Term Care, *Nursing Home Care in the United States,* 94th Cong., 2d sess., March 1976, p. 24.

33. Ibid.

34. Ibid., p. 13.

35. Ibid., p. 15.

36. *Catastrophic Health Insurance,* p. 26.

37. National Council of Organization for Children and Youth, *America's Children 1976* (Washington, D.C.: Government Printing Office, 1976), p. 45.

38. *Medicaid for the Youth–The EPSDT Program in the South* (Atlanta, Georgia: Southern Regional Council, October 1976), pp. 24–25.

39. U.S. Congress, House, Subcommittee on Oversight and Investigation, *Department of Health, Education and Welfare's Administration of Health Programs: Shortchanging Children,* September 1976; and M. Elaine Gilliard, *Medicaid for the Young: The Early and Periodic Screening, Diagnosis and Treatment Program in the South* (Atlanta, Georgia: Southern Regional Council, 1976).

40. *Department of Health, Education and Welfare's Administration of Health Programs: Shortchanging Children,* p. 3.

41. *Medicare-Medicaid Administrative and Reimbursement Reform,* p. 175.

42. Ibid., pp. 172–175.

43. "Rampant Medicine Fraud Alleged," *The Houston Post,* 7 August 1976, p. 10A.

44. Reported in *The Houston Post,* 14 June 1976, p. 1.

45. Ribicoff, *The American Medical Machine,* p. 21.

46. See Davis, *National Health Insurance, passim.*

47. See Milton Roemer, *The Organization of Medical Care Under Social Security* (Geneva: International Labor Organization, 1969), pp. 60–65; and Raul Tunley, *The American Health Scandal* (New York: Harper & Row, 1966).

48. Gordon R. Trapnell, Consulting Actuaries of Washington, D.C., 1977.

49. Davis, *National Health Insurance,* p. 73.

50. Ibid.

51. On the many deficiencies of this bill, see Davis, *National Health Insurance,* pp. 85–89.

7

EMPLOYMENT, POVERTY, AND ECONOMIC HARDSHIP

Employment opportunities are closely linked to the degree of economic well-being of a society. If every person needing employment were able to obtain a job offering remuneration sufficient to meet his or her needs, the economy would be healthier, there would be fewer social tensions, and fewer citizens would require government aid to survive. America has long suffered a job crisis, which has contributed very substantially to severe social problems and the need for welfare programs. The job crisis takes four forms: (1) large numbers of unemployed; (2) large numbers of part-time workers who want full-time work; (3) large numbers of persons holding jobs below their skills; and (4) large numbers of people employed in jobs that do not pay a living wage. Some of the latter jobs are part-time or part-year, but many are full-time, year-round positions that simply pay poverty-level wages. Over eight million full-time, year-round workers earned less than $5,000 in 1973. In 1975, 12.9 million persons worked full-time, year-round and still earned less than $7,000.[1]

The United States has not approached full employment since 1944, when the official unemployment rate was 1.2 percent (see Table 7.1). Between 1950 and 1974, official unemployment averaged about 5 percent.

TABLE 7.1

Average unemployment 1929, 1933, 1944, 1947–1976

Year	Number (in thousands)	Percent of labor force
1929	1,550	3.2
1933	12,830	24.9
1944	670	1.2
1947	2,311	3.9
1948	2,276	3.8
1949	3,637	5.9
1950	3,288	5.3
1951	2,055	3.3
1952	1,883	3.0
1953	1,834	2.9
1954	3,532	5.5
1955	2,852	4.4
1956	2,750	4.1
1957	2,859	4.3
1958	4,602	6.8
1959	3,740	5.5
1960	3,852	5.5
1961	4,714	6.7
1962	3,911	5.5
1963	4,070	5.7
1964	3,786	5.2
1965	3,366	4.5
1966	2,875	3.8
1967	2,975	3.8
1968	2,817	3.6
1969	2,832	3.5
1970	4,088	4.9
1971	4,993	5.9
1972	4,840	5.6
1973	4,304	4.9
1974	5,076	5.6
1975	7,830	8.5
1976	7,288	7.7
1977 (April)	6,568	6.9

Source: *Employment and Earnings* (January 1974), p. 24. Data includes fourteen- and fifteen-year-olds prior to 1947. *Social Security Bulletin,* April 1977, p. 212.

In 1975, unemployment exceeded the crisis point when it averaged 8.5 percent, the highest unemployment since the Great Depression. By official figures, in each month of 1975 some 7.9 million Americans sought jobs unsuccessfully. The job situation improved little in 1976, averaging 7.7 percent with an 8.1 percent unemployment rate in December of 1976. Estimates are that some 18 million persons were unemployed at some time during 1974, and this figure rose to 20.4 million in 1976. Considering both workers and their dependents, "60–70 million Americans in 1976 . . . were hit by unemployment, with its income loss, anxiety, social and civil aggravation, and even humiliating sense of rejection by the civilization in which they live."[2] In 1976, 8.6 million persons were unemployed for fifteen weeks or longer, and 3 million persons never found a job. In most other Western nations, an unemployment rate of 2.5 to 3.0 percent would be considered a national crisis. Indeed, between 1962 and 1973, the unemployment rates in Japan, France, the United Kingdom, Sweden, and Germany averaged 1.8 percent (see Table 7.2).[3] Since 1973, unemployment has increased in many Western nations, but has generally remained far below American rates.

While the official unemployment rate in America is ominous enough, it covers up two important facts. First, many groups of Americans suffer much higher unemployment than the national average. For example, unemployment among black males averaged more than 13 percent in 1976. Among young black males, unemployment averaged 25 percent. Black unemployment has remained above 7 percent in all but two years since 1954. Unemployment among black females has averaged about 10 percent since 1960. Women make up about 45 percent of all the unemployed. Teenage unemployment is also extremely high. It has not been below 10 percent since 1954 and, in 1976, was 18.7 percent, with 36 percent of black teenagers unemployed.[4] Persons between the ages of sixteen and twenty-four represented about half of the officially unemployed. Unemployment in many major cities, especially in central cities, is also much higher than the national average.

The second problem with the official statistics is that they do not reflect true unemployment.[5] Actual unemployment is substantially higher. The official statistics do not include: (1) those working part-time who want full-time employment; (2) those working part of the year, but wanting year-round employment; (3) those who have become so discouraged that they have quit looking for work; and (4) those with physical or mental handicaps who would like to work. The first three categories have included some two million persons per year in the mid 1970s. Thus, true

TABLE 7.2

Unemployment rates in seven countries, 1964–1974

Year	Belgium[a]	France[b]	Germany[a]	Italy[c]	Netherlands[a]	Sweden[c]	United Kingdom
1964	2.2	1.1	0.8	2.7	0.6	1.6	1.6
1965	2.4	1.4	.7	3.6	.7	1.2	1.4
1966	2.7	1.4	.7	3.9	1.0	1.6	1.4
1967	3.7	1.8	2.1	3.5	2.0	2.1	2.2
1968	4.5	2.1	1.5	3.5	1.9[e]	2.2	2.4
1969	3.6	1.7	.9	3.4	1.4	1.9	2.4
1970	2.9	1.7	.7	3.2	1.1	1.5	2.5
1971	2.9	2.1	.8	3.2	1.6	2.5	3.4
1972	3.5	2.3	1.1	3.7	2.7	2.7	3.8
1973	3.6	2.1	1.2	3.5	2.7	2.5	2.6
1974	4.1[f]	3.4[g]	2.6	2.9	3.2[f]	2.0	2.7

Source: U.S. Department of Labor, Bureau of Labor Statistics. Reported in *Hearings on H.R. 50,* Part 2, p. 49.
[a] Based on registered unemployment.
[b] Official estimate based on registered unemployment statistics and estimate of the unregistered unemployment.
[c] Based on labor force sample survey.
[d] Great Britain.
[e] Beginning in 1968, series altered to include married women who are not heads of households.
[f] September, not seasonally adjusted.
[g] October, seasonally adjusted.

unemployment in 1975 was at least 10 to 11 percent.[6] The Department of Labor estimates that there are somewhere between five and seven million handicapped persons who could also be placed in the job market.[7] If handicapped persons were included in official figures, unemployment rates even in the mid-1970s would have almost doubled. There are also millions of housewives and elderly people who would enter the job market if opportunities were available.

As devastating as the unemployment figures are, an alternative measure known as the subemployment rate shows even more severe hardship resulting from inadequate job opportunities. Subemployment includes those who are unemployed, those who have given up looking for a job, those working part-time who want full-time work, and those working full-time who cannot earn enough to escape poverty. Subemployment afflicts a staggering number of Americans. Table 7.3 shows a subemployment index for 1972 compiled by Vietorisz, Mier, and Harrison. The data show

TABLE 7.3

Subemployment, 1972

Subemployment category	Number of subemployed individuals	Percent subemployed	Cumulative number of subemployed individuals	Cumulative percent subemployed
Unemployed workers	4,840,000	5.3%	4,840,000	5.3%
Discouraged workers	4,462,000	4.9	9,302,000	10.2
Involuntary part-time workers	2,624,000	2.9	11,926,000	13.1
Full-time workers earning less than $2.00/hr.	6,100,000	6.7	18,026,000	19.5
Full-time workers earning $2.00 to $3.85/hr.	18,801,000	20.6	36,827,000	40.1
Labor supply	91,003,000	—	—	—

Source: Reprinted by permission from "Full Employment at Living Wages" by Thomas Vietorisz, Robert Mier, and Bennett Harrison, in volume no. 418 of *The Annals of the American Academy of Political and Social Science,* March 1975, p. 104.

that some eighteen million Americans were subemployed, if only the un-employed, discouraged, involuntary part-time, and full-time workers earn-ing less than $2.00 an hour are considered. If full-time workers earning $2.00 to $3.85 are added, subemployment affected 36.8 million workers. Subemployment for minorities would be even higher. Since 1972, of course, the employment situation has gotten worse, not better.

These figures make terribly obvious the catastrophic job crisis in America. Millions of Americans cannot prosper through the job market and thus are forced to turn to the government for aid, live a life of crime, or suffer a desperate poverty.

THE JOB SHORTAGE

Why is there such a critical job shortage in the United States? This is a complex question, but some of the reasons are quite apparent. The num-ber of jobs in a society corresponds to the size of the population and the resources and consumption patterns of that society. As the population of a society and its consumption patterns increase, so should the number of jobs. In general, this has been the case in America—as the population has increased, so has the labor force and the number of available jobs. Table 7.4 shows, for example, that, in 1950, there were some 62 million persons in the civilian labor force and some 59 million jobs. In every year from 1950 to 1974 the civilian labor force increased. Only in 1961 and in 1975 did the labor force increase while the job market declined. This, of course, caused high unemployment in 1961 and 1975. In August 1976, there were some 96.7 million persons in the civilian labor force and some 89 million jobs, resulting in an unemployment rate of about 7.6 percent.

A number of factors can upset the balance between population and jobs. Automation (or simply mechanization) is an obvious example. Auto-mation, simply put, is the replacement of workers with machines and/or advanced technology. Automation has seriously reduced the number of jobs in our society. For example, in the textile industry in recent years, new electrokit looms produce the same amount of fabric with 25 percent fewer workers.[8] Similarly, technological advances led to a 47 percent in-crease in steel production between 1960 and 1974, but employment in the steel industry declined by 15 percent.[9] The situation in many other indus-tries has been similar. For example, between 1967 and 1972:

- crude-ore mining increased 3 percent, but jobs in this industry de-creased 25 percent;

- production of man-made fibers increased 75 percent, jobs increased 18 percent;
- sugar manufacturing increased 16 percent, jobs decreased 10 percent;
- aluminum production increased 26 percent, jobs decreased 3 percent;
- copper manufacturing increased 61 percent, jobs increased 27 percent;
- car production increased 35 percent, jobs increased 6 percent.[10]

TABLE 7.4

Civilian labor force and unemployment rate, 1950–1976 (in millions)

Period	Total labor force	Employed	Unemployed	Unemployment rate
1950	62,208	58,920	3,288	5.3
1955	65,023	62,171	2,852	4.4
1960	69,628	65,778	3,852	5.5
1961	70,459	65,746	4,714	6.7
1962	70,614	66,702	3,911	5.5
1963	71,833	67,762	4,070	5.7
1964	73,091	69,305	3,786	5.2
1965	74,455	71,088	3,366	4.5
1966	75,770	72,895	2,875	3.8
1967	77,347	74,372	2,975	3.8
1968	78,737	75,920	2,817	3.6
1969	80,733	77,902	2,831	3.5
1970	82,715	78,627	4,088	4.9
1971	84,113	79,120	4,993	5.9
1972	86,542	81,702	4,840	5.6
1973	88,714	84,410	4,304	4.9
1974	91,011	85,936	5,076	5.6
1975	92,612	84,783	7,830	8.5
1976 (August)	96,690	89,367	7,323	7.7

Source: *The Social Security Bulletin*, January 1977, p. 77.

Perhaps the premier example of the effects of automation is farming. In 1870, 50 percent of the population were farmers; in 1975, only 4 percent of the population lived and worked on farms. To counterbalance the effects of automation, it may be necessary to create labor-intensive jobs or shorten the workweek (we will return to these points).

Industries can also retard the growth of the job market by holding back on production. Industries frequently cut back on production to keep their products in limited (sometimes even scarce) supply and thus their prices high. Even during boom periods, 10 percent of all factory capacity in America is idle. During periods of economic slump, such as 1974–1975, one-third of all factory capacity stands idle. If industries produced at full capacity, many products would be much cheaper and more readily available to the public. Increased consumption and production would also generate more jobs. Increased production in the housing, transportation, and food industries would be particularly beneficial. The problem is that industries operating at full capacity generally have to accept a lower margin of profit per unit sold. Industry can often make the same profit by selling fewer units at higher prices and thus may have little incentive to increase production. The other side of the problem is that if production increases much faster than wages, consumers will not have the money to purchase all the increased goods. When this happens, the result is recession. Thus, a balance must be created between production and wages or wealth. The severe maldistribution of wealth described in Chapter 2 is a major obstacle to achieving a healthy economy.

Imports also frequently harm the job market by making it difficult for American industries to compete with products manufactured in foreign countries at very low labor costs. Industries that do try to compete with foreign imports often try to keep their costs low by paying American workers extremely low wages. This is true of the textile industry, where wages are generally extremely low (and were low even before imports began to cause problems).

American industry has added to the import problem in several ways. The most critical has been the decision of many American industries to move their operations to foreign countries to avoid American taxes and to reduce their labor costs. Ironically, United States tax laws have often given corporations an incentive to move outside the United States, which only aggravates the job problem created by imports. In recent years, American corporations have purchased or established foreign corporations that produce electronic equipment, leather goods, rubber products, and even "American" cars. In 1973, three of the top ten imported cars in the United States were made by American corporations abroad. Rarely are any of the savings American corporations realize by moving overseas passed on to American consumers.

The most obvious solution to the import problem is, of course, not practicable. The United States cannot outright bar foreign-made imports, because other countries would retaliate by barring our exports. Protective tariffs are often used, but this tends to provoke similar tariffs against American products and creates markets insulated from competition. Multination agreements requiring some balance in trade between nations have proven to be moderately effective.

One last problem is that, in recent years, governmental policies to stimulate the job market have been fairly unsuccessful, but political leaders have refused to face this fact. For example, one recent attempt by the government to stimulate the job market has been the traditional technique of providing extra tax breaks for businesses. The assumption is that an additional tax break, in the form of a business-investment credit, will lead to increased business investment and thereby produce more jobs. Studies reveal, however, that the tax-incentive option has generally failed to bolster the job market substantially.[11] Of the 2,091,000 Americans added to the job rolls between November 1973 and November 1976, 1,325,000 were hired by various local, state, and federal governments. Only 766,000 workers were added to the private sector. The problem is a dual one. Many businesses simply pocket the extra profits made possible by an additional tax cut and do not increase production or investment. Second, even if businesses do increase investments and thus output, the overall effect is not desirable if the public does not have the buying power to absorb the increased goods or services. As noted, both low wages and the maldistribution of wealth retard the public's buying power. The money spent on the business-investment credit (or most likely not collected because of it), could have been much better spent on more direct ways of dealing with unemployment, such as job programs (see Chapter 8). It is cheaper to create jobs directly, and employment increases consumer buying power.

Some of the problems that cause unemployment, then, are fairly obvious and could be directly dealt with by the government. Clearly, there are many jobs that need to be done and there is no evidence to support the notion of a natural economic or ecological ceiling on the number of jobs a society can create. Estimates of how many jobs are currently needed vary considerably. Conservative estimates suggest that we need an additional ten to twelve million jobs and the upgrading of twenty to thirty million other jobs.[12] Some experts believe we need to generate as many as fifty million new jobs over a five-year period.[13] Be the estimates conservative or liberal, the challenge of creating enough jobs to serve the needs of the public is an enormous one.

FULL EMPLOYMENT VERSUS UNEMPLOYMENT

Since creating a great many more jobs will clearly not be easy, it is important to investigate more carefully the costs and benefits of full employment versus unemployment. Let's begin by examining some of the effects of unemployment.

Unemployment

One of the most immediate effects of unemployment is that it reduces the nation's gross national product (GNP), which retards economic growth and shrinks tax revenues. The GNP is the dollar value of all goods and services produced in a nation in a given year. With increasing population, GNP growth is necessary to keep the economy healthy. During several periods before 1953, real economic growth was a healthy 4.5 to 5.1 percent a year. However, because of higher unemployment, real economic growth averaged only 3.3 percent during the period from 1953 to 1974. Economists estimate that every one percent of unemployment causes a loss of $50 billion in GNP. It has been estimated that, during the 1953–1974 period, deficient economic growth cost an estimated $2.1 trillion in total national production.[14]

The tax-revenue loss caused by unemployment is also severe. It is estimated that each one percent of unemployment causes a loss of between $12 to $15 billion in tax revenues per year. Between 1953 and 1974, unemployment and the consequent loss of production resulted in a loss of over $920 billion in government outlays at all levels for goods and services.[15] Economist Leon Keyserlings points out that the 1976 federal deficit of some $75 billion was almost entirely due to unemployment. Keyserlings noted that if full employment had been in effect in 1976, tax revenues would have been at least $50 to $55 billion higher, unemployment compensation about $15 billion lower, and welfare outlays about $5 billion less. Deficits primarily result, then, not from excessive government spending or lax tax laws, but from a sick economy.

Unemployment and underemployment, of course, greatly increase welfare costs. In 1975, there were 5.4 million heads of poor families. Only 20 percent of these heads had full-year jobs, and some of these jobs were part-time. Another 31 percent of all poor heads had part-year jobs, and some of these were part-time. About half of all poor heads were without jobs. In fiscal 1976, unemployment compensation alone cost $19.8 billion. The AFDC program, food stamps, and other welfare programs almost entirely support unemployed or underemployed adults and their dependents. Congressman William Lehman (D.-Fla.) has calculated that once unemployment exceeds five million, every additional million costs $14 billion in unemployment compensation and welfare outlays.[17]

Unemployment also causes crime. Many poor people turn to crime because they see no viable opportunities in the job market. *The 1971 Manpower Report of the President* reached the following conclusions:

> Many people in the slums, especially young black men, see illegal activity as an alternative to menial jobs paying low wages and offering no hope of achievement. A recent study in Harlem estimates that roughly 2 out of every 5 of the adult inhabitants had some illegal income in 1966 and that 1 out of 5 appeared to exist entirely on money derived from illegal sources.
>
> Part of the study consisted of a series of intensive interviews conducted in 1968 with unemployed young people aged 18 to 24 in Harlem. Many of these black youths subscribed to such generally accepted values as education and training, employment in meaningful and responsible work, and dependence on one's own resources. Furthermore, they were interested in goals such as having a successful career, accumulating money, and achieving status and prestige through possessions. But in many instances, they found the accepted means of realizing these goals too ridden with frustration or out of their reach and viewed illegitimate activities as a much easier way of achieving some measure of economic success and status in the immediate community.
>
> The absence of employment opportunities which could lead to a radical improvement in life styles and movement out of the slums seemed to be the basic reason why jobs, even those which pay above the minimum wage, were sometimes regarded disdainfully. . . . Hustling was often regarded as a logical and rational option. The market for gambling, numbers, prostitution, and narcotics is large and highly profitable, and the possibility of "being on one's own" competes powerfully with the opportunities available in the regulated middle-class world.[18]

Numerous empirical studies document a strong correlation between unemployment and the incidence of crime. Delinquency, property crimes, violent crimes including homicides, and admissions to prisons have all been shown to vary with unemployment. Cross-national studies of the United States, Canada, England and Wales, and Scotland between the years 1920–1940 and 1947–1973 have substantiated a positive relationship between unemployment and the incidence of crime. Additionally, one of the main reasons that ex-convicts have such a high rate of return to prison is that most cannot find employment. About 50 percent of all ex-cons are unemployed.[19]

A lack of job opportunities also undermines many government programs, including most federal and state job-training programs. Between 1972 and 1976, the federal government averaged spending about 4.8 billion per year on employment programs for the poor. Some of the major programs included the Neighborhood Youth Corps (NYC), Work Incentive Program (WIN), Job Corps, the Manpower Development and Training Act (MDTA), and Job Opportunities in the Business Sector (JOBS). Evaluations of these programs indicate only modest successes, because, while the programs can better prepare the poor for jobs and thus make them more successful workers, they cannot expand the job market (see Chapter 8).[20] When jobs are scarce, job training is no guarantee of actually finding a job. Rather, viable jobs are simply shuffled among those poor who have had the advantage of a training program. If there were more jobs available, the job programs would gain greater credibility and would be much more successful. Trainees generally know whether their training will lead to a decent job and, if this seems in doubt, they are likely to view the program with skepticism and regard their training less seriously.

A scarcity of jobs also causes resistance to civil rights goals, such as employment gains for blacks, other minorities, and women. In a slack job market, minorities and women generally cannot be placed in good jobs or given promotions without displacing someone else—most probably a white male. When minorities and women are advanced over others with more seniority and service, resentment naturally runs high. Economist Bernard E. Anderson's research has shown that, in recent years, blacks have made substantial economic gains when the economy was prospering and job opportunities were opening up. But, despite civil rights laws, blacks have not made substantial gains during periods of economic slack.[21] A full-employment economy does not guarantee minority and female progress, but substantial progress is unlikely to occur without a viable job market.

This raises another point. It is traditional in America to believe that people can obtain work if they only try and that those who obtain jobs do so because of their skills. The severity of unemployment in the mid 1970s made this argument untenable. It is also generally believed that people are compensated for their labors in relation to their abilities on the job. Thus, those who obtain good-paying jobs are the most skilled and are paid according to their skills. As noted in Chapter 3, economist Lester Thurow's research suggests that, in many instances, one's abilities have little to do with job compensation or, in some cases, even with one's ability to obtain a job. Thurow argues that there are just so many good-paying jobs in our society. In most instances, the abilities required to do these jobs are widespread among the public, but employers choose only the most educated for the positions (and those from "better" backgrounds), because they assume these individuals will be the easiest to train and work with. Those without the "right" characteristics are passed over and must accept low-paying jobs. Thus, Thurow argues, it is not the productivity of the employee that determines compensation, but the characteristics of the job market and the employee selection process.[22] This argument seems to have real merit. It suggests that expansion of good jobs in our society is critical to improving the economic condition of many citizens—especially minorities and women.

One last effect of unemployment is its physical and psychological impact on the jobless. A recent study by Dr. M. Harvey Brenner, conducted for the Joint Economic Committee of Congress, concluded that the strain of joblessness caused by a 1.4 percent rise in unemployment in 1970 led to a substantial number of physical and mental breakdowns, murders, and suicides between 1970 and 1975. The study concluded that at least 26,440 deaths from stress-related diseases, 1,540 suicides, and 1,740 homicides resulted from the strain of involuntary unemployment (see Table 7.5). The total mortality rate was 51,570 persons.[23] Studies of the human effects of unemployment in France and in the United States during the Great Depression reached similar conclusions.[24]

Full Employment

The problems caused by unemployment make terribly obvious some of the advantages of full employment.[25] Most obviously, under full employment, the unemployed could find work, GNP and tax revenues would increase, standards of living would improve, and welfare costs would go down. Additionally, many who have not been able to find jobs would be able to find work and, in a tight labor market, more unskilled workers would be trained by employers for better jobs. The wage rate of low-skill workers would also improve, because more job opportunities would be open to them and employers would have to compete for workers. A tight job market would also increase the number of good jobs available to minorities and women.

Equally important, families would not be destroyed by welfare laws and economic problems. More children would be able to grow up in healthy homes where the advantages of education and honest labor would

TABLE 7.5

Cumulative input of the 1.4 percent rise in unemployment during 1970

Social stress indicator	Stress incidence 1975	Change in stress indicator for a 1.4 percent rise in unemployment	Increase in stress incidence due to the rise in unemployment
Suicide	26,960	5.7%	1,540
State mental hospital admission	117,480[a]	4.7	5,520
State prison admission	136,875[b]	5.6	7,660
Homicide	21,730	8.0	1,740
Cirrhosis of the liver mortality	32,080	2.7	870
Cardiovascular-renal disease mortality	979,180	2.7	26,440
Total mortality	1,910,000	2.7	51,570

Source: U.S. Congress, Joint Economic Committee, *Estimating the Social Costs of National Economic Policy: Implications for Mental and Physical Health, and Criminal Aggression,* October 1976, p. vii.
[a] 1972 data, age 65 and under
[b] 1974 data

be more obvious. This might improve children's performance in school and reduce delinquency and crime.

While few political or business leaders will openly admit to being opposed to job opportunities, especially when the alternative is public assistance, many businesses gain substantially from high unemployment and perceive no reason to support policies that will create full employment. Quite obviously, high unemployment keeps wages down—if people are desperate enough, they will take any job they can obtain. When jobs are scarce and insecure, workers make fewer wage or work-condition demands. Corporations are also able to obtain tax breaks and other incentives from states and localities for locating their businesses in the area, and they can ward off taxes and regulations by threatening to move their plants to more generous and lax states. Pollution standards can be opposed on the grounds that workers will have to be laid off or even plants closed. And minority and women's rights will be pushed less vigorously when it becomes clear that progress for them would mean displacing nonminority or male workers.[26] Thus, the benefits of high unemployment are large for some industries, and they will use various deceptive rationales to justify their opposition to policy decisions designed to bring about full employment.

Obtaining Full Employment: The Humphrey-Hawkins Approach

Since the 1940s the federal government has given lip service to the goal of establishing and maintaining full employment in America. In 1946 Congress passed the Employment Act, which, at best, only expressed the sentiment that full employment should be a national goal. One of the backers of a genuine full employment act, Senator Albin Barkley (D.-Ky.), sagely predicted that the bill's effect would be no more profound than to guarantee "anyone needing a job the right to go out and look for one." In the 1970s sentiment again began to rise for a comprehensive federal policy to achieve full employment. The major bill under consideration by Congress in the mid-1970s has been the Full Employment and Balanced Growth Act (or Humphrey-Hawkins bill, after its sponsors).

In response to critics, the Humphrey-Hawkins bill had to be revised numerous times between 1975 and 1977. An analysis of the early version of the bill and the points raised by critics is quite insightful. Later, we will examine a watered-down version of the bill, which finally won the endorsement of President Carter.

As originally drafted, the Humphrey-Hawkins bill was a genuine full-employment proposal involving comprehensive federal planning and coordination to produce millions of new jobs and stimulate the improvement of millions more. The bill would have required in-depth analysis of the nation's economy and coordinated fiscal planning to achieve balanced economic growth (growth without excessive inflation) and full employment. Most importantly, the bill would have established a right to gainful employment at fair compensation for all adults seeking work. The goal established by the bill was 3 percent unemployment within four years after passage of the bill.

The bill also proposed specific programs to reduce unemployment resulting from cyclical, structural, regional, and youth factors, as well as unemployment caused by discrimination. The bill was designed to bring about an estimated ten to twelve million additional jobs within four years, so that unemployment would be reduced to 3 percent. If these policies did not reduce unemployment to the 3 percent level, the government would establish enough public-service jobs to meet that goal. However, the expectation was that two-thirds to three-fourths of all new jobs would be in the private sector.

This version of the Humphrey-Hawkins bill was considered rather controversial, because it would have attempted to manage economic growth by careful analysis and planning rather than allowing supposedly natural economic forces to determine investment decisions. The provision for public-sector jobs also stirred some opposition. Criticisms of the bill were exaggerated. Basically, what the bill attempted to do was to stimulate the growth of the private sector with well-planned and coordinated economic strategies. The bill reflected a great deal of confidence in the ability of the private sector to productively grow with some aid and thus create a healthy economy with more and better job opportunities. The bill, however, went considerably beyond tokenism. It recognized that unemployment results from a wide range of conditions in society, and it required not only efforts to overcome these problems, but continual monitoring to determine if reforms were working and if new problems needed to be dealt with to create or maintain a tight labor market.

Arguments that the bill would have interfered with natural economic forces were rather disingenuous. Since the Great Depression, the federal government has been deeply involved in the economy. Among other boards, commissions, and agencies, the Council of Economic Advisors (CEA) and the Federal Reserve Board (FRB) attempt to formulate monetary and economic policies to promote healthy economic growth. The federal tax laws literally bulge with policies designed to aid economic growth and even to assist specific industries, and the government provides an especially lucrative interest rate (known as the prime rate) for the nation's largest businesses. Most government regulation of big business could just as accurately be called government protection.[27]

Equally important, since the Great Depression, the federal government, including both major parties, has attempted to moderate violent up and down shifts in the economy by using Keynesian techniques to keep the economy on as even a keel as possible. Through the manipulation of interest rates, taxes, and government spending, the government tries to increase production when the economy is in a slump and limit production when inflation rises too quickly. The fact that Democrats and Republicans alike readily accept the necessity of using such techniques underscores their firm belief that capitalism is extremely unstable without government intervention.

As originally conceived, the Humphrey-Hawkins bill would certainly have expanded the government's role in managing the economy. More importantly, however, the bill would have attempted both to coordinate existing government policies and to ferret out problems undermining these policies. Through tax reform, it would also have attempted to balance economic investments. At present, this is a major problem. The tax laws provide incentives for investors in some sectors of the economy (e.g., real estate) that are already so lucrative that investors are naturally drawn to them. Other areas of the economy that may need stimulation very badly, however, can be seriously neglected. Humphrey-Hawkins would have attempted to correct this problem.

The creation of public-service jobs to make up for slack in the private sector was really not all that controversial an idea. During the 1930s, the federal government instituted public job programs to ease the nation out of the depression. During the 1970s, a number of job programs were being used to help alleviate unemployment. In January 1977, for example, the federal government was spending $2.5 billion to support 310,000 public-service jobs in state and local governments, $2 billion to finance a variety of state and local construction projects, $1.25 billion to help state and local governments provide public services without raising taxes or laying off workers, and $900 million to help state and local governments run manpower programs (see Chapter 8).[28] Humphrey-Hawkins would simply have required an expansion of such programs if other efforts could not stimulate enough jobs in the private sector. There is certainly no shortage of jobs needing to be done in our society. Among other things, the central cores of many major cities need to be rebuilt, the railroads are in a state of ill repair, thousands of sewage- and waste-treatment plants need rehabilitation, and there are far too few teachers (for a reasonable pupil-teacher ratio) in the nation's schools. With pressing needs such as these, there is no reason for make-work projects.

Estimates of the net cost of creating public-service jobs vary somewhat, but most are reasonable. Congressman Hawkins estimated that the gross cost of creating even as many as four million public-service jobs would be about $40 billion a year. However, social-service costs would drop $20 billion a year and tax revenues would increase by $10 billion. The four million public-service jobs would generate another 1.5 million private-sector jobs. Thus, for a net cost of $10 billion, 5.5 million new jobs could be created.[29] Ten billion is about half the cost of the 1975 federal tax-reduction program and a small proportion of a federal budget that exceeds $458 billion in 1978. The House Budget Committee estimated that the gross cost of creating roughly 3,581,000 jobs would be $36 billion. Reduced services and increased tax revenues would produce a net cost of $11.3 billion.[30]

The last major criticism of the original Humphrey-Hawkins proposal was that it would cause inflation. In the past, many economists did believe that full employment pumped so much money into the economy that competition for goods caused an extremely rapid rise in prices, thus creating inflation (this was generally measured by what economists call the Phillips Curve). More recent studies, however, show little correlation between employment rates and inflation. In the mid-1970s both inflation and unemployment were very high. During periods of very low unemployment, such as 1952–1953 and 1965–1967, inflation rates were also low. Economist Glen Cain, in testimony before Congress, reported that "if one were to correlate unemployment and the inflation rate for the twenty-eight years from 1948 to 1975, one would find a correlation that is negative, but it is so low and so unreliable that the prudent person would call it a zero correlation."[31]

A major reason for the breakdown of the relationship between inflation and employment seems to be that the forces causing inflation in recent years have had little to do with employment rates. Many economists believe that recent inflation has been substantially caused by such factors as economic concentration or oligopoly. Robert Lekachman, for example, argues that "inflation is not a simple matter of translation of higher wages into higher prices. Rather, it is an aspect of the distribution and concentration of market power among suppliers and sellers, abroad and here at home, who are in a position, within generous limits, to set their own prices for the goods and services that they sell. In both recession and expansion, sellers with market power have chosen to charge more, even if, as a result they sell less."[32] There is plenty of evidence to support Lekachman's contentions.

In the early 1970s the 100 largest corporations controlled 52 percent of all industrial assets in the nation.[33] The five largest corporations (Standard Oil, General Motors, Texaco, Ford Motors, and Gulf Oil) alone control 10 percent of the nation's industrial assets. The top 100 corporations constitute only a small portion of the some 200,000 manufacturing corporations in America, but they receive almost 60 percent of all after-tax profits. The top 200 receive 70 percent, and the top 500 receive 80 percent of all profits. In any given year the top ten corporations alone receive about 25 percent of all after-tax profits.[34]

This level of concentration exists in other areas of the economy as well. The fifty largest banks, out of 13,500, control 48 percent of all banking assets. These banks also have leverage control over thousands of major corporations and control billions in trust-fund dollars, including pension funds. Eighteen of 1,790 insurance companies control two-thirds of all insurance assets. Thirty-three corporations out of 67,000 in the fields of transportation, communications, electricity, and gas control over 50 percent of all assets.[35]

Concentration is actually increasing. As Greenberg points out: "The 100 largest firms in 1968 held a larger share of manufacturing assets than the 200 largest in 1950; the 200 largest in 1968 controlled as large a share as the 1000 largest in 1941."[36] The government, of course, has a hand in all this. Between 1948 and 1968 the government approved the merger of some 1,200 manufacturing companies, each with assets of $10 million or more, with other firms. As head of the Federal Trade Commission, Casper W. Weinberger testified about the impact of these mergers:

> Overwhelmingly these original companies have been well established, healthy firms making good profits. These are precisely the kinds of companies—the viable middle tier—which we would expect to grow in the normal way and therefore present a real competitive challenge to the top corporations. The disappearance of healthy, medium, middle-size firms is a matter of concern not only for competition but for social and political institutions.[37]

One result of this intense concentration is that the American economy has become highly oligopolistic. Many economists consider an industry to be a shared monopoly, or oligopoly, when four or fewer firms control 50 percent or more of all sales in an area of the economy. Oligopoly currently affects a substantial proportion of the total market, and it affects industries that have a substantial impact on American consumers. In 1972 the Census Bureau divided all manufacturers into 422 individual product lines; 110 were found to be oligopolistic by margins of 50 to 97 percent. *Consumer Reports* calculates that "industries in which four firms or fewer control 50 percent or more of sales account for 64 percent of all manufacturing sales."[38] Areas of the economy that are controlled by four or fewer firms include motor vehicles, telephone equipment, soaps and detergents, glass, gypsum products, tires, computers, cigarettes, typewriters, photographic equipment, industrial chemicals, copper, and numerous other areas of the food industry.

Oligopolistic industries are pretty much impervious to market forces. Within what Lekachman calls "generous limits," they can set prices where they want them, during periods of boom or bust. Two studies are instructive. Economist John Blair studied sixteen pairs of products, one from an oligopolistic industry, the other from a more competitive industry. "Blair found that during the two recessions of the 1950s, the wholesale price index of every product produced in a competitive industry declined, responding to slack demand. But the price indices of thirteen of the sixteen products produced in concentrated industries actually rose, defying the law of supply and demand."[39] Economist Gardiner Means examined price structures between September 1973 and September 1974, a period of falling demand and rising prices. "Means found that wholesale prices increased less than 5 percent in competitive-dominated industries, including farm, leather, lumber, and textiles. But the rise in concentrated-dominated industries was 27 percent."[40] Typical of concentrated industries is the practice of target pricing, where the corporation sets a goal of 15 to 20 percent profit on its investment in a line of production and achieves it by keeping the price high enough to meet the goal regardless of fluctuations in supply and demand.

The food industry provides an excellent example of how oligopoly raises prices. Between September 1972 and September 1974, food prices increased an unbelievable 35 percent. Everything from the weather to blight was blamed. But, in fact, considerable evidence indicates that oligopoly within the food manufacturing and retail market was the major cause.[41] Four or fewer firms control 50 percent or more of all sales in the following food markets: breakfast cereals, bread and prepared flour, baking, fluid milk, dairy products, processed meats, sugar, roasted coffee, and canned goods.

The retail market is also controlled by a few giant firms such as Safeway, Kroger, and Colonial. While food prices were skyrocketing the manufacturers and retailers were making extraordinary profits. For example, Del Monte's profits increased 43 percent during the first nine months of 1974; Pillsbury's increased 32 percent; Safeway's increased by 51 percent; Kroger's by 94 percent; and Colonial's by 37 percent.

While precise data are not available, it is clear that oligopoly in the food market costs the public billions annually. The Federal Trade Commission estimates that oligopoly in just thirteen food lines costs citizens $2.1 billion in overcharges annually.[42] Economist Fredric M. Scherer attempted to calculate the total cost of oligopoly in all manufacturing areas to consumers in 1974 and came up with an estimate of $87 billion.[43]

Oligopolies, then, cause inflation in two ways: they inflate prices and they react to falling demand for their products by raising rather than lowering prices. Prices are raised to obtain the same level of profit with lower sales. This practice increases prices even during economic slumps and flames inflation.

The government has done little in recent decades to ensure competition in the marketplace. Not only has the government consistently approved mergers, it has also failed to deal with oligopoly. The Anti-Trust Division of the Department of Justice is small and understaffed, and the legal powers entrusted to it are fairly impotent. Additionally, both major parties seem actually afraid to take on the powerful industrial giants, regardless of how much evidence there is that they hurt the economy. Richard Barber, former counsel to the Senate Subcommittee on Anti-Trust, reported that President Johnson's response to his own task force's recommendation that such industrial giants as GM, IBM, and U.S. Steel should be dismantled was to deny that the task force had even made a report. Richard Nixon's reaction to a similar recommendation from his task force was in the same spirit. He denied that the task force even existed.[44]

Inflation has also been caused by the tremendous increases in fuel costs brought about by OPEC's quintupling of prices and by the excessive profits allowed to major energy producers in America. Like nonexistent energy policies, a lack of food planning has also contributed to inflation. And, as we note in more detail below, the economic policies used in recent years to curb inflation have actually produced, rather than reduced, inflation.

The early versions of the Humphrey-Hawkins bill contained a variety of techniques to deal with these problems. By strengthening the antitrust laws and seeking to revitalize competition in the market, the bill sought to diminish inflation caused by economic concentration. Additionally, Humphrey-Hawkins would have authorized a battery of techniques to deal with inflation, including better analysis of the economy, improved fiscal and monetary policies, strategies to eliminate shortages, export licensing, and stockpiling of scarce commodities.

Does all this mean that an approach like Humphrey-Hawkins would not have caused inflation? Not really, but any inflation created by such a bill should be temporary. Any rapid increase in the job force is likely to greatly increase the money supply and put pressure on consumer goods. Additionally, many of the new entrants into the work force may not be skilled enough initially to produce sufficient goods or services to offset the cost of their employment. However, once the initial influx of new workers has passed, the money supply should stabilize, reducing inflationary pressures. Similarly, once new workers become more skilled, their productivity should increase enough to offset their wages. Economist Bradley Schiller augments this point:

Expansion of demand will, indeed, lead to higher prices, but . . . the stepped up rate of inflation is only a temporary phenomenon. As new workers are absorbed into the production process, the pressure on prices is abated. Hence, what the Phillips Curve may portray on an aggregate level is the rate of inflation necessary to evoke the required labor force adjustment. It should not necessarily be understood to mean that the same high rate of inflation will continue once the adjustment is made. Not only may the price rise be temporary, but it is an integral feature of the adjustment mechanism. Hence, we might be able to say that a 5 percent rate of inflation is necessary to reduce the unemployment rate from 4.5 to 3.5 percent, but we have no firm reason for anticipating continued high rates of inflation once the lower level of unemployment is reached.[45]

A couple of final points about the relationship between employment and inflation should be made. When employment and inflation did correlate with one another in our society, federal decision makers generally attempted to fine tune the economy by playing unemployment off against inflation.[46] When inflation was too high, interest rates and taxes were raised and government spending reduced to "cool off" the economy. These measures reduced business expansion and production, reduced hiring, and even led to workers being laid off. With reduced production and less money available because of unemployment, purchasing decreased. With lower product demand, prices declined, bringing down inflation. Similarly, if the economy needed to be "heated up," interest rates and taxes could be lowered and government spending increased. This would stimulate production, employment, and purchasing.

There are two major problems with this type of economic strategy. First, because of extensive oligopoly and monopoly in our society in recent years, the strategies not only do not work, they create inflation. Attempts to "cool off" the economy only reduce production and create shortages—they do not bring down prices. As Leon Keyserling points out:

Deficient economic performance brings tremendously lower rates of productivity growth, which increases per unit production costs, and this—with or without justification—leads to more rapid price increases. The deficient economic performance, continued in the name of restraining inflation, causes many shortages which add to the inflation, outstanding examples being housing, medical care, utility services, and food. The prevalent monetary policy, designed to restrain inflation, is in fact highly inflationary. . . .[47]

Second, even in a simpler time when these policies did work to some extent, they were (and continue to be) immoral. Workers were simply pawns to be employed when it was convenient and thrown out of the market when it was deemed necessary. Surely such policies show a lack of concern for the human consequences of economic decisions. During the Ford administration, unemployment rates as high as 7 and 8 percent were considered "tolerable" to limit inflation, even when the evidence showed that the strategy did not work. Not only will such policies no longer work in our economy, the considerable increase in welfare programs since the late 1960s means that when people leave the job market, they frequently end up on unemployment compensation or welfare. Thus, both government and private industry must pay a very high price for unemployment. Since the increase in welfare programs involves decisions that are unlikely to be overturned, it behooves our society to develop rational policies for expanding and insuring employment.

Many economists believe that, even in a nonoligopolistic economy, there is no immutable relationship between employment and inflation. Schiller makes this point:

> A fixed rate of inflation is not associated with any given level of unemployment or with efforts to reduce unemployment by any given amount. Policymakers have a variety of options available at all times to effectuate an improved tradeoff between inflation and unemployment. By changing the pattern of demand or improving the function of the labor market, policymakers can achieve lower rates of unemployment with little pressure on prices. To formulate the goal of price stability as an alternative to fuller employment is to ignore other options and rob the poor.[48]

While the original version of Humphrey-Hawkins would have decidedly been a positive step toward full employment, it was in many ways a very modest bill. For example, the bill would have allowed four full years for traditional means to stimulate enough private-sector jobs to bring unemployment down to 3 percent. Only if this failed would any public-sector jobs have been created. Those public-service jobs created would have been low-skill, low-wage jobs. The bill also accepted 3 percent as full employment, a standard that would undoubtedly have left many of the hard-core poor unemployed. This is especially true because the bill continued to rely on standard measures of the work force, which, as we noted earlier, seriously underestimate unemployment.

The bill also failed to consider shortening the workweek to increase the number of jobs. Because of automation, it may be necessary in the future to reduce the workweek to, say, thirty-six hours, without reducing pay. This would considerably increase the number of jobs. Nor did the bill deal with the problem of job exporting by American corporations. Youth were provided for in a special section of the bill, but were excluded from the basic "right" to a job. Only persons twenty years old and over were considered to have a "right" to a job. Indeed, the right to a job was only a goal or promise under the bill; no one could have sued for a job.

But, most importantly, the bill contained two flaws that could have been fatal. It failed to give Congress or the executive the authority to impose wage and price controls, even in concentrated industries. Because efforts to deal with monopoly in recent years have proved unsuccessful, price controls might be a necessary alternative to antitrust legislation. Without these controls, all efforts to control inflation might fail. Second, the bill made no provision for the redistribution of wealth in society. With acute maldistribution of wealth, the public might not be able to consume increased production, which would plunge the country into recession.

Humphrey-Hawkins: The Carter Version

Despite its modesty, the original version of Humphrey-Hawkins could not win support from President Carter or a majority of the members of Congress. Most business lobbies, such as the National Association of Manufacturers and the Business Roundtable, opposed the bill, because, for reasons noted earlier, these groups have never favored full employment. President Carter endorsed Humphrey-Hawkins during his 1976 campaign for the presidency, but once in office refused to give it his support. In the fall of 1977, Carter and the sponsors of Humphrey-Hawkins agreed to a compromise version of the bill. The Carter-backed version is more ambiguous and does not require the government to act as the employer of last resort if unemployment cannot be reduced by other means. The basic provisions of the Carter-backed version are:

Commitments

1. The federal government will accept an obligation to achieve full employment, balanced growth, and price stability.

2. It will be recognized that all persons able, willing, and seeking work have a right to useful paid employment at fair rates of compensation.

3. Inflation will be regarded as a major national problem, probably requiring new methods of control. New methods might include stronger antitrust laws, stockpiling of critical materials, a reexamination of regulatory policies, and productivity and supply incentives.

Economic planning

1. As part of the annual economic report, the president will be required to develop a five-year plan, which, on a yearly basis, establishes numerical targets for employment, unemployment, production, real income, and productivity.

2. The bill establishes an interim goal of 4 percent unemployment among workers sixteen and older, with 3 percent for adults twenty and over. Achievement of these goals would be expected within five years of passage of the bill.

3. The president will be required to submit a budget compatible with achieving the goals stated in the five-year plan.

4. The president will be allowed to modify the unemployment goals and timetable if, at least three years after enactment, they seem unreasonable.

5. The Federal Reserve Board will be required to specify how its monetary policies would help achieve the goals specified in the president's plan.

Programs

1. The president will be required to spell out the policies needed to achieve his or her goals.

2. The bill lists a number of program options the government might want to consider as means of improving employment. Included are public-works programs, public-service employment, special programs for depressed areas, and special youth programs.

3. The government will be required to create some jobs directly (such as public-service employment) if other types of programs do not create enough new jobs.[49]

This new version of Humphrey-Hawkins is much weaker than previous versions. The government is not required to create enough public-service jobs to bring employment down to 3 or 4 percent if all else fails, the goals depend on each president, and they can easily be modified. The bill is also quite vague about how objectives would be achieved. Certainly a president who wants to create full employment would find the bill quite helpful, but no president would be seriously obligated by it. At the least, the bill would increase the importance of unemployment as an issue, would obligate all presidents to give the issue some consideration, and would probably make the government's economic policies somewhat more consistent. It is likely, however, that the bill will be further amended during congressional debate, and any bill actually passed by Congress may be even less capable of creating a full-employment economy.

CONCLUSIONS

The United States is now, and has long been, in the grip of a severe job crisis. Millions of Americans are unemployed or employed in jobs that do not pay a living wage. Improving the economy is one of the key steps in any real antipoverty campaign. As long as the employment crisis continues, poverty will persist, because welfare programs are never likely to be broad enough to cover all the poor or generous enough to support adequately those eligible for welfare aid. More importantly, employment opportunities are a much better alternative than welfare programs—both for the poor and for the broader society.

The fact that real full-employment bills have never been able to obtain support from Congress and the president is quite instructive. This failure reflects the priorities of government and reveals who has power and influence in the political process. Those who prosper from unemployment (or are unconcerned about it) are much more powerful than are those who suffer its consequences. But unemployment is not necessary, nor is it ever actually good for society. Although those who focus exclusively on their short-term interests may not perceive the fact, unemployment spawns all kinds of problems and severely limits a society.

Debates like that over the Humphrey-Hawkins bill should illuminate one point: all governments select the form of economy they will have and largely determine the conditions of that economy. The choice determines who and how many will prosper. Economic systems, in other words, are not fixed, nor are they infallible. If a particular choice of economic system ill serves some of the public, those ill served are not at fault. Recognition of these facts would be a first step toward a healthier political, economic, and social system.

NOTES

1. U.S. Bureau of Census, "Money Income and Poverty Status of Families and Persons in the United States: 1975 and 1974 Revisions (Advance Report)," *Current Population Reports,* Series P-60, no. 103

(September 1976), p. 27; and Bradley R. Schiller, *The Economics of Poverty and Discrimination* (Englewood Cliffs, N.J.: Prentice-Hall, 1976), p. 70.

2. See *Hearings Before the Subcommittee on Equal Opportunities of the Committee on Education and Labor*, Part 5, March 1976, p. 168. These hearings were on the Humphrey-Hawkins bill and were in five parts. The bill is numbered in the House as H. R. 50. Further footnotes to these hearings will be cited as *Hearings on H. R. 50.*

3. *Hearings on H. R. 50,* Part 2, March 1975, p. 49.

4. Testimony of Alan Gartner, *Hearings Before the Subcommittee on Equal Opportunities of the Committee on Education and Labor*, Part 1, February 1975, p. 67-68.

5. Economists have developed a variety of measures of true unemployment. Most of them show significantly higher rates of unemployment than the government's figures. For a review and critique of many of these measures, see Stanley Moses, "Labor Supply Concepts: The Political Economy of Conceptual Change," in Stanley Moses, ed., *Planning for Full Employment, The Annals of the American Academy of Political and Social Science,* March 1975, pp. 26-44.

6. Testimony of Leon H. Keyserling, *Hearings on H. R. 50,* Part 1, February 1975, p. 14.

7. Alan L. Sorkin, *Education, Unemployment and Economic Growth* (Lexington, Mass.: D.C. Heath, 1974), pp. 8-9.

8. Steve Babson and Nancy Brigham, "What's Happening to Our Jobs?" *Popular Economic Press,* 1976, p. 6.

9. Ibid.

10. Ibid, p. 7.

11. Study by Joint Council 16 of the International Brotherhood of Teamsters, reported in *The Houston Post,* 1 December 1976, p. A17.

12. Thomas Vietorisz, Robert Mier, and Bennett Harrison, "Full Employment at Living Wages," in Stanley Moses, ed., *Planning for Full Employment, The Annals of the American Academy of Political and Social Science,* March 1975, p. 104.

13. Testimony of Leon Keyserling, *Hearings on H. R. 50,* Part 5, p. 166.

14. Testimony of Leon Keyserling, *Hearings on H. R. 50,* Part 1, p. 14.

15. Ibid., pp. 14-15.

16. Ibid., p. 15.

17. Testimony of William Lehman, *Hearings on H. R. 50,* Part 5, p. 3.

18. *The 1971 Manpower Report of the President.*

19. See Daniel Glaser and Kent Rice, "Crime, Age, and Unemployment," *American Sociological Review,* October 1959, pp. 679-686; Belton M. Fleisher, "The Effects of Unemployment in Delinquent Behavior," *Journal of Political Economy* 71 (1963): 545-555; U.S. Bureau of

Prisons, "Correlation of Unemployment and Federal Prison Population," *U.S. Bureau of Prisons Report,* March 1975; M. Harvey Brenner, "Effects of the Economy on Criminal Behavior and the Administration of Criminal Justice in the United States, Canada, England and Wales, and Scotland," in *Economic Crisis and Crime: Correlations Between the State of the Economy, Deviance and the Control of Deviance* (Rome, Italy: United Nations Defense Research Institute, 1976).

20. Jon H. Goldstein, *The Effectiveness of Manpower Training Programs: A Review of Research on the Impact on the Poor,* a staff study prepared for the use of the Subcommittee on Fiscal Policy of the Joint Economic Committee, Congress of the United States, November 1972. See also Sar A. Levitan, Garth L. Mangum, and Ray Marshall, *Human Resources and Labor Markets* (New York: Harper & Row, 1976), pp. 340–350.

21. Bernard E. Anderson, "Full Employment and Economic Equality," in Moses, ed., pp. 127–137.

22. Lester C. Thurow, *Generating Inequality: Mechanisms of Distribution in the U.S. Economy* (New York: Basic Books, 1975).

23. U.S. Congress, Joint Economic Committee, *Estimating the Social Costs of National Economic Policy: Implication for Mental and Physical Health and Criminal Aggression,* October 1976.

24. See Arthur M. Okum, *The Battle Against Unemployment* (New York: Norton, 1972), p. viii; and Wm. Kapp, "Socio-Economic Effects of Low and High Employment," in Moses, ed., pp. 60–71.

25. See A. Dale Tussing, *Poverty in a Dual Economy* (New York: St. Martin's Press, 1975), pp. 188–189.

26. See Robert Lekachman, "The Spector of Full Employment," *Harper's,* February 1977, pp. 35–40.

27. See Grant McConnell, *Private Power and American Democracy* (New York: Vintage Books, 1966), and Theodore Lowi, *The End of Liberalism* (New York: Norton, 1969).

28. "Job Programs: How Well Do They Work?" *The Congressional Quarterly,* February 19, 1977, pp. 302–307.

29. Cited in the testimony of Elmer L. Winter, *Hearings on H. R. 50,* Part 4, pp. 57–58.

30. Rep. Conyers and Ottinger, *Congressional Record,* H2044.

31. Testimony of Glen C. Cain, *Hearings on H. R. 50,* Part 4, p. 45.

32. Lekachman, "The Spector of Full Employment," p. 39.

33. Thomas R. Dye and L. Harmon Zeigler, *The Irony of Democracy: An Uncommon Introduction to American Politics* (North Scituate, Mass.: Duxbury Press, 1975), p. 110.

34. Edward S. Greenberg, *Serving the Few: Corporate Capitalism and the Bias of Government Policy* (New York: Wiley, 1974), p. 38.

35. Figures from Dye and Zeigler, *The Irony of Democracy,* p. 110; and The AFL-CIO Platform Proposals, Presented to the Democratic and Republican National Conventions of 1976, Washington, D.C.

36. Greenberg, *Serving the Few,* pp. 38, 39.

37. U.S. Congress, Senate, Antitrust Committee, Subcommittee on Antitrust and Monopoly, *Economic Concentration, Part 8: Hearings on The Conglomerate Merger Problem,* 91st Cong., 2d sess., 4, 5, 6 November 1969; 28 January, 5, 18, 19 February 1970, p. 4815.

38. "The New Monopolies: How They Affect Consumer Prices," *Consumer Reports,* June 1975, p. 378.

39. Ibid., p. 379; see also John M. Blair, *Economic Concentration* (New York: Harcourt Brace Jovanovich, 1972).

40. Ibid.

41. See Jim Hightower, *Eat Your Heart Out: How Food Profiteers Victimize The Consumer* (New York: Crown, 1975).

42. See Fredrick J. Perella, Jr., *Poverty in American Democracy* (Washington, D.C.: United States Catholic Congress, 1974), p. 182.

43. Ibid.

44. Richard Barber, *The American Corporation* (New York: Dutton, 1970), pp. 177–179.

45. Bradley R. Schiller, *The Economics of Poverty and Discrimination* (Englewood Cliffs, N.J.: Prentice-Hall, 1976), p. 62.

46. On the Phillips Curve, see Bradley R. Schiller, *The Economy* (Englewood Cliffs, N.J.: Prentice-Hall, 1975), Chapters 8 and 11.

47. Testimony from *Hearings on H. R. 50,* Part 5, p. 177.

48. Schiller, *The Economics of Poverty and Discrimination,* p. 65.

49. See Mary Eisner Eccles, "Backers Defend Revised Humphrey-Hawkins Bill," *Congressional Quarterly,* November 26, 1977, pp. 2475–2476.

8

WELFARE REFORM

As previous chapters should have made clear, poverty is complex in its origins and manifestations. It is difficult to overcome because of the diversity of elements involved—sexism, racism, crime, illiteracy, poor health, lack of self-confidence, economic orthodoxy, the reality of political power and elite advantage in America, public misconceptions about the poor, bad housing, inadequate public transportation, and an ailing economy. With so many factors, interests, and points of power involved, the most likely reform is symptomatic—patchwork measures designed to alleviate only some of the most severe deprivations. Comprehensive reform must overcome so many hurdles that the most severe deficiencies of welfare programs in 1977 were almost precisely those identified in literally dozens of government and private studies in the late 1960s.[1]

With due regard for the barriers to reform legislation and the difficulties of making even the best legislative efforts work, this chapter suggests and evaluates various methods of alleviating poverty in America. It is instructive to begin by reviewing some of the deficiencies of current welfare programs. Extant programs suffer from the following major problems:

- Welfare programs are far too numerous and often fail to mesh; thus, they suffer from duplication and lack of coordination, which sometimes results in their actually having a negative impact on the poor.

- Much of the overlap, waste, and ineffectiveness of welfare programs is attributable to the fact that they are administered by too many levels of government (federal, state, and local).

- Because each state has considerable latitude over the number of state and federal dollars its poor will receive, there are extreme interstate variations in welfare aid. In many states, welfare aid is so low that it is a major cause of poverty.

- Welfare assistance is narrow in coverage, unresponsive to the needs of many poor persons, and often detrimental in its impact. The most obvious example is the categorical nature of welfare programs, which allows the neglect of needy single persons, couples without children, and intact, male-headed families. Frequently this inadequate response to the needs of the poor leads to destruction of the family unit.

- Multiple benefits, high tax rates on some earnings, and exclusion of some working poor from in-kind programs such as Medicaid often discourages work.

- Benefits under the major cash welfare program (AFDC) are generally inadequate and unresponsive to changes in the cost of living.

- Welfare programs lack horizontal equity—those with the same need do not receive the same degree of aid.

- Welfare programs lack vertical equity—those with the greatest need do not receive aid before those with less severe needs.

One option to these deficiencies would be to reform existing programs. The AFDC program, for example, could be completely federalized, a national minimum for all recipients could be established with only cost-of-living variations, coverage could be expanded to all needy persons, work incentives could be improved, and benefits could be pegged to changes in the consumer price index.

In the absence of more fundamental reform, even modest changes in many welfare programs would be an improvement—although far from the ideal. The most severe drawback of this type of incremental reform is that tinkering with one or more programs would not consolidate the welfare effort. An unnecessarily large number of programs would continue to exist. As long as there are multiple programs to deal with the poor, there will be overlap, waste, and inefficiency. Secondly, only drastic reform could improve many of the programs. The food-stamp program, for example, is administratively very expensive, because the stamps must be printed, shipped to distributors, dispersed to recipients, and redeemed from retailers. The stamps also frequently embarrass and stigmatize recipients.

Similarly, the Supplemental Security Income (SSI) program is severely deficient—at best, it provides very low benefits and, to be even modestly adequate, requires state supplementation. The Social Security program (OASDI) is also flawed, because it is based on a highly regressive tax, provides inadequate benefits to many recipients, and provides benefits to many persons who do not need them. Because OASDI is financed by a distinct tax on employees and employers, it creates the illusion (discussed in Chapter 5) that recipients pay during their working years for the benefits they later receive. This causes even the richest citizens to feel entitled to OASDI in their old age.

Fundamental reform of the welfare system would:

- create conditions to enable as many persons as possible to earn their own living in the job market;
- seriously reduce the number of welfare programs;
- relieve the states of all welfare costs;*
- make welfare aid automatic; administratively simple, comprehensive, and adequate for decent living standards without intrusion into the personal lives of the poor;
- be designed to prevent and break the cycle of poverty rather than just administer to the poor.

AN IDEAL REFORM PACKAGE

An ideal welfare reform package would have three parts: (1) a series of programs designed to create full employment; (2) a comprehensive

---

* The states should be relieved of all welfare costs for two reasons. First, many of the states are severely burdened financially and need to be relieved of some of their obligations. Second, the number of poor persons in a state frequently has nothing to do with that state's economy or past efforts on behalf of the poor. For example, many of the poor residents of northern states migrated there because of severe economic and racial conditions in the Deep South.

health-care program; and (3) one cash-aid program to take the place of all existing cash-aid programs and all in-kind programs.

Job expansion to create full employment would have to rely on measures like those implicit in the Humphrey-Hawkins bill to stimulate and improve the economy, improve manpower and educational programs, and expand child care (see Chapter 7). Comprehensive health care could be achieved through a national health-insurance program, such as the one proposed by the Kennedy-Corman bill (see Chapter 6). The best single cash-assistance program would be one based on the concept of the negative income tax (NIT), perhaps involving tax reform.

'What a novel idea. Applying it to the poor, too.'

Sanders in *The Milwaukee Journal*

The negative income tax (NIT) is an idea generally accredited to economist Milton Friedman.[2] Since its introduction by Friedman in 1962, it has been proposed in many forms.[3] Basically, however, the idea is a simple one. All NIT proposals involve some basic cash floor for poor individuals and families. For example, a proposal could specify that a penniless family of four would receive a basic cash benefit of $2,500. A family that had earnings below the floor would receive a grant large enough to bring them up to the floor and no more.

To encourage the poor to earn more than the floor, recipients could receive some type of matching aid for money earned above the floor up to some cutoff or break-even point. For example, a break-even point might be established at $7,500 for a family of four. A family that earned $3,500 ($1,000 more than the floor) would receive some proportion of the deficit between earnings and the break-even point ($7,500–$3,500). The rate at which the deficit would be funded is generally called the tax rate. Most proposals call for a tax rate of 0.50. Thus, the family that earned $3,500 would receive 50 percent of the deficit between $7,500 and $3,500 ($4,000), which would be $2,000. This $2,000 would give the family a total income of $5,500.

NIT proposals, then, provide a basic floor of income for all families, a cutoff point for aid, and work incentives based on a funding scheme for those earning above the floor but below the break-even point. The attractions of such a program are fairly obvious. A comprehensive program could eliminate all other aid programs, it would completely federalize the welfare system, it would aid all the poor regardless of their personal characteristics, it would not penalize marriage or work, it would be uniform, and it would be automatic and simple. A family whose income was low enough for benefits would receive them with limited intervention into their personal lives.

There are, however, a few problems with the NIT. The major one is that the implicit goals of the NIT may conflict. The floor has to be set high enough to provide adequate benefits to those who cannot work, but it cannot be set so high as to discourage work. The break-even point must also be set high enough to encourage work and to aid low-income working families. But the overall cost of such a program must be kept reasonable. While these are genuine problems, they can be dealt with.

Three points should be kept in mind. First, with the exception of the aged and the disabled, the NIT would, for the most part, be an income supplement, even for the poorest families. In 1974, over 50 percent of female-headed poor families and almost 75 percent of male-headed poor families had some earnings from employment.[4]

Second, for nonworkers, the benefit level does not have to be as high as that of working families. The reason is that work itself is expensive. Transportation, child care, clothing, and food costs all tend to increase with employment. One study, for example, showed that, in July 1974 $619 in earnings were required to match a net of $448 in food stamps and

AFDC benefits to a family of four in New York.[5] Thus, the floor for non-workers could be set 10 to 20 percent lower than the base for worker families. Third, current welfare programs have become so expensive in recent years that, if NIT could eliminate most welfare programs, sums as high as $25 to $30 billion could be spent without exceeding current expenditures, even if only welfare programs were reformed. If a NIT system was also substituted for OASDI, sums in excess of $100 billion could be spent.

Some have questioned the feasibility of any plan that would pay a livable base to families whether they worked or not. The question raised is whether a guaranteed base could be established without encouraging many persons to avoid the job market or even drop out of the job market and just draw the base. To deal with this question, two major studies have been carried out in recent years.[6] One study was conducted in urban areas of New Jersey and Pennsylvania and the other in rural areas of the Midwest and South. Both studies showed that a guaranteed base could be offered without substantially altering work habits and that the work-incentive provisions were viable. In both the rural and urban studies husbands worked only slightly fewer hours than did the controls (about 6 percent fewer), and few husbands dropped out of the work force. Wives did tend to work less (about 15 percent), as did dependents. These latter findings may not be altogether negative, depending on particular family situations. The important point, however, is that when poor families were offered a sizable payment, they chose to continue their efforts at self-support at nearly the same levels as those not offered a payment. The NIT, then, does seem to be a viable idea.

The Family Assistance Plan (FAP)

The first attempt to establish a NIT plan as a substitute for the traditional welfare approach was the Family Assistance Plan (FAP) recommended to Congress by President Nixon in 1969. The original plan would have provided $500 each for the first two persons in a family, and $300 for each additional member. To encourage work by recipients two provisions were made. First, under the plan, able-bodied adults would have been required to accept a job or, if needed, job training. Exceptions were allowed for mothers of small children, the ill, aged and incapacitated and their caretakers, mothers in a family where the father worked, and those who were already employed full-time.

Second, families could earn up to $720 without losing any benefits and they could receive a supplement for earnings above the base but below a break-even point that varied by family size. The tax rate was set at 0.50. Table 8.1 shows the cash benefits that a family of four would have been entitled to, according to the family's income. A family of four with no earnings would have received $1,600. A similar family earning $2,000 would have received an additional $960, half the difference between earnings and the break-even point. If the family earned as much as $3,920, they would have received no cash benefits. Because the benefits would have been very low for most families, the proposal was later amended to provide an $800 food-stamp subsidy for recipient families. The Nixon administration estimated the costs of the cash benefits under FAP at $6 billion.

TABLE 8.1

The Family Assistance Plan: basic benefits for a family of four

Earned income	New benefit	Total income
$ 0	$1,600	$1,600
500	1,600	2,100
1,000	1,460	2,460
1,500	1,210	2,710
2,000	960	2,960
2,500	710	3,210
3,000	460	3,460
3,500	210	3,710
3,920	0	3,920

Source: U.S. Congress, House, "Welfare Reform: A Message from the President of the United States," House Document No. 91-146, *Congressional Record* 115, no. 136, 91st Cong., 1st sess., H7239-7241.

Although the FAP stirred considerable controversy and was twice passed by the House of Representatives, it was finally rejected by Congress in 1972. While opinion varies, it seems clear that the bill failed for three major reasons. First, it would have provided inadequate benefits to most recipients. The benefits provided by the proposal were so low that thirty states were providing higher benefits than the FAP proposed. Second, the FAP was designed only for families with children. Third, the proposal failed to eliminate or coordinate existing welfare programs. Even with all its drawbacks, the FAP was still an important stage in welfare history in America, because it was the first proposal to advocate a guaranteed income for the poor. Most importantly, it was recommended by a conservative president.

Allowances for Basic Living Expenses (ABLE)

The demise of FAP led to a much more sophisticated and comprehensive NIT proposal developed by the Joint Economic Committee of Congress. [7] In 1974 the committee proposed a NIT plan based on cash grants, tax reform, and tax credits. The plan was entitled Allowances for Basic Living Expenses (ABLE) and was estimated to cost about $15.4 billion if fully operational in 1976, with about half the cost in the form of tax relief to low-income working families.

Cash supplements to the poor would have been based on the following ABLE grants:

- married couple filing jointly $2,050
- head-of-household filer   1,225
- single filer   825
- dependent age eighteen or over   825
- 1st and 2nd child   325
- 3rd, 4th, 5th, 6th child   225
- 7th child or more   0

The tax structure would have been reformed in several ways. First, the personal exemption deduction of $750 per person would have been converted to a $225 credit per person against tax liability. This would have lowered the taxes of the poorest families and raised the taxes of the highest-income families, because the value of a tax deduction varies with income and is worth a great deal more to a high-income family than to a low-income family. The tax deduction, in fact, is frequently completely worthless to those with very low earnings.

Second, for those in the lowest income levels who owed no taxes, the $225 credit per family member would have become a positive grant. A family would have paid no taxes and would have received a check from IRS for the amount of the tax credits. Third, the tax code would have been amended to allow the Internal Revenue Service to administer both grants and tax credits.

Table 8.2 shows the benefits under ABLE to an intact family with two children. A penniless family would have paid no taxes, would have

TABLE 8.2

Benefits and taxes for a father, mother, and two children at varying earning levels under ABLE

Annual earnings	Federal income tax liability	Tax credits	Net federal income tax liability	Social Security tax	ABLE grant	Net cash income
$ 0	$ 0	$900	+ 900	$ 0	$2,700	$ 3,600
500	0	900	+ 900	29	2,464	3,835
1,000	0	900	+ 900	58	2,229	4,071
1,500	0	900	+ 900	88	1,994	4,306
2,000	0	900	+ 900	117	1,758	4,541
2,500	0	900	+ 900	146	1,523	4,777
3,000	0	900	+ 900	176	1,288	5,012
4,000	0	900	+ 900	234	817	5,483
5,000	0	900	+ 900	292	346	5,954
6,000	124	900	+ 776	351	0	6,425
7,000	595	900	+ 305	410	0	6,895
8,000	1,066	900	166	468	0	7,366
9,000	1,314	900	414	526	0	8,060
10,000	1,490	900	590	585	0	8,825
15,000	2,510	900	1,610	772	0	12,618
20,000	3,820	900	2,920	772	0	16,308
25,000	5,340	900	4,400	772	0	19,788

Source: U.S. Congress, Joint Economic Committee, Subcommittee on Fiscal Policy, *Income Security For Americans: Recommendation of the Public Welfare Study* (Washington, D.C.: Government Printing Office, 1974), p. 14.

received a $900 grant from IRS, paid no Social Security tax, and received a $2,700 ABLE grant for a total cash income of $3,600. As income increased, the family would have received a lower grant from IRS or, at the $6,000 income level, would have started to pay taxes, would have contributed more to Social Security, and would not have received an ABLE grant. ABLE grants, in fact, would have been given only to the poorest families, while much of the relief for the working poor would have resulted from tax relief and/or tax grants. As noted, the tax rate for those in the highest income brackets would have increased some.

Under ABLE, the AFDC program would have been terminated. State supports for AFDC would have continued for two years if recipients would have been worse off under the ABLE program. The food-stamp program would also have been terminated. The SSI program would have been continued, as would OASDI.

The ABLE proposal was far superior to the FAP and would have been a considerable improvement over existing programs. It would have been uniform, it would have federalized welfare, it would have covered all the poor, it would not have penalized families or work, it would have built on private efforts, it included some tax reform, it was simple in administration, its costs were reasonable, and it would not have intruded unnecessarily on the privacy of the poor.

Its liabilities were significant but curable. The most serious problem was that its benefits were too modest for families that had no private earnings. Since the proposal was estimated to cost only $15.4 billion in 1976, there was latitude to expand the benefits without exceeding current costs. Second, ABLE unnecessarily left some programs such as SSI in operation. It would have been extremely simple to amend ABLE to cover SSI recipients. Third, as drafted, ABLE was not very responsive to short-term poverty. Benefits for one year were based on earnings during the past year. This could have been changed to a monthly evaluation based on current-year earnings.

Shortly after the Joint Economic Committee put forth the ABLE proposal, the Ford administration formulated a plan entitled the Income Supplement Program (ISP). Like ABLE, ISP proposed a NIT program, consolidation of some programs, and tax breaks. Like ABLE, the plan provided $3,600 in cash assistance to a penniless family of four. However, because of extremely high inflation and unemployment during Ford's administration, all reform proposals were set aside.

CONTEMPORARY EMPLOYMENT AND TRAINING PROGRAMS: AN APPRAISAL

Regardless of how enlightened reform of welfare programs might be, no reform can truly succeed if the economy is not healthy enough to meet the needs of both consumers and workers. Without a full-employment economy, the expense of maintaining all the unemployed, unemployables, and subemployed at a decent income level would simply be prohibitive. Since any attempt to reform welfare must expand and improve the job market, the techniques currently used and those most likely to be used in any attempt to reach these goals should be evaluated. The evidence indicates that these programs can be a vital part of an antipoverty strategy.

Contemporary employment and training programs evolved in a piecemeal fashion throughout the 1960s and were subjected to a major overhaul in 1974. The programs were inititially authorized by the Area

Redevelopment Act (ARA) of 1961, the Manpower Development and Training Act (MDTA) of 1962, and the Equal Opportunity Act (EOA) of 1964. Because of serious employment problems, the Emergency Employment Act was passed in 1971 to supplement existing programs. In 1974 the Concentrated Employment and Training Act (CETA) revamped the federal government's approach to employment and training programs, but did not basically alter a commitment to and reliance on such programs.

Table 8.3 shows the myriad programs developed over the years and their costs. In 1961 the programs cost $235 million. By 1975 the cost had risen to $6.3 billion. As Table 8.3 indicates, the programs were barely beginning in the first half of the 1960s; only a half-dozen programs were in operation in 1964. By 1967 the programs were developing much faster, with the Job Corps, the various Neighborhood Youth Corps (NYC) programs, and Operation Mainstream (OM) in full operation. By 1973 a full range of programs were in operation. As might be expected, costs almost doubled between 1970 and 1973.

The Comprehensive Employment and Training Act (CETA) of 1974 substantially revised the government's approach. Rather than the federally run programs of the preceding twelve years, a system of grants was established whereby state and local governments could plan and run their own programs—programs that hopefully would be better designed to meet the special needs of a given region or community. This flexible, locally planned approach replaced MDTA, Neighborhood Youth Corps, Operation Mainstream, and most of the other manpower programs. Under CETA, state and local elected officials are responsible for identifying groups that need aid, for deciding what type of aid they need, and for establishing or subcontracting to provide that aid. All these activities are still subject to federal oversight.

As of August 1977, CETA had eight titles.[8]

- *Title I:* Establishes a program structure in which grants can be made to states and local units of government to allow them to develop manpower services such as training, employment, counseling, remedial education, subsidized private employment, and training allowances.

Eighty percent of the funds appropriated for Title I are distributed to states and local governments on the basis of the number of unemployed persons and the proportion of low-income families in each prime sponsor's area, as well as its proportionate share of employment and training funds received in the previous year.

- *Title II:* Authorizes special public-service employment funds for areas

TABLE 8.3
Employment and training programs: 1961–1976 (in millions)

	1961	1964	1967	1970	1973	1974	1975	1976
Total	$235	$450	$1,775	$1,596	$4,952	$4,666	$6,294	$8,559
Department of Labor								
U.S. Employment Service	126	181	276	331	431	390	462	452
MDTA—institutional	—	93	221	260	358			
Job Corps	—	—	321	144	188			
Jobs	—	—	—	86	104			
Jobs—optional	—	5	53	50	73			
NYC—in-school	—	—	57	58	73	1,419	3,102	3,295
NYC—summer	—	—	69	136	220			
NYC—out-of-school	—	—	127	98	118			
Operation Mainstream	—	—	9	42	82	Concentrated Employment		
Public Service Careers	—	—	—	18	42	and Training Act		
Concentrated Employment Program	—	—	1	164	129			
Work Incentive Program	—	—	—	—	177	218	202	198
Public Employment Program	—	—	—	—	1,005	598	58	3,250
Program administration, research, and support	8	23	118	143	209	162	179	194
Department of Health, Education & Welfare								
Vocational Rehabilitation	54	84	215	—	636	755	819	830
Work Experience	—	—	120	—	—	—	—	—
Other Programs								
Veterans' programs	14	12	19	—	292	351	457	440
Other training and placement programs	8	15	116	—	382	377	297	303
Employment-related child care	26	37	53	—	433	398	604	498

Source: Constructed from data in Sar A. Levitan, Garth L. Mangum, and Ray Marshall, *Human Resources and Labor Markets* (New York: Harper & Row, 1976), pp. 252 and 270.

that have unemployment in excess of 6.5 percent. Like Title I, these funds are administered by state and local governments under federal supervision.

- *Title III:* Authorizes the Secretary of Labor to provide special employment and training services to such groups as Indians, migrant and seasonal farm workers, offenders, youth, and others determined to have special disadvantages in the labor market.

- *Title IV:* Provides continuing authority for the Job Corps, originally authorized by the Economic Opportunity Act of 1964.

- *Title V:* Establishes a National Commission for Manpower Policy to serve as an advisory board to examine employment questions and make recommendations to the Secretary of Labor and the Congress.

- *Title VI:* This title was added to CETA in 1974 by the Emergency Jobs and Unemployment Assistance Act. It provides for a temporary program of emergency public-service employment specially designed to help ease high unemployment during the mid-1970s.

- *Title VII:* Contains definitions and administrative procedures necessary to assist in the orderly management of the act.

- *Title VIII:* Establishes a Young Adult Conservation Corps to be administered by the Department of Labor. Authorizes year-round, conservation-related jobs on public lands for persons aged sixteen through twenty-three. Maximum job duration is twelve months, with compensation at least at the minimum wage.

In early 1977 employment and training expenditures under CETA and other programs were averaging about $9 billion a year.[9] This included about $2.5 billion a year to support 310,000 public-service jobs in state and local governments. Most of these jobs were in public schools, health and public-safety departments, and state and local government offices. Two hundred and sixty thousand of these jobs were funded under Title VI of CETA and the remaining 50,000 jobs were financed under Title II. All persons aided under Title II are required to be unemployed for thirty days before they can become eligible for aid. This provision is designed to guarantee that only the neediest persons obtain aid. Similarly, under Title VI, a substantial proportion of all jobs are reserved for persons unemployed fifteen weeks or longer.

Under Title I another $900 million was being spent to provide work experience and public-service employment by state and local governments under CETA grants. Job-training programs were being conducted under Title I grants, under Work Incentive Program (WIN) grants, and under Vocational Rehabilitation. The total cost of job training was about 1.1 billion.

In addition, in 1976 the Congress passed a $2 billion emergency public-works program (after two vetoes by President Ford) to finance a variety of state and local construction projects. The construction programs mostly involved sewer and street repair, and construction of public buildings. The states were provided another $1.25 billion to help them avoid layoffs and to maintain existing levels of unemployment. The Environmental Protection Agency received $480 million for additional grants for construction of waste-treatment works.

Since it is frequently charged that public-works jobs primarily involve leaf raking and litter collection, it is instructive to examine how the $2 billion for public works was allocated in 1976. The breakdown was as follows:[10]

Project type	Number of projects	% of total	Grants (in millions)	% of total
Public safety	133	6.7	$ 97.7	5.0
Hospitals	49	2.5	62.4	3.2
Schools	268	13.5	372.8	19.1
Recreational buildings and parks	94	4.7	78.8	4.0
Other public buildings	469	23.6	481.1	24.6
Industrial development	47	2.3	50.2	2.6
Miscellaneous or multiple buildings	88	4.4	91.4	4.7
Water, sewer, drainage	475	23.9	405.7	20.7
Streets, roads, bridges	224	11.3	179.2	9.2
Miscellaneous or multiple civil works	123	6.2	119.4	6.1
Miscellaneous or multiple facilities	18	0.9	16.8	0.8
Total	1,988	100.0	$1,955.4	100.0

These figures indicate that the funds were not spent for frivolous projects. While a considerable proportion of the funds were spent on brick and mortar, 42 cents of every dollar spent went for worker salaries. The feasibility of these types of projects to create jobs and to finance badly needed facilities is indicated by the number of projects that communities requested funding for, but were denied because of fund limitations. Over 2,000 communities asked for nearly $3 billion to build public schools; almost 3,000 communities asked for $2.7 billion to construct public buildings; almost 4,000 communities sought $3.4 billion to build water, sewage, and drainage systems; and some 2,500 jurisdictions asked for $1.8 billion in order to build and repair streets, roads, bridges, highways and sidewalks.

These types of expenditures not only finance worthwhile projects, they create many more jobs than do stimulus techniques such as tax cuts. Secretary of Labor Ray Marshall has estimated that it requires $5,000 in direct expenditures to produce a job, but it requires $20,000 in tax cuts to put one person to work.[11] These findings also indicate that the $19.8 billion spent on unemployment compensation in 1976 could have been put to much better use. Unemployment funds could finance thousands of local construction projects, which would directly and indirectly create millions of jobs.

In May 1977, Congress passed the several parts of an economic-stimulus package proposed by President Carter early in 1977. One part of the package included $7.9 billion under Titles II and VI of CETA to increase the number of public-service jobs in state and local governments from 310,000 to 750,000. Under Title I of CETA, $1.4 billion was authorized for youth employment and training programs and $59.4 million for community-service employment for older Americans. Appropriations for public-works projects were increased from $2 to $6 billion, and $632 million was set aside for antirecession aid to help state and local governments maintain basic services during periods of high unemployment. Beginning July 1, 1977, another $2.25 billion was made available over the next five quarters to provide further aid to state and local governments, so that they would not have to lay off employees or cut back on services.

As part of Carter's stimulus package, a $34.2 billion tax-cut bill extending over three years was also passed in May 1977. Some $5 billion of the tax cut was for a tax credit to small and medium-sized firms that hire new workers. Most of the tax cut was designed to put more money into the economy to increase consumer buying power.

In August 1977, a bill containing a number of youth-employment programs was signed into law. The bill established Title VIII of CETA, which created the Young Adult Conservation Corps, and a number of one-year demonstration programs designed to focus on structural and aggregate unemployment among youth. The demonstration programs, to be administered under a new part C of CETA Title III, were designed to upgrade youth job skills and to provide jobs, job information, and supportive services. Part of the funds would support guaranteed jobs for economically disadvantaged high school students, including youth community-improvement projects. Funding for these programs was authorized under Carter's economic-stimulus package passed in May 1977.

Evaluating Job Training Programs

While public-works expenditures can definitely finance worthwhile programs and create good jobs, the question remains as to whether job training programs have any real value. Can they train people for good jobs and help them obtain viable employment?

Studies of training programs differ in their sophistication and conclusions, but all agree that a large proportion of the unemployed can be trained for jobs and that the job training programs generally have a positive, worthwhile impact on enrollees.[12] Jon H. Goldstein recently surveyed and critiqued studies of the five largest programs (MDTA, NYC, Job Corps, Jobs, and WIN) for the Joint Economic Committee. His basic conclusions were as follows:[13]

1. Most studies estimated positive and relatively large internal social rates of return for MDTA.

2. Disadvantaged persons do experience earnings increases as a result of exposure to job training.

3. Every study estimated an improvement in the economic position of the disadvantaged large enough to recoup the social cost incurred in training.

4. The evidence examined supports the widely held belief that on-the-job training is superior to institutional training, but this evidence is neither extensive nor conclusive.

5. The effectiveness of training is very likely to vary directly with the demand for labor in the local labor market.

6. Disadvantaged and low-income persons have responded to training and have become more self-sustaining.

What the training programs cannot do, however, is actually create jobs. If the base of jobs does not expand, training programs can help only some part of the unemployed obtain jobs. Training may also help those who obtain jobs to perform better in the job market and may increase their job earnings somewhat.

Levitan, Mangum, and Marshall point out a few basic lessons that evaluators have learned from the job training programs.[14]

1. Basic literacy is almost essential as a prerequisite to employment in the United States, and techniques for teaching it to adults in conjunction with skill training had to be and have been developed.

2. Training is also useful and often essential for those whose work experience is unusually limited, especially when the employer expects the individual to have some advance experience or exposure.

3. A variety of supportive services and a sympathetic but challenging atmosphere are necessary to train the really disadvantaged.

4. Training will be taken seriously when it is evident that it leads to attractive jobs; when training clearly does not lead to jobs, it will justifiably be perceived as a frustrating waste of time. A direct linkage to employment or a demonstrated high placement rate in desirable jobs is essential.

Job programs, then, can help the unemployed, but they must be fairly sophisticated and clearly worthwhile to enrollees if they are to accomplish anything beneficial.

Even in the slack job markets of the mid-1970s the training programs were showing some successes. In 1975 the Department of Labor reported that, of the 658,000 individuals who left programs operated under Titles I, II, and VI of CETA, 202,300 (31 percent) left for unsubsidized employment. Another 198,000 (30 percent) left to enter school, the armed forces, or to pursue other activities expected to improve their employability. Thus, positive terminations totaled 61 percent of all persons who left the program.[15]

The Job Corps completed its tenth year of operation in 1975. The program is designed to assist disadvantaged youth between the ages of sixteen and twenty-one to gain the education and job skills necessary for employment. Ninety percent of all terminees from the program were placed in 1975. Of the 29,336 terminees, 20,408 found new jobs and 8,928 returned to school, qualified for additional training, or entered the armed forces.[16]

The least successful of all job programs is WIN. In 1975, 840,000 persons registered with WIN. Only 555,000 registrants were appraised for entry into the program, and only 328,000 were certified available for active participation in WIN employment or training components. Some 171,000 registrants obtained a job in 1975, two-thirds of whom received no training. About 53,000 of those who obtained a job were able to earn enough to leave the welfare rolls.[17]

Given the fact that the WIN training facilities are small, that child-care services are limited, that there are few real penalties for refusal to participate in the program, that employers are frequently reluctant to hire AFDC recipients, and that jobs have been so scarce in recent years, it is little wonder that WIN has had such modest successes.

In summary, job training programs have, for the most part, been successful and can be a vital part of an antipoverty strategy. They can help the unemployed obtain basic skills, improve self-confidence, and provide the opportunities necessary for job attainment. The training can be effective only if it actually leads to a job, and it cannot be a substitute for methods to improve the overall health of the economy. Without full employment, the programs will help only a small percentage of the poor and will have little impact on the overall extent of poverty in America.

CHILD CARE

Any viable strategy to eradicate poverty must include an expanded child-care program as part of a full-employment plan. For poor families, child care is often necessary to permit family heads to enter the job market or educational or training programs. Child care would also provide supervision for many children who are currently left unattended for all or part of a day by parents who must work and cannot afford to hire anyone to look after them.

Good child care is also necessary if the cycle of poverty is to be broken. Child-care centers can provide poor children with the educational stimulation and training often lacking in their environment. In addition, they can provide the poor child with at least one nutritious meal per day and with health care. A poor child able to receive all these services at an early age would be significantly less likely to enter public school with nutritional and health deficiencies, and several years behind his or her middle-income peers educationally.

Child care need not be thought of as substituting institutional supervison and education for parental care. In fact, as Fein and Clarke-Stewart argue, a goal of good child care should be "minimal attenuation of the sense of responsibility the family should have for the child."[18] Parents can be included in child-care programs and taught to work with their children; or, alternatively, if educational stimulation is the only needed service, parents can be taught how to instruct their own children in the home environment.

Extended child care is also necessary for many families who are not actually below the poverty level. Many persons (mostly women) cannot obtain the education or training they need to pursue a career because they cannot afford child care. With substantial increases in female-headed families and increases in the number of women who want to enter the job market, child care needs to be made more universally available. In 1950 only about 25 percent of all married women were in the work force; in 1975 their rate of labor-force participation reached 44 percent.[19] Thirty-seven percent of all women with children under six were in the labor force, as were 52 percent of women with only school-age children.[20] A total of 26 million American children had working mothers. Most women who are in the job market are there out of economic necessity. A recent study found that:

> Of the 26.5 million women in the labor force as of March 1975, 42.2 percent were single, widowed, divorced, or separated, and ... manifestly needed jobs to support themselves. Of the 21 million women in the civilian labor force who had husbands present, about 50 percent had husbands with incomes within $7,000 and about 16 percent had husbands with incomes under $5,000. All in all, about 70 percent of all women wage earners worked out of compelling economic necessity, and a very large portion of these lived in families with low income or even in poverty.[21]

Increases in the number of female-headed families have contributed dramatically to the increase in women in the work force. In 1975 there were 7.2 million female-headed families, containing 10.5 million children under eighteen years of age.[22] Forty-one percent of all black children lived in homes in which the father was missing, as did 11 percent of all white children.

The majority of all poor families with children are headed by a female. Forty-five percent of all poor families are headed by a female—36.3 percent of poor white families and 66.3 percent of poor black families. There were a total of 10.9 million children in poor families in 1975, one of every six children in America. Thirty-six percent of all females heading poor families in 1975 were in the job market.[23]

There are, therefore, some ten million children in poor families who would benefit substantially from sophisticated child care. With the proper attention, these children would not have to start life with the handicaps that doom many of them to a lifetime of poverty. There are millions of other children whose parents would have a better chance to advance themselves economically if child care were more widely available. Below, we examine the government's role in child care and suggest reforms that should be a part of any comprehensive antipoverty strategy.

Day Care

The federal government provides child-care services through a variety of agencies. Day-care assistance is provided under some eight to ten acts and by at least five federal agencies. Since the federal government does not collect detailed statistics on all child-care expenditures, no one knows exactly how much money is spent on day care or how many families are served.[24] Table 8.4 shows the United States Senate's Committee on Finance's best estimates for a range of child-care services provided during fiscal years 1975 to 1977, including estimates for day care.

While the Appalachian Regional Commission, the Community Services Administration, the Department of Housing and Urban Development, the Department of Interior, and the Small Business Administration either directly provide funds for day care or help finance day-care centers, most day-care support is provided by the Department of Health, Education and Welfare (HEW). Under Title XX of the Social Security Act, HEW provides states with funds for providing day care to actual, former, or potential recipients of AFDC. The federal government pays 80 percent of the cost of day care for these recipients. Children may be placed in centers that provide services ranging from custodial to developmental, or in family day-care homes. Usually the states contract with an agency to provide these services. Table 8.4 indicates that, during fiscal years 1975 to 1977, Title XX funds for day care averaged $635.8 million per year, serving an average of 785,500 children yearly, at an average federal cost of $845 per child.

HEW also provides day care under a number of other programs. For example, under Title IV-A of the Social Security Act, the states must allow an AFDC recipient to deduct the cost of child care as a work expense in determining income for welfare purposes (see Chapter 5). During fiscal years 1975 to 1977, this deduction cost the federal government an average of $77.5 million yearly. An average of 142,000 children a year received child-care support under this program, at an average yearly cost of $545 per child.

Also under Title IV-A, AFDC recipients who are placed in jobs or given training under the Work Incentive Program (WIN) are eligible for any needed day-care assistance. Day care is provided throughout training and for the first ninety days of employment. After ninety days, the family may qualify for day-care assistance under other provisions of the Social Security Act. Most child care provided under WIN is for care within the child's own home or in the home of a relative. Additionally, over half of all WIN care goes to families with children aged six or above. Thus, most WIN families need only part-day or part-year services. In fiscal years 1975 to 1977, WIN day-care expenses averaged $55.2 million yearly, served an average of 83,000 children yearly, at an average cost of $723 per child. The allocation for day care under WIN has been particularly deficient. Many mothers who desire employment or job training cannot obtain it because day-care funds for their children are not available.

Under Title IV-A the federal government provides some matching funds to the states for a variety of child welfare services. Some of these funds are used by the states to provide day-care assistance, usually on a short-term basis, to needy families. During fiscal years 1975 to 1977, an average of $3.8 million per year of all child welfare aid was spent on day care. An average of 19,000 children per year received assistance, at an annual cost of about $200 per child.

Between fiscal years 1975 and 1977 the four HEW programs provided an average of 1,027,500 children a year with day-care services. The average yearly cost was $772.3 million. The average number of children provided day care by the other programs listed on Table 8.4 was 127,800 at an average yearly cost of $50.5 million. The yearly average of children served by all the programs was 1,155,300 at an average yearly cost of $822.8 million.

These figures clearly reveal that too little support is provided for day care. In 1976 there was a monthly average of 7.9 million children in AFDC families, with 3.4 million female-headed families.[25] If only half these children were provided with day care, 3.95 million would have needed assistance. But, of course, if day care is thought of as more than just a means of freeing parents for employment or training, day care or special educational programs would have to be made available to some eight to ten million children. As we shall see, another million or so poor children are provided with preschool educational assistance, but most poor children are untouched either by day care or preschool educational aid.

Of the day care that is provided, some is not designed to optimally benefit the child. Day care that provides only custodial care is deficient and shortsighted. Early educational, medical, and nutritional intervention

TABLE 8.4

Department of Health, Education and Welfare estimate of national child-care funding, fiscal years 1975–1977: federal child-care expenditures[a]

Agency/program	Federal obligations (millions)			Children served (thousands)			Federal cost per child (dollars)[b]			Matching state contributions (millions)		
	FY 75	FY 76	FY 77	FY 75	FY 76	FY 77	FY 75	FY 76	FY 77	FY 75	FY 76	FY 77
I. Department of Agriculture Child Care Food Service Program	$ 42.3	$ 75.4	$ 120.0	452	460	580	$94	$164	$207	None required		
II. Appalachian Regional Commission	12.8	12.3	9.3	61.7	58.6	46.8	207	209	197	$6.9	$7.8	NA
III. Community Services Administration Community Action Agency Program	2.5	2.5	2.5	NA[c]	NA	NA	NA	NA	NA	None required		
IV. Department of Health, Education and Welfare												
SSA, Title XX, Social Services[d] (child care)	487.0	611.8	808.6	525.8	1,026.1	798.6	926	596	1,013	162.4	203.9	269.5
SSA, Title IV-A, Work Expense Allowance (child care)	72.6	75.4	84.4	136.0	145.0	144.9	534	520	582	59.4	61.4	71.6

SSA, Title IV-A, WIN	57.4	51.1	57.1	79.1	83.8	85.0	726	770	672	5.7	5.1	5.7
SSA, Title IV-B, Child Welfare	2.0	4.7	4.7	19.0	19.0	19.0	105	247	247	42.0	62.6	62.6
Head Start	412.8	427.1	447.6	349.0	349.0	349.0	1,183	1,224	1,283	82.6	85.4	89.5
ESEA, Title I-A, Preschool and Kindergarten Programs	120.0	128.0	136.0	367.0	367.0	367.0	327	349	371	None required		
ESEA, Title I-A (Supplement), Migrants	10.1	10.6	14.4	37.7	37.7	37.7	268	283	382	None required		
ESEA, Title VI-B, Education for the Handicapped State Grant Program	7.0	7.0	7.7	260.0	260.0	260.0	27	27	30	None required		
ESA, Title VI-C, Early Education for the Handicapped	11.2	14.0	14.0	8.3	14.0	14.0	1,350	1,000	1,000	1.1	1.4	1.4
HEW total	($1,180.1)	($1,329.7)	($1,574.5)	(1,781.9)	(2,301.6)	(2,075.2)	($ 662)	($ 578)	($ 759)	($353.2)	($419.8)	($500.3)
V. Department of Housing and Urban Development Community Development Block Grant Entitlement Program	27.4	37.8	42.7	54.8	75.6	85.4	None required					

TABLE 8.4 (cont.)

Agency/program	Federal obligations (millions)			Children served (thousands)			Federal cost per child (dollars)[b]			Matching state contributions (millions)		
	FY 75	FY 76	FY 77	FY 75	FY 76	FY 77	FY 75	FY 76	FY 77	FY 75	FY 76	FY 77
VI. Department of Interior Bureau of Indian Affairs:												
Kindergarten Program	2.3	2.5	2.7	2.5	2.4	2.4	935	1,056	1,125	None required		
Parent-Child Development Program	.5	.7	.7	.2	.2	.3	2,634	2,462	2,222	None required		
BIA total	($2.8)	($3.2)	($3.4)	(2.7)	(2.6)	(2.7)	($1,056)	($1,203)	($1,244)			
VII. Department of Labor[e]												
VIII. Small Business Administration	2.2	2.0	NA	NA	NA	NA	None required					
IX. Department of Treasury	225.0	261.0	756.0	NA	NA	7,000	NA	NA	108	None required		
Total federal expenditure	$1,495.1	$1,723.9	$2,508.4	$2,353.1	$2,898.4	$9,567.3	$ 635	$ 596	$ 262	$360.1	$427.6	$500.3

Source: U.S. Congress, Senate, Committee on Finance, *Child Care: Data and Materials*, 93rd Cong., 2nd sess., October 1974, unnumbered appendix prepared in 1977.
[a] Expenditures for the following are excluded even though some may provide full- or part-day child care: (a) grants for training educational and/or day-care personnel; (b) research and development funds; (c) administrative grants; (d) health program funds for children; (e) summer programs for teenagers; (f) programs for teenagers before and after school (Neighborhood Youth Corps, Department of Interior recreation programs); (g) grants to school systems for postkindergarten children; (h) parent training and home intervention programs (e.g., Department of Agriculture extension programs for improved family living).
[b] Federal cost per child is an average derived from reported estimates of children served and obligations. Total average cost is underestimated due to several programs for which child estimates were unavailable.
[c] NA = not available.
[d] Until 1976, these funds were authorized under Title IV-A of the Social Security Act.
[e] All DOL programs included in the 1974 edition of this table have been incorporated into CETA. Specific program expenditures were not identifiable.

into the lives of poor children is one of the most efficient strategies for breaking the cycle of poverty. Given the rapidly changing status of American families and the role of women in society, widely available comprehensive day care for all families with fees pegged to family income would be advisable. Standards for day care should also be designed to allow "good" quality care for large numbers of children rather than "excessively expensive" care for only a few.[26] Expenditures of only $4 to $6 billion could increase day-care services fivefold, with an excellent long-term antipoverty potential.

Preschool Educational Programs

The best known of the federal preschool programs is Head Start. Established in 1965, Head Start was initially hailed as the most insightful antipoverty strategy on the horizon. It was broadly designed to improve the conceptual, perceptive, and verbal skills of poor children, to increase their sense of dignity and self-worth, to expand their curiosity, to help them develop self-discipline, to provide them with medical and dental care, and to develop in poor children and their parents a responsible attitude toward society. Initially the program was designed to serve 100,000 children during the summer of 1965. Enthusiasm for the program was so high, however, that 561,359 were enrolled, many in hastily assembled programs.[27]

The initial enthusiasm for the program continued for several years. However, by 1969 the first evaluations of the impact of Head Start began to appear.[28] Most of the studies were disappointing—the major impacts anticipated had not occurred. Some of the initial expectations had been overly optimistic, especially the expectation that three to four years of educational neglect could be compensated for in only one or two eight-week summer terms. The studies showed that the physical conditions of Head Start children tended to be considerably better than that of children from similar backgrounds who had not been in the program, but educational gains tended to be small, especially for children who had not participated in year-round programs.[29] The most critical of the studies, known as the Westinghouse Report, showed worthwhile gains for students in full-year programs, but only minor gains from the eight-week program—gains that tended to fade as the child completed the first two years of public school.[30]

While the Westinghouse study was considered controversial from the start because of dissension among the research staff over some of the assumptions the research was based on and because of methodological problems involved, the negative findings were basically accepted at face value and cost Head Start much of its support in Congress. In fiscal years 1975 through 1977, Head Start served only 349,000 children yearly, over 200,000 fewer than during its first year of operation.

In recent years, however, studies have shown that the Head Start program has improved considerably in its impact. Educational experts have speculated that the improvements probably result from experience-related innovations in teaching techniques in Head Start programs and the development of more sophisticated methodologies to measure program impact.[31] It seems reasonable that teaching techniques would improve with experience and that experience would be required to fully understand the children's needs and how to respond to them.

A recent symposium sponsored by the American Association for the Advancement of Science which evaluated ninety-six longitudinal studies of Head Start participants reported particularly heartening results.[32] All of the ninety-six studies showed that Head Start has significant positive impacts on children. As Bernard Brown of the Office of Child Development concluded, the studies provide "compelling evidence that early intervention works, that the adverse impact of a poverty environment on children can be overcome by appropriate treatment."[33] The studies showed that Head Start is very successful in cutting down the rate of school failure, in improving IQ scores, in improving reading achievement, and in helping children gain self-confidence. The studies showed that major educational gains do not fade out and, even more encouraging, that a "sleeper effect" often showed up several years after the program and helped Head Start recipients become more academically competent even into the junior-high-school years. The more exposure children had to Head Start, the more gains they tended to make and maintain.

These highly positive results suggest the great value of preschool educational programs as a method of combatting poverty. Unfortunately, funding for Head Start and other preschool programs is very modest. As Table 8.4 shows, during fiscal years 1975–1977, an average of $429.2 million per year was spent on Head Start, with only 349,000 students per year served. By law, 90 percent of all students in a Head Start program must be from poverty families. Ten percent must be children with handicaps. If the unlikely assumption is made that all the students enrolled in Head Start in recent years were from poverty families, only 15 percent of all those students qualified for Head Start by their family's income have been served.

Four additional programs are operated by the Office of Education under the Elementary and Secondary Education Act (ESEA). These include child-care or preschool education programs designed to meet the needs of educationally deprived children from poverty areas (see Table 8.4), as well as programs for migrant children and children who are handicapped, neglected, or delinquent. In fiscal years 1975–1977, these four programs cost an average of $160 million per year and served an average of 676,800 children yearly.

All the federal programs to provide day care or preschool education have served, on the average, some 2.2 million children in recent years at an average yearly cost of $1.8 billion per year. If poverty is to be alleviated, the number of children served must be expanded considerably.

THE BETTER JOBS AND INCOME PROGRAM: THE CARTER PROPOSAL*

In the fall of 1977, President Carter forwarded to Congress his $30.7 billion proposal for reforming the welfare system. Carter's proposal called for comprehensive reform, reflecting a clean break with the prevailing welfare system.

Carter's plan emphasized a dual strategy: the poor would be divided into those who could work as opposed to those who could not. Those designated as capable of work would be expected to accept a public- or private-sector job, which the government would supplement if wages fell below levels established for varying family sizes. Many workers would also receive some tax relief (the cutoff point for a family of four would be $15,650). Those unable to work would be eligible for a negative income tax program that would provide a guaranteed income based on family size. The NIT program and the jobs program would cover all the poor, including two-parent families, single persons, and childless couples.

The Jobs Component

To provide employment for the poor, the plan proposed the creation of 1.4 million public-sector jobs, some 300,000 of which would be part-time. This program would replace the 700,000 public-sector jobs authorized in 1977 under various titles of CETA. All the jobs created would pay the minimum wage. To qualify for one of the public-sector jobs, an individual

---

* This description was written in the fall of 1977. Undoubtedly the bill will change in many ways as it is considered by Congress.

would have to be unemployed for five weeks. All holders of the newly created jobs would be required once every twelve months to engage in a thorough search for private-sector employment.

The Department of Labor anticipated that the newly created jobs would be in the following areas:

Number of jobs

200,000:	construction and repair of recreational facilities;
200,000:	home services for the elderly and sick;
150,000:	child care;
150,000:	public safety;
150,000:	paraprofessionals and teachers' aides;
125,000:	recreational programs;
100,000:	neighborhood cleanup and pest control;
100,000:	improvement of school facilities;
75,000:	cultural activities;
50,000:	environmental monitoring;
50,000:	home weatherization;
25,000:	waste treatment and recycling;
25,000:	facilities for the handicapped.

Those expected to accept employment would include parents with children above fourteen and those healthy, nonelderly adults with no children. Single parents with children aged seven to fourteen would be expected to work full-time if child-care facilities were available, part-time if they were not. Single parents with preschool children would be exempt from the work requirement. Some 42 percent of the public-sector jobs would be intended for heads of AFDC families.

Earnings of workers would be supplemented in two ways. Using a NIT principle, worker salaries would be supplemented, with grants varying by earnings and family size. A family of four, for example, would be eligible for a work benefit of up to $2,300. For every dollar earned over $3,800, the benefit would be reduced 50 cents, disappearing when earnings reach $8,400. If, for example, the head of a four-person family earned $5,000, he or she would receive a supplement of $1,700 ($2,300 minus 50 percent of earnings in excess of $3,800), providing a total income of $6,700. Similarly, if the head earned $6,000, the supplement would be

$1,200, giving the worker a total income of $7,200. To help single parents get into the work force, up to 20 percent of earned income could be deducted for child-care expenses (up to $150 per month for one child and up to $300 for two or more children).

Additionally, many low-income workers (the major exceptions being those holding the public-sector jobs created under the plan and families without children) would receive some tax breaks. Families with children could claim a 10 percent tax credit on earnings up to $4,000. Above $4,000 in earnings an additional credit of 5 percent could be claimed up to a cutoff point at which the family ceases to be eligible for cash assistance. The various supplements were designed to make employment more attractive than welfare and to encourage workers to earn above the threshold point. The denial of the tax credit to those holding the public-sector jobs was designed to encourage them to obtain employment in the private sector.

The Guaranteed Income Component

Those not expected to work would receive a cash grant under a NIT plan. The grant would replace the AFDC, SSI, and food-stamp programs. The cash grants would vary by family size and would be quite small. A family of four would receive a total grant of $4,200, some $1,615 less than the poverty threshold for a nonfarm family of four in 1977. (In 1977 only twelve states, mostly in the South, paid less than $4,200 a year to a four-person family.) An aged, blind, or disabled individual would receive $2,500; a couple would receive $3,750. A single individual would receive only $1,100. A couple without children would receive $2,200.

The cash grants were designed to be very modest for two reasons. Most obviously they were meant to force as many adults as possible to work. Second, the low grants were designed to encourage the states to supplement the grants. To encourage state supplements, the federal government would pay 75 percent of the first $500 in supplements for a family of four, and 25 percent of all additional supplements.

State Relief

Aid to states to help them reduce their welfare costs would be phased over a four-year period. During the first year the states would receive $2.1 billion in relief, guaranteeing to each state a 10 percent reduction in welfare costs. During the second year the states would be required to maintain only 60 percent of their current expenditures—this would drop to 30 percent during the third year and to 10 percent in the fourth. Thus, over a number of years, the states would receive considerable aid.

The Positive Features

The attractions of Carter's proposal are numerous. The proposal would:

- achieve some important program consolidation;
- provide a base of uniform benefits;
- eventually federalize welfare;
- cover all the poor;
- not penalize families;
- simplify administration;
- reduce attempts to regulate the lives of the poor;
- provide some tax relief to many low-income workers.

Since those unable to find a job would qualify for assistance (which would include many persons not presently covered by welfare programs), the government might feel some obligation to keep the economy healthier than normal to hold down the welfare rolls. Additionally, since all the poor would be covered by the bill, the number of citizens eligible for Medicaid would probably increase substantially. This would probably increase congressional support for national health insurance.

The Negative Features

Despite its many merits, the problems with Carter's approach are substantial. There are numerous deficiencies, but four deserve emphasis. First, the benefits to nonworkers are much too low. Since the benefits cannot be supplemented with food stamps or SSI, both of which will be abolished, poverty may well be institutionalized for those who cannot work. Depending on the states to supplement the cash grants will only perpetuate the inequities that currently exist. Some states will provide decent supplements, others will provide modest assistance, and some will do little or nothing.

Since Carter's proposal only calls for a total of 1.4 million public-service jobs and is vague about how the job market would be expanded, millions of able-bodied persons would undoubtedly continue to be left out of the job market. Thus, in the absence of full employment, Carter's guaranteed income would simply perpetuate a spiral of poverty for many persons. Maintenance at a very low guaranteed income would, in all probability, become a substitute for serious efforts to expand and improve the economy.

Some simple alterations in Carter's plan could deal with this problem. A distinction can be made between those who can realistically be expected to work and those who cannot. The bill does this to some extent by providing higher benefits to the aged, disabled, and blind. This principle could be expanded to all others who cannot work and their benefits could be raised to a livable level. Benefits to those who are unemployed but expected to find employment could be raised above the subsistence level without removing the employment incentive.

If additional funds are needed, the relief to the states could be sacrificed. The states could be required to continue their current levels of funding, at least until the unemployment situation improved considerably. Basing relief to the states on the unemployment rate within the state would give the states an added incentive to work on this problem.

The second drawback to the Carter approach is that the jobs to be created under the bill would be quite inadequate. Since the jobs would pay only the minimum wage, some employers (particularly state and local governments) might replace higher-paid workers with welfare recipients, thus further disrupting the job market. Since many (if not most) of the jobs would have to be supplemented, it would make more sense to simply pay a decent wage. Welfare recipients would have more incentive to work, other jobs would not be jeopardized, and workers would have the dignity of earning their own living.

Third, there is too little emphasis on child care. Rather than expand federal and state child-care efforts, the proposal allows deductions to low-income workers, so that they can pay for child care. This requires that the parent incur considerable expense to start work. Further, it is too nondirected to stimulate the child-care market and fails to set any standards for child care. Since the evidence indicates the great value of quality child care and preschool education, the optimal value of child care should be obtained by direct federal expenditure.

Fourth, the fundamental flaw with Carter's proposal is that it is not directly coupled with a forthright program to correct permanently some of the deficiencies of the economy—namely, unemployment, subemployment, and inflation. Carter's proposal was originally submitted to Congress without any backup economic package, except a temporary tax cut and an expansion of job programs under CETA. Carter's intention seemed to be to improve the economy with rather traditional techniques and build on this progress with his welfare-reform package. But Carter's plans were clearly too modest. His goal of reducing unemployment to 6 percent by the end of 1977 was not met, and thus he had to admit that the economic problems plaguing our society are too complex and too chronic to respond to halfhearted remedies.

Faced with solid evidence of the failure of traditional economic approaches, Carter reluctantly endorsed a watered-down version of the Humphrey-Hawkins bill in the fall of 1977. But, as noted in Chapter 7, it is not clear how effective the much-altered bill will be even if passed by Congress. The goals of the revised Humphrey-Hawkins bill are modest, and many of the problems that would have been addressed under the original version (e.g., poor schools, inadequate transportation systems, lack of economic planning) are not likely to be illuminated and addressed under the revised bill. If the revised version of Humphrey-Hawkins is passed, economic problems should receive some attention. A well-intentioned president might use the Humphrey-Hawkins programs quite effectively. A president unconcerned about problems of poverty and unemployment, on the other hand, would be little obligated by the bill. But if the Humphrey-Hawkins bill is not passed, economic problems are likely to improve very little, and may even get worse. If the economy does not improve, Carter's welfare plan will be extremely expensive and millions of Americans will have to survive on the modest benefits provided by the NIT.

CONCLUSIONS

Understanding the problems that plague our nation's current approach to alleviating poverty is not very difficult, nor is it very hard to devise viable alternatives. The patchwork of ill-related programs presently in effect all too clearly reflects prejudice and ignorance of the poor and underscores the desire of many in power to rationalize away the problem and preserve the economic status quo.

A coordinated three-step program to create full employment, reform the health-care industry, and provide a guaranteed livable income to those unable to work would be the most ideal approach to poverty eradication. It is quite clear that such a coordinated approach will not be pursued, although, under the Carter administration, each of these programs may be dealt with over a five-to-eight-year period. Carter's refusal to support a genuine full-employment proposal like the original version of Humphrey-Hawkins is likely to severely hamper his battle against poverty, and will certainly place severe financial strains on his poverty program if it is passed by Congress.

Thus, while Carter's welfare reform would be a significant step in the battle against poverty (especially if the bill is altered in the ways mentioned above), it still reflects the traditional refusal to face up to the serious deficiencies of the American economic system. Until these deficiencies are dealt with, no reform is likely to be very successful.

NOTES

1. See the excerpts and citations in Theodore R. Marmor, ed., *Poverty Policy* (Chicago: Aldine-Atherton, 1971); Christopher Green, *Negative Taxes and The Poverty Problem* (Washington, D.C.: The Brookings Institution, 1967); Robert J. Lampman, *Ends and Means of Reducing Income Poverty* (New York: Academic Press, 1971); and Michael C. Barth, George J. Carcagno, and John L. Palmer, *Toward an Effective Income Support System: Problems, Prospects, and Choices* (Madison, Wisconsin: Institute for Research on Poverty, 1974).

2. Milton Friedman, *Capitalism and Freedom* (Chicago: University of Chicago Press, 1962), Chapter 7.

3. See Marmor, *Poverty Policy;* Kenneth E. Boulding and Martin Pfaff, *Redistribution to the Rich and the Poor: The Grants Economics of Income Distribution* (Belmont, Ca.: Wadsworth, 1972); Green, *Negative Taxes and the Poverty Problem;* and Joseph Pechman and P. Michael Timpane, eds., *Work Incentives and Income Guarantees* (Washington, D.C.: The Brookings Institution, 1975).

4. U.S. Congress, Joint Economic Committee, Subcommittee on Fiscal Policy, *Income Security for Americans: Recommendations of the Public Welfare Study,* 93rd Cong., 2d sess., December 1974, p. 112.

5. Ibid., p. 61.

6. Both studies were conducted by the Institute for Research on Poverty at the University of Wisconsin, Madison and are examined in U.S. Department of Health, Education, and Welfare, *Rural Income Maintenance Experiment* (Washington, D.C.: Government Printing Office, November 1976).

7. U.S. Congress, Joint Economic Committee, Subcommittee on Fiscal Policy, *Income Security for Americans;* and Brock Adams, "Welfare, Poverty, and Jobs: A Practical Approach," *Challenge,* September–October 1976, pp. 6–12.

8. See U.S. Department of Labor and U.S. Department of Health, Education and Welfare, *Employment and Training Report of the President* (Washington, D.C.: Government Printing Office, 1976), pp. 87–90.

9. "Jobs Programs: How Well Do They Work?" *Congressional Quarterly* 35, no. 8 (February 19, 1977): 302–307.

10. See *The National Journal,* February 12, 1977, p. 247.

11. "Jobs Programs . . . ," *Congressional Quarterly,* p. 305.

12. See the bibliography in Jon H. Goldstein, *The Effectiveness of Manpower Training Programs: A Review of Research on the Impact on the Poor,* a staff study prepared for the Joint Economic Committee, Congress of the United States, November 20, 1972, pp. 68–70.

13. Ibid., pp. 1–15.

14. Sar A. Levitan, Garth L. Mangum, and Ray Marshall, *Human Resources and Labor Markets* (New York: Harper & Row, 1976), p. 350.

15. *Employment and Training Report of the President,* 1976, p. 102.

16. Ibid., p. 109.

17. Ibid., p. 117.

18. Greta G. Fein and Alison Clarke-Stewart, *Day Care in Context* (New York: Wiley, 1973), p. xx.

19. U.S. Bureau of the Census, "A Statistical Portrait of Women in the U.S.," U.S. Department of Commerce, *Current Population Reports,* Special Studies, Series P-23, no. 58, p. 26.

20. Ibid.

21. *Hearing Before the Subcommittee on Equal Opportunities of the Committee on Education and Labor,* Part 5, March 1976, p. 167.

22. "A Statistical Portrait of Women in the U.S.," p. 1.

23. See Table 2.4 in Chapter 4.

24. See U.S. Congress, Committee on Finance, *Child Care: Data and Materials,* 93rd Cong., 2d sess., October 1974, pp. 22–28.

25. U.S. Department of Health, Education and Welfare, *Public Assistance Statistics 1976,* No. (SRS) 77-03100, Ness Report A-2 (January 1977), p. 7.

26. See Dennis R. Young and Richard R. Nelson, *Public Policy for Day Care of Young Children* (Lexington, Mass.: Lexington Books, 1973), p. 7. Day Care is a highly developed social service in many Western European countries. See Alfred J. Kahn and Sheila B. Kamerman, *Not For the Poor Alone: European Social Services* (New York: Harper & Row, 1975); and Bodil Rosengren, *Pre-School in Sweden* (Stockholm: The Swedish Institute, 1973).

27. See Gilbert Y. Steiner, *The Children's Cause* (Washington, D.C.: The Brookings Institution, 1976), p. 30.

28. See Ada Jo Mann, Adele Harrell, and Maure Hurt, Jr., "A Review of

Head Start Research Since 1969," presented at the 1977 Annual Meeting of the American Association for the Advancement of Science, Denver, Colorado, February 23, 1977.

29. Ibid.

30. V.G. Cicirelli et al., *The Impact of Head Start: An Evaluation of the Effects of Head Start on Children's Cognitive and Affective Development.* Vols. 1 and 2. A report presented to the Office of Economic Opportunity pursuant to Contract B89-4536, June 1969. Ohio University, Westinghouse Learning Corporation, 1969.

31. See Bernard Brown, "Long-Term Gains from Early Intervention: An Overview of Current Research," presented at the 1977 Annual Meeting of the American Association for the Advancement of Science, Denver, Colorado, February 23, 1977.

32. The results are reviewed by Bernard Brown, ibid.

33. Ibid., p. 9.

9

EPILOGUE

The continuation of poverty in the United States reflects the political priorities of this country, the biases and deficiencies of the American political and economic systems, and the extent to which American political leaders have become the victims of their own efforts to miseducate the public about economic and political realities. In simple truth, in a country as rich as the United States, poverty is unnecessary. However, within the current limitations of American capitalism, some poverty is absolutely inevitable.

Capitalism assumes that unemployment is both unavoidable and requisite to keep the economy healthy and that the existence of millions of low-paying, even poverty-wage, jobs is essential to business success. As we attempted to show in Chapter 7, unemployment and underemployment are not essential to a healthy economy; in fact, they are quite dysfunctional. Political leaders refuse to accept these facts, because those most directly harmed by unemployment and underemployment rarely have any real influence in the political process. On the other hand, those who profit from a labor surplus and the cheap labor a surplus provides wield a great deal of power.

Many Americans even refuse to recognize the extent and type of poverty in America. Rather than accept the fact that poverty in this country results primarily from racism, sexism, and a scarcity of genuine opportunity, many attempt to delude and comfort themselves with the belief that the poor are the victims of their own weaknesses. Elaborate myths about the poor are perpetuated by the mass media, written into textbooks, and transmitted from one generation to the next. The poor are depicted as able-bodied males who could earn a living if they would only accept available jobs, spend their money wisely, and abstain from drink and loose living. Those who live off welfare, of course, never work, but still manage to live in style. They drive Cadillacs, eat steaks while luxuriating in front of their color tv's, and winter in Florida. If the welfare check becomes too skimpy to cover all their vices, they slink down to the local welfare office and invent another needy aunt or procreate another illegitimate child, who, like themselves, will spend his or her life on welfare. And the poor,

"You Must Have The Wrong Address — We're
A Very Prosperous People"

From *The Herblock Gallery* (Simon & Schuster, 1968).

of course, are mostly blacks—in other words, genetically programmed for sloth, sin, and simplemindedness.

While these myths have no basis in fact, they are powerful because they serve an important function. If given credence, myths about the poor make it legitimate to dismiss poverty as the consequence of personal inadequacies and indolence. If we had to admit that poverty results from factors other than deficiencies of the poor, we would then have to look elsewhere for its causes. Looking elsewhere might lead to an objective evaluation of the biases of our social and political system and of the strengths and weaknesses of our economic and political system—something we very much fear doing. The powerful who prosper so well in the system have long hammered home the message that the system is flawless—error lies with those who fail to prosper in the system. The myths even provide a scapegoat for the public. When inflation is high, when taxes hurt, when services are poor, blame can be attached to the poor and the funds they receive. So long as the poor are blamed, the real causes of these problems are not scrutinized.

One consequence of these attitudes toward poverty is that our government's approach to the problem is quite illogical and wasteful. We spend billions, but never actually meet the needs of the poor or break the cycle of poverty, because there is no overall design to assistance programs. Each program was created separately to deal with a particular problem or a particular clientele, the natural consequence of a refusal to accept poverty as a legitimate issue requiring coordinated solutions. Since poverty is not considered a legitimate problem, the government primarily responds only to the needs of those it is most difficult to rationalize ignoring—children, women with dependent children, and the aged. This approach proliferates poverty programs, but is too fragmented to really deal with the needs of the poor or the root causes of poverty.

The continuation of poverty is, of course, quite harmful to our society. Poverty is a major cause of crime and delinquency, it creates blight, it keeps millions of people from realizing their human potential and contributing fully to society, and it harms the economy by reducing real economic growth and tax revenues while increasing the cost of social programs. The horrible conditions of the poor cast shame on our society and make hypocrites of those who refuse to acknowledge the problem's origins. The social, political, and economic costs of poverty affect everyone and keep us from creating a more humane, productive, safe, and creative society.

As noted in Chapter 3, the government plays a large role in the lives of all citizens who prosper in our society, including the rich and the middle class. If big business, the rich, and the middle class need aid, why should we expect those who have been the victims of racism, sexism, and economic exploitation to make it wholly on their own? It would not be a departure from current economic practices for the government to aid the poor and, further, if the aid were designed to help the poor obtain jobs and to upgrade the jobs held by many low-income workers, the economy would be given a substantial boost.

Solving the problem of poverty will require an honest and critical appraisal of the failures and limitations of this country and its economy. It will also require a genuine concern for all citizens. Until we take these steps and make these changes, we will not—sadly and ironically—be able to eradicate poverty from the richest and most powerful nation on earth.

INDEX

INDEX